SOCIAL WORKERS
as
GAME CHANGERS

SAGE was founded in 1965 by Sara Miller McCune to support the dissemination of usable knowledge by publishing innovative and high-quality research and teaching content. Today, we publish over 900 journals, including those of more than 400 learned societies, more than 800 new books per year, and a growing range of library products including archives, data, case studies, reports, and video. SAGE remains majority-owned by our founder, and after Sara's lifetime will become owned by a charitable trust that secures our continued independence.

Los Angeles | London | New Delhi | Singapore | Washington DC | Melbourne

SOCIAL WORKERS
as
GAME CHANGERS

Confronting Complex Social Issues through Cases

LAURA LEWIS
Mercyhurst University

Los Angeles | London | New Delhi
Singapore | Washington DC | Melbourne

FOR INFORMATION

SAGE Publications, Inc.
2455 Teller Road
Thousand Oaks, California 91320
E-mail: order@sagepub.com

SAGE Publications Ltd.
1 Oliver's Yard
55 City Road
London, EC1Y 1SP
United Kingdom

SAGE Publications India Pvt. Ltd.
B 1/I 1 Mohan Cooperative Industrial Area
Mathura Road, New Delhi 110 044
India

SAGE Publications Asia-Pacific Pte. Ltd.
3 Church Street
#10–04 Samsung Hub
Singapore 049483

Printed in the United States of America

Library of Congress Cataloging-in-Publication Data

Names: Lewis, Laura, 1958- author.
Title: Social workers as game changers : confronting complex social issues through cases / Laura Lewis, Mercyhurst University.

Description: Thousand Oaks : SAGE, [2018]
Identifiers: LCCN 2016039110 | ISBN 9781506317052 (pbk. : alk. paper)

Subjects: LCSH: Social service—United States. | Social service—Practice—United States. | Social justice—United States. | United States—Social policy.

Classification: LCC HV91 .L3966 2018 | DDC 361.30973—dc23 LC record available at https://lccn.loc.gov/2016039110

This book is printed on acid-free paper.

Acquisitions Editor: Nathan Davidson
Editorial Assistant: Alex Helmintoller
Production Editor: Veronica Stapleton Hooper
Copy Editor: Michelle Ponce
Typesetter: Hurix Systems Pvt. Ltd.
Proofreader: Barbara Coster
Cover Designer: Michael Dubowe
Marketing Manager: Shari Countryman

17 18 19 20 21 10 9 8 7 6 5 4 3 2 1

Contents

Acknowledgments

The support and generous assistance of many people has made the first edition of this book possible. This book found a home with a publisher thanks to Ray Engel believing in its value and connecting me with Kassie Graves, an acquisitions editor at SAGE at the time, who also saw its potential. Kassie's helpfulness in working with me during the first part of the process is much appreciated. The baton was passed to Nathan Davidson, acquisitions editor, who was terrific to work with. He provided great support and excellent feedback. Others at SAGE who have also been extremely helpful are Heidi Dreiling, editorial assistant, Veronica Stapleton Hooper, project editor, Michelle Ponce, copy editor, Shari Countryman, marketing manager, and cover designer Michael Dubowe.

Phillip Belfiore, vice president of academic affairs at Mercyhurst University during much of the time this work was in progress, realized the value of faculty engagement in research and its contribution to the classroom. His support was so important. Brian Ripley first suggested the format used for this book during a conversation a number of years ago. While our work together ended, and I took a different direction, Brian's idea sparked what turned into this book.

Over the past 18 years, I have had the privilege of working with a great many exceptional students. It is because of my work with them that I embarked on writing this book. I have learned much from them during the journey we traveled together. Their enthusiasm and desire to be change agents serves as continuous inspiration. It is my deepest hope that society will make significant progress in addressing the issues discussed in this book, and it is today's students who will be leaders ensuring progress continues to be made.

Emily Shanahan, a social work major, served as my research assistant the past 2 years and was outstanding. I so appreciate Emily's willingness to step in whenever asked to secure background information, proof drafts, and provide thoughtful feedback. Eileen Wilmot also read a case and provided helpful feedback. Thanks to her, as well. While I don't have the names of all reviewers, I want to thank them as a group. I definitely found their feedback helpful and used it to improve the cases.

Katie Clemons and Mandy Fauble each worked with me and wrote cases for this book based on their experience in the field. I am pleased that they took on this opportunity and produced cases that enriched the book and that will serve the readers well. I owe a debt of gratitude to Moe Coleman. Moe and Ray Engel were and are exceptional mentors, and I treasure their friendship and the guidance they have offered along the way.

My two children, Jack and Katie, have brought joy and richness to my life. As is the case with my students, their desire for a more just society gives me hope. There are no words to express the gratitude to my life partner and soul mate, Randy. He was supportive at every step and contributed a great deal to the final product thanks to his willingness to critique the cases, continuously pass along current materials on issues discussed in the book, letting me bounce ideas off of him, and providing moral support.

PUBLISHER'S ACKNOWLEDGMENTS

SAGE wishes to acknowledge the following peer reviewers for their editorial insight and guidance.

Karen Brown, *Western Connecticut State University*

Margaret A. Elbow, *Texas Tech University*

Charles Garvin, *University of Michigan*

Troy D. Harden, *Northeastern Illinois University*

Mavis Braxton-Newby, *California State University East Bay*

Barbara Levy Simon, *Columbia University School of Social Work*

Marcia Spira, *Loyola University Chicago*

Paul H. Stuart, *Florida International University*

Lester H. Wielstein, *California State University, Sacramento*

About the Author

Laura Lewis serves as the chair of the Applied Sociology and Social Work Department at Mercyhurst University in Erie, Pennsylvania. She primarily teaches policy, social welfare analysis, human behavior in the social environment, senior seminar, and contemporary social problems. She helped initiate a mentoring program and teaches the accompanying course. When not serving as chair, Laura served as the field study coordinator and has supervised students in the field throughout her teaching career. In 2010, she was the recipient of the university's Teaching Excellence Award. Much of her research and public scholarship has been in the area of poverty, but she has presented on a variety of other topics such as spirituality, the use of simulations to inspire social change, the use of case studies, and system readiness to address problem gambling. A chapter-length case study she wrote, "The Expansion of Human Services in Allegheny County 1968–1995," is published in *Public Policy Praxis: A Case Approach for Understanding Policy and Analysis,* in Clemons, R., & McBeth, M., 2001, 2009, and 2016 editions (Routledge). In 2016, an article on a research study she conducted, "Problem Gambling: 'Behind the Eight Ball,'" was published in Taylor & Francis Online. In 2009, after authoring a report, *The High Costs of Poverty in Erie County: It Affects Us All,* Laura worked with other leaders to launch Erie Together, a community-driven collective impact movement addressing poverty in Erie County. She continues to serve as the Mercyhurst University partner in strategic planning, oversight, and fund-raising for Erie Together. In 2001, Laura received the Social Worker of the Year for the Northwest Division of the Pennsylvania-NASW, and in 2006, she was chosen to be among Mercy Center for Women's Dynamic Dozen in recognition of her service to women and the community. She has been an active member of numerous nonprofit boards and community committees. When unable to water-ski or spend time on the water, she enjoys trail running, with a few 50Ks under her belt, and hiking.

Introduction

I have been a fan of using case studies since I started teaching 18 years ago, in part because as a student I enjoyed them. My experience, which is consistent with research on case studies, is that students are more invested when teaching methods require them to be engaged in figuring out how to deal with challenging dilemmas. This is exactly what cases do and why the case method is widely used in social work education. If you like hands-on, active learning, being able to relate concepts to your personal and future professional life, provocative examples that make you think, and gaining a deeper understanding of issues that challenges how you think about them, this is the book for you.

Social Workers as Game Changers is unique in that the cases included in the book aim to significantly increase your knowledge base about broad social justice issues (that call for looking at larger systems and policy) while at the same time increasing your capability to fulfill—and sense of efficacy about fulfilling—the important role social workers can and do play in addressing challenging social issues. The cases illustrate the interrelationship between the micro, mezzo, and macro levels and facilitate not just recall of facts but higher-level learning and greater long-term understanding. These cases will allow you to argue from facts; force you to evaluate, analyze, and synthesize; and create more engaged and informed classroom discussions. Experience tells me that you'll even have fun dealing with them.

Each of the 11 case studies is a stand-alone case and varies slightly in style to maximize your interest and learning. Your professor may choose to use some and not others, but you might find you want to read them all. The order of the cases in the book is random and does not signify importance or level of difficulty. In some cases, the social worker is a very prominent character. In other cases, while the social worker is not prominent, as noted above, the issue itself is very relevant to social justice and the field of social work.

Each case is framed around factual background information. That is, each case begins with an engaging fictional (but very realistic and often a composite or real-life scenario) story about exactly the sort of situations and issues social workers will have to confront in their jobs. About halfway through the story, just as you've gotten invested in the characters, you are provided with crucial content about the issue at hand before returning to the story. In one sense, the two parts of the cases could each stand alone. The case that surrounds the factual filling would work without it. The information about these significant social problems could be read just by itself. But I believe you will find that they work better together. There are questions for each case that allow and require you to demonstrate that you understand pertinent information about the topic and also questions that challenge you to think critically about vital issues, weigh the advantages and disadvantages of competing solutions, explore policy alternatives, and grapple with realities such as the unintended consequences of any decision. It is suggested that you review the questions before reading the case so you can keep them in mind and take notes that relate to them.

In sum, the cases are designed to be interesting and educational; to allow or force you to be active participants in your education rather than just passive mugs waiting for the professor to pour from his or her jug of wisdom and knowledge. Yes, your professor will be there to guide you, to explain things, to make sure you see the connections between, for example, the code of ethics, core competencies and the case challenges, dilemmas, and real-world situations—but you'll also have to grapple with them yourself. In the field you will have to deal with complexity and ambiguity. You will have to think critically and will need to operate from well-understood principles. You will need to have up-to-date fact-based approaches and well thought through values. Practicing with cases will help you do that.

Following is a quick introduction to each of the cases.

UNDERSTANDING THE COMPLEXITIES, COSTS, AND BENEFITS SURROUNDING IMMIGRATION POLICY: TOUGH DECISIONS FOR FAMILIES AND POLICY MAKERS

This case introduces you to Santana and Adriana, who are inseparable teenage friends. Santana was born in the United States to undocumented immigrants, and Adrianna, without legal documents, came to the United States with her father at the age of 10. Both of their families face major challenges as a result of their status. This case brings to light the dilemma faced by far too many people who are seeking a better life for themselves and their children. The complexity of the immigration issue is evident in this case. You will read about the history of immigration policy in the United States, the current situation, and the key arguments being made regarding economic and social costs and benefits of competing immigration policies. This case provides you with the knowledge to begin to consider how the United States might go forward in more effectively addressing immigration.

COMMUNITY ORGANIZING CONCEPTS AND PRINCIPLES: REBUILDING HOLYOKE FROM THE GROUND UP

Gina Travor, a community organizer, knows it won't be easy, but she is confident that residents in Holyoke, a troubled low-income city neighborhood in Middleton, can come together to make significant improvements in their neighborhood. Too many people outside of Holyoke see only the negative aspects of this neighborhood, such as high teen pregnancy rates, soaring high school drop-out rates, crime, drugs, dilapidated buildings, and trashed vacant lots. This case explores key concepts and principles of community organizing and focuses on the importance of having a community-driven plan inclusive of residents' voices that are too often unheard. It is up to you to help Gina determine how to best develop the plan.

ACHIEVING RACIAL EQUALITY: EDUCATION, HOUSING, HEALTH, AND JUSTICE . . . A LONG WAY TO GO

The two Norby boys, and their friend James, are captivated by the stories Nana Jo Nickels tells them about the lives of their great-great-great grandparents who were slaves, great-great and great grandparents who were sharecroppers, and her own experiences with discrimination. The Norby boys' mom, Jewell, wanting to believe society has moved beyond blatant racial prejudice, ends up being the victim of ugly comments made about her by her coworkers because of her skin color. The background in the case provides an overview of how some policies and practices have brought about improvements in regard to decreasing discrimination but documents that, as structured, the system today still results in significant inequalities and lack of opportunity for Blacks. Specifically, the racial disparity that still exists in the areas of education, housing, bank lending, health, and criminal justice are discussed. The intersection of race and class is also highlighted. The reader is left with the challenge of determining where we go from here in addressing the racial disparity.

END-OF-LIFE CARE, COSTS, CONCERNS, AND CONFLICT: TOO MUCH OF THE WRONG KIND OF CARE?

Katie, a medical social worker in the intensive care unit, often feels conflicted about choices that doctors or family members make regarding end-of-life interventions that she believes are merely prolonging suffering. However, she doesn't allow her concerns to interfere with effectively working with patients and their family members as they struggle with end-of-life decisions. The background section covers research on medical treatments at the end of life, costs of treatments, public opinion and value conflict regarding end-of-life care, and progress made and key challenges still faced. It also presents recommendations for end-of-life health care that doesn't prolong life at all costs but is instead focused on comfort, dignity, and as much choice as possible. What needs to happen to better ensure that more people will have a "good death"?

MENTAL ILLNESS: COMMUNITY SUPPORTS AND COMMUNITY DILEMMAS

Brent and Regan are members of a crisis intervention team responding to a man named Simon, whose life has been forever changed by his diagnosis of schizophrenia. Simon was a football player who joined the army, got married, and had a son and still lives in the same town where he grew up. While in the army, Simon developed schizophrenia, and it led to the loss of his job, wife, a relationship with his son, and ultimately, his ability to be in touch with reality. Brent and Regan must struggle to make sense of how to help Simon when they are called to see him in a local park. In the background section, you will learn about serious mental illness and how society has attempted to provide both institutional and community-based care to those who are impacted most significantly. When you complete the reading, you will have learned that most adults with serious mental illness recover and live satisfying lives in their communities. You will also better understand the dilemmas we face in helping adults who continue to struggle with their illness and need substantial support while balancing preservation of their civil rights and promoting the dignity and worth of all people.

PERPLEXING CHALLENGES IN CHILD PROTECTIVE SERVICES: LIFE ON THE FRONT LINE

Sean, a child welfare worker, is doing his best to juggle his many cases and the curveballs that typically includes. Two children on his case load must be moved immediately to a new foster home, and two more children are in need of a long-term option. In the latter case, the children have a loving mother, but she is too developmentally delayed to adequately care for them. How will Sean handle these challenges? The background section includes the history of the Children's

Administration, information on the prevalence and consequences of child abuse, the relationship between poverty and abuse or neglect, a summary of the Adverse Childhood Experiences Study, and an overview of federal legislation that informs the current practices of child welfare workers and situations such as those Sean is facing. This information will be of use as you determine how you might address certain challenges.

SOCIETY'S EVOLVING UNDERSTANDING OF CHEMICAL ADDICTION AND THE SUBSEQUENT CHANGES IN POLICY AND TREATMENT APPROACHES: THE STRUGGLE TO STAY CLEAN

Carolyn's childhood was filled with trauma ranging from witnessing her father physically abuse her mother to being molested herself by a relative. Drugs gave her an escape from her pain, or so it seemed in the beginning. Encounters with the law, jail time, and having her children removed from her care provided motivation for Carolyn to get clean. Staying clean, though, was harder than she imagined for both psychological and physical reasons. Both her friend and her social worker have to struggle with how best to help and the roles they should and should not play. The background section provides the scope of the issue of substance use and abuse, an overview of the 40-plus years "war on drugs," the swinging pendulum on our approach to addressing illicit drug use, and the factors informing this approach. With the information in this section in hand you will be better prepared to discuss and evaluate policy choices relative to efforts to address substance abuse effectively.

UNDERSTANDING THE DRAW OF GANGS, CONSEQUENCES FOR NEIGHBORHOODS, AND DETERMINING AN EFFECTIVE RESPONSE: THE NORTH SIDE CREW

Chandrika Greene, a strong student academically and basketball standout, was being recruited by Division I colleges until the evening of January 20. After a grueling practice, she and some friends were walking home when shots were fired, and Chandrika was hit by a bullet intended for someone else. Her friend Silvia was also struck by a bullet that ricocheted off a cement wall. This was not the first shooting of innocent bystanders in this area of the city. In the past 5 months there had been multiple drive-by shootings resulting in the deaths of two known gang members and one nongang member. This case discusses the scope of gang membership and the theoretical explanations for, and research on, why youth join gangs. It asks, what can be done to address the escalating violence?

EMINENT DOMAIN, URBAN RENEWAL, AND NIMBY: IS THERE A WIN-WIN SOLUTION?

The Stevenses had not thought too much about the use of eminent domain to access property just one block from where they lived, as the area had become quite rundown over the years, and the development that had occurred as a result of eminent domain resulted in an economic and cultural boost for the city. But when the city starts planning to redevelop their block and threatens to use eminent domain if necessary, they and their neighbors are none too happy and must figure out how to save their homes. Is this just a case of Not in My Back Yard (NIMBY)? The issue of the use of eminent domain is explored through this case. The background for the case provides an overview of the early use of eminent domain, the relationship between eminent domain and urban renewal, and the current controversy over the use of eminent domain. The information in the case is useful in trying to determine in what circumstances the use of eminent domain is within the scope of its intent and for the greater good.

HOMELESSNESS AND THE HOUSING FIRST DEBATE: WRESTLING WITH THE ISSUES

A public forum at the city council meeting provides an opportunity to debate the future of A Brighter Tomorrow, an ongoing program designed to address the issue of chronic homelessness in Middleton. At the heart of the debate is whether the city should support a *Housing First* approach, aimed at placement of the chronically homeless in stable housing or rely on a *continuum of care* philosophy requiring the homeless to meet certain standards before being granted a publicly funded home. Tight budgets and differing views of fairness lead to a lively forum. The background section provides an overview of the problem of homelessness, the causes of and possible solutions to the problem, explores the paradigm shift in addressing chronic homelessness, and examines the effectiveness of the Housing First approach. Enough dollars aren't being freed up to house all homeless individuals who would take advantage of the shelter offered. How do we determine who should get priority and what services are critical to ensure people don't return to homelessness?

EXAMINING THE ELEMENTARY AND SECONDARY EDUCATION SYSTEM IN THE UNITED STATES AND ONE FAMILY'S DILEMMA: FIGHT OR FLIGHT

Lavonda Jenkins wants her academically gifted young son to have a better future but is not sure if he will receive the preparation necessary at Worthington Elementary, the city school he is currently attending. There are some positive signs of change at Worthington, but will they come soon enough for Julius? Then, by luck of the draw, after not being selected for 2 years, Julius's name is drawn in the annual lottery, and he has the opportunity to attend Oakesdale Charter School. While this is what Lavonda had wanted, changed personal circumstances, a meeting with the principal at Worthington Elementary, and her research leaves Lavonda unsure of the best course of action. The background section in the case discusses school funding and the educational system in the United States. It begs the question, How do we better provide a quality education for all children regardless of socioeconomic status?

INSTRUCTOR OPTION: WRITTEN ANALYSES FOR CASE STUDIES

For all or some chapters, a written analysis could be required of the students. Assigned analyses will help the students process the case in advance of discussing it in class. If this option is used, instructors may choose to revise the student preparation questions that accompany each case, but this is not essential. The preparation/discussion questions at the end of each chapter could also be used for assignments, and as with these case analysis assignments, be used either as group or individual tasks. Even if not used as written assignments, it is recommended that the instructor have the students read the questions prior to reading each case to help them maximize what they get from the case. The instructor can use them and these assignments to help prepare lecture and discussion notes.

The following are suggested instructions to be provided to students for each of the case analyses:

- Your goal is to take a position and then provide evidence, using specific examples from the case, to support your position.

- Attempt to convince the reader that your position is the one that should be taken. You do not need to do outside research to write your analysis—just draw from the case study.
- In writing the analysis, it is not necessary to define the concepts discussed in the case in the paper.
- Make sure not to retell the story.
- Avoid using first person (e.g., "I think," "I feel," "I believe").

For each case analysis:

There is a question specific to each case provided for the instructor that students can be assigned to address in their written analysis. It is suggested that the analysis be an approximately two- to three-page (page length will vary by case), typed, double-spaced essay. The analysis should reflect the standards and expectations of college-level writing.

Chapter 1

Understanding the Complexities, Costs, and Benefits Surrounding Immigration Policy

Tough Decisions for Families and Policy Makers

" If I get caught sneaking out again, my uncle might make good on his threat to send me to Guatemala," Santana whispered to Adrianna.

"Well, we'll just have to be more careful then," replied Adrianna. "I don't see how you can handle your uncle's oppressive rules; you can hardly take a breath without asking for permission."

Santana just laughed. She figured it was pointless to defend her uncle by telling Adrianna that they should not be sneaking out anyway. Mature beyond her 13 years, Santana was extremely grateful to Uncle Felix for taking her and her younger sister, Izzie, into his already crowded home when their mom was detained and then deported. Eight months had passed since that horrible day when she came home from school to find her aunt waiting with the bad news. Santana had no doubt her mom would do everything she could to get back to her daughters. She would first have to figure out a way to somehow piece together enough money to pay a coyote[1] to assist her in crossing the borders from Guatemala to the United States. She did not want to think about how long that might take or even if her mom would get across safely. Though she missed her mom, putting up with Uncle Felix's rules

---

[1] Term used for person who, for a fee, assists in the transport (smuggling) of undocumented immigrants across the U.S. border.

was not that bad, as they really were not terribly unreasonable. Santana knew that his tendency to be a bit overprotective was due to his cultural beliefs and because he cared about her. He was as close to a father as Santana had since her dad had died when she was seven. And Santana was well aware of the promise Uncle Felix made to her father to watch out for his two children.

"Let's get back to studying," was Santana's response to her best friend whom she shared so much with: clothes, secrets, and the loss of a parent to cancer. What they did not share was immigration status. Born in the United States to undocumented immigrants, Santana was a U.S. citizen, while Adrianna came to the United States with her father at the age of 10 after her mom died. Adrianna had two younger siblings who remained in Mexico with her grandparents.

"Okay, okay, I only have an hour until I need to prepare dinner so let's get at it," said Adrianna, who knew she would never have made it this far in school if Santana had not befriended her, helped her with her English, and tutored her in every subject except math, which she excelled in.

Adrianna had arrived at Ridgeway Elementary halfway through the fourth grade year, knowing little English and still in the throes of grief after the painful loss of her mom to brain cancer. Something about the depth of sadness Adrianna exuded that first day she arrived at school caused Santana to gravitate to her, and soon they were inseparable. They balanced each other, Santana being the more responsible and serious of the two while Adrianna was always looking for ways to have fun.

Ten minutes back into studying, Santana's mind started to wander. She had been having nightmares about her mom's potential journey back into the United States. There was no doubt that her mom would either try to come back to her daughters or maybe decide to bring her daughters back to Guatemala. Santana did not know which one scared her more. Her parents had come from an impoverished village where one-room concrete homes with tin roofs and dirt floors were the norm. What kind of future would this hold for her and Izzie? The United States was her home and the only country she had ever lived in. Her English was better than her Spanish, and she was proud to be a U.S. citizen. On the other hand, could her mom safely navigate her way back to the outskirts of Middleton to be with her daughters?

The stories her mom shared with her over the years, and subsequently that she had passed on to Adrianna, kept running through her head. Santana's mother, Marissa, had told Santana that she had not wanted to leave Guatemala and that it had taken Santana's father, Miguel Gomez, their entire first year of marriage to convince her that they had to leave to build a better life for the children they planned to have. He promised her that in time they would return, but at the time, he could not make a living in Guatemala. Miguel was not naïve; he knew life would still be hard at first in the United States, but he also knew he could find work and both provide for his immediate family and send money back home to help his parents.

Thoughts of her father mingled with fears for her mother. Santana knew that her dad was not yet a teenager when he had started spending close to 5 months of most years as a migrant worker in the United States, following the crops from California to Colorado. His work in the fields, alongside his father and two brothers, allowed his family to live comfortably for the remainder of the year. During the years they didn't make the trip to the United States, her dad's family often could not scrape up the money to pay for basic necessities. Over the years, as the number of Border Patrol agents increased, along with other surveillance, the trip became more expensive and more dangerous. One year, shortly before marrying Marissa, while crossing the border from Mexico into the United States, four of the men in the vehicle Miguel rode in died from heat stroke. Their coyote had arranged for them to ride in the back of an old produce truck. It turned out to be an unseasonably hot period, and the combination of poor ventilation, too little water, and no stops to get out for air (as they had been promised) turned the back of the truck into a death trap for some of the 20 men crammed in. The men had been given orders to remain silent whenever the truck stopped. Finally, after one exceptionally long stop, the men knew something was very wrong and could not handle the sauna-like conditions any longer. Their pleas and banging to get out went unheeded for what seemed like hours, and, as some of the men lost consciousness, the fear that they were all doomed intensified. Miguel considered it a miracle that Border Patrol spotted the abandoned vehicle before they all succumbed to the heat. Though disappointed about being sent back home, it seemed like a small price to pay at that point. Despite this brush with death, Miguel knew that he would journey to the United States again. He simply concluded he must travel back and forth much less often, and that moving to the United States permanently was the best option of providing for the family he dreamed of having.

"Santana!" shouted Adrianna.

"What is it, what's wrong?" a startled Santana asked.

"Why don't you tell me? You were staring out the window, and I had to call your name three times before you responded."

Fighting back tears, Santana told Adrianna what was consuming her thoughts, not that Adrianna could not have guessed. "I miss my parents. They were always yelling at us or each other, but that is just how they communicated, and when Dad got sick I saw how much they cared for each other. Uncle Felix and Aunt Margareta do their best, but I need my mom. It is not fair. Did I ever tell you that my parents did try to get papers to enter the United States legally? Mom said it was almost a year before they heard back that they were so far down the waiting list it would be years and maybe decades before they would be considered. My mom said after that news, she and Dad had countless arguments before she finally gave in, agreed to cross the border, and enter the United States without proper documentation. All she insisted on was that he find a job, and then she would follow."

Adrianna had heard bits and pieces of the story before but knew her friend needed to talk. So, she listened as Santana continued on about how her father, Miguel, had traveled to the United States, secured a job in construction with the help of Marissa's older brother, Felix, and then sent money to pay for Marissa to make the trip. Seven months after Miguel landed a job in Texas, Marissa, now eight months pregnant with Santana, followed. At great cost, Miguel had made sure that he hired someone he could trust to ensure safe passage for his pregnant wife.

"I really better finish up these few algebra problems," was Santana's signal that she had said all she wanted for the time being, so they both got back to their homework. Within minutes, Santana's mind had gone to thinking about her best friend's situation and conversations they had not so long ago.

Adrianna's story differed from Santana's in that her father had left his family in Mexico while he worked in construction in the United States. He returned for visits a couple of times a year during the first few years of Adrianna's life. During one of those visits, Adrianna's twin sisters were conceived. After her third birthday, the visits became less frequent. Adrianna had no way of knowing that the infrequency was due to beefed-up security at the border following the September 11, 2001, attacks on the World Trade Center. All she knew was that she missed her father. He came home for a longer than usual stay when she was 8 years old, after her mom was diagnosed with cancer.

Santana had seen Adrianna cry more than a few times as she retold the story of how, when her dad was home in Centro, a village just outside Mexico City, and her mom was still healthy enough to enjoy life, the five of them were always together playing, dancing, and singing. This only lasted a short while. Reflecting back, Adrianna thinks maybe it was 5 to 6 months of happy memories before her dad was gone again, right after her ninth birthday, this time not to return until after Adrianna's mom had died. Adrianna had confided in Santana that sometimes she still felt anger at her dad for leaving them that last time. Now at 13, she knew her dad had left because there was no work in their village, and he wanted to be able to support his family and send money so her grandparents could get her mom the care she needed. But, as a 9-year-old, she had convinced herself that if her dad had stayed, her mom would have gotten better and not died. Despite what logic told her, she still felt a degree of resentment.

Increasingly, in the past few months, Santana had observed Adrianna lash out in anger at her dad, Mr. Torrez, when things were not going her way. Mr. Torrez's response, or more accurately lack of response, is what surprised Santana. She could see the hurt on Mr. Torrez's face, but he let Adrianna get away with, what Santana considered, horribly disrespectful behavior. Santana wondered if he too blamed himself for not being able to save his wife from cancer and maybe felt guilty about leaving two of his three children in Mexico. Santana did not say anything after the first time she witnessed Adrianna yelling at her father, but following the second time, after she knew Adrianna had calmed down, asked, "What the heck was that about?"

"I get my temper from my mom. Oh, I know it's not fair, and that he's doing the best he can, but he wasn't there for me so many nights when I was scared when mom was dying, and he's not there for me too often now. You know, when I'm not with you, I'm often alone here since he takes overtime work whenever it's offered. Why can't I just have a normal family?"

Santana knew well enough that when Adrianna got going like this, it was better to just let her go, which is exactly what she did when this interaction occurred a couple of months ago. Sure enough, Adriana continued, "Yeah, I feel like crap for yelling at my dad, but sometimes I just want to explode. Not only is Mom gone but also my little sisters need me, and while I know I could go back and live with my grandparents, my dad needs me, too. I can't talk to him about missing my sisters because he feels so bad that he couldn't bring us all to the United States with him. I hate that I sometimes resent him for that, too. Of course I want the opportunities I will have here that I wouldn't get back home, but, at the same time, I feel guilty because I don't know if we can ever get my sisters here."

At the time Adrianna shared this, Santana had not known what to say, and thinking about it today she felt just as helpless. Santana knew she could not bring her dad or Adrianna's mom back, but she believed that a country as great as the United States could figure out a better immigration policy. From her perspective, it just did not make sense that a country can stand for justice and freedom but have policies in place that lead to families being torn apart, especially those of people like Mr. Torrez and her mom, who were working hard, paying taxes, and contributing to the economy. Santana knew that both her mom and Mr. Torrez had been praised by their employers for their work ethic, yet they both lived in fear of being deported. For Santana's mom, that fear had become a reality. Why would the U.S. government spend $5 billion a year to find, detain, and deport people like our parents and have policies that end up separating children, who are citizens, from their hardworking parents?

"Earth to Santana, earth to Santana," Adrianna was sarcastically chanting. "Are you done with your algebra?"

"Dang, I just can't focus," responded Santana when she realized her mind had been wandering again.

"Well, I need to go fix dinner for Dad and me. It's my turn, and I want to surprise him with a dish my mom used to make."

Santana was reminded of one of the things she liked about her friend. Adrianna might hold some resentment toward her dad, but, on the other hand, she wanted to make him happy as well. Pulled out of her funk by Adrianna's enthusiasm, Santana responded, "Why don't I help you? I haven't eaten at your place for a while, and it sounds better than what we'll probably have."

"Great," said Adrianna with a smile, "and afterward maybe we can sneak out and go to Javier's party for a while." Santana just chuckled.

BACKGROUND INFORMATION

Stories abound that illustrate pride in the sacrifices and contributions our immigrant ancestors made, which resulted in the United States becoming a prosperous nation. While more experts agree that new immigrants remain essential to ensuring that the United States remains competitive in the 21st century, there is a marked divide in public reaction toward immigrants who are here legally versus those who are here without legal documentation. The focus of this section is on background information that can help inform individuals how to best address the complex and contentious issue of illegal immigration, which is certainly an issue with no easy solutions.

Becoming informed about the issue of illegal immigration is very difficult given the polarized perspectives that we hear from political leaders, which are too often driven by ideology rather than based on empirically sound research. Of course, a review of the research findings can be frustrating as well because the results from different scholars sometimes counter each other. Added to these factors are too many instances where talk show hosts have presented blatantly inaccurate information (Uwimana, 2010). This simply perpetuates myths, feeds into prejudice, and makes political compromise difficult.

This section provides valuable information that needs to be considered if the United States hopes to create a sound immigration policy. Although this is not an in-depth and comprehensive review of all the factors that come into play, it will cover the scope of the issue, past and current legislative attempts to address the issue, and research on the economic costs and benefits associated with undocumented immigrants. Within this discussion, the reader can glean ideas for potential future directions our nation might take as we continue to struggle with how to create a more effective immigration system. Throughout this section the question to continually ask is if, and how, this information might inform future policy.

Demographics

The demographic data should not be overlooked as it provides valuable information to consider in determining policy solutions. According to the Pew Hispanic Center, there were approximately 11.3 million undocumented immigrants living in the United States in 2014. After two decades of continual increasing numbers of undocumented immigrants living in the United States, from 3.5 million in 1990 to 12.2 million in 2007, the number has stabilized (Passel & Cohn, 2015). What did increase significantly from 2010 to 2014 was the number of unaccompanied minors who were apprehended while trying to cross the border. In 2014, over 68,000 children were detained. This increase came not from young Mexicans but youth from other Central American countries and is said to be the result of the spike in gang- and drug-related violence (BBC, 2014). In 2015, the number of children apprehended dropped to 35,000 (Karaim, 2015).

Just as immigrants with proper documentation come from all over the world, the same is true with undocumented immigrants. It is estimated that 62% of unauthorized immigrants are from Mexico, and another 13% are from El Salvador, Guatemala, Honduras, the Philippines, India, Korea, Ecuador, Brazil, and China (Hoefer, Rytina, & Baker, 2011). Approximately 55% to 58% of undocumented immigrants entered the United States unlawfully, and the remaining (40% to 45%) of undocumented immigrants have overstayed their visa (Alden, 2010). Recently, the biggest wave of new immigrants is Asian. The large majority are legal; only 13% to 15% of them are here without legal documents (Semple, 2012).

There is universal agreement that economic opportunity has long been the primary reason why people have chosen to leave their birth countries for a foreign land where they are unlikely to be received with open arms. Families are often faced with the difficult decision of leaving some members behind in hopes of finding employment and being able to meet basic needs. For example, Liana (2012) reports that the majority of Mexicans say that they do not want to leave their homes and only do so because they cannot find jobs that will allow them to take care of their families. They would prefer to stay and work in their home country, but with unemployment high and salaries low, the opportunity simply does not exist.

Of the estimated 11.3 million undocumented immigrants, approximately 8 million of them are in the workforce. This equates to about 5.1% of the total U.S. workforce (Krogstad & Passell, 2015). Often the positions filled by undocumented workers are in low-wage service sector areas (e.g., maids and housekeepers, maintenance), farm labor, and construction.

Recent Trend in Undocumented Hispanic Immigrants ▬

As noted above, there has been no net growth in the number of undocumented Hispanic immigrants entering the United States since 2007, and in fact there has been a decrease. This trend is attributed to a variety of factors. The economic recession experienced in the United States that resulted in fewer jobs being available is thought to have played a key role. Increased and stricter deportation rules and tougher border enforcement are also factors that account for this trend (Semple,

2012). The dangers[2] that future undocumented immigrants face have increased, not only due to growing difficulty in crossing the border because of beefed-up surveillance and the border fence but also due to the heightened risk of the illegal immigrants being kidnapped, murdered, or raped because of the violent drug cartels operating along the border (Walser, McNeill, & Zuckerman, 2011).

One more reason is the fact that the birthrates in Mexico have plummeted in the last 50 years. Today, the growth rate among Mexico's working-age population is 500,000 per year, which is half the rate during the early 1990s when record levels of unauthorized immigrants were crossing the border (Hinojosa-Ojeda, 2010). Regardless of other factors, the decreased population will continue to impact new entrants into the United States from Mexico.

There are factors that could counter the current trend. For example, the political turmoil in other Latin American countries tends to increase the desire to emigrate. A resurgent U.S. economy could also play a role in increasing the desire to emigrate.

Why Not Just Get a Green Card and Enter the United States Legally?

As noted above, it is estimated by various credible sources that between 40% and 45% of undocumented immigrants did not enter the United States illegally; they entered lawfully with a visa and then overstayed that visa. The other 55% to 60% of undocumented immigrants did enter the United States unlawfully (Alden, 2010).

There are various pathways available to become a legal permanent resident (often referred to as a green card holder) of the United States. Family sponsorship is the pathway sought by the majority followed by the specialized work pathway. Under the current system, the majority of individuals who seek legal permanent residence through family sponsorship will have to wait for years, after they have a visa petition filed, before they can start the green card application process. Years of waiting will turn into a decade or even two for many as the United States issues about 226,000 family-sponsored green cards per year. In 2012, about 4.3 million people under family sponsorship were waiting in line for their green card (Bergeron, 2013). Bergeron (2013), an analyst with the Migration Policy Institute, estimates at this rate it will take 19 years to clear the backlog of people in the pipeline, and that is only if no more families are added.

Pulitzer prize-winning journalist Jose Vargas came to the United States from the Philippines at age 12 and has been living here without proper documents for

---

[2] The proportion of border-crossing fatalities to border-crossing apprehensions increased from 2005 to 2011 (Moreno, 2012).

[handwritten in left margin: One visa should last a lifetime, unless Critical Crime is Committed]

over 20 years. He notes that the current quota system is not proportional to each country's population, resulting in approximately the same number of green cards for a country such as Moldova, with a population of 3.5 million, as Mexico, with a population of 122 million (Vargas, 2012).

The employment pathway is not necessarily quick and easy either. One must have an employer in the United States, and then then those with more specialized, crucial jobs skills are given top priority. Temporary work visas are often sought as a first step toward getting permanent legal residency.

[handwritten margin note: Employment Pathway.]

[handwritten margin note: Family sponsored visa cards.]

Impact of Unauthorized Immigrants on the U.S. Economy

Throughout our history, immigrants have played an essential role by creating wealth and prosperity in our nation. But what about today's immigrants who are in our country without proper documentation? We often hear that undocumented immigrants don't pay taxes, are a drag on our economy, and take jobs away from natives. Organizations for stricter immigration laws, such as Federation for American Immigration Reform (FAIR) and Center for Immigration Studies (CIS), provide findings indicating significant net costs resulting from unauthorized immigrants (Grayson, 2012; Martin & Ruark, 2011). Martin and Ruark (2011) reporting for FAIR indicate undocumented workers cost taxpayers $29 billion at the federal level and $84 billion at the state level. At the federal level, taxes paid by undocumented workers offset costs by one third, but their findings indicate that at the state level much less was recouped.

There is also sound research that paints a very different and more complicated picture. The Immigration Policy Center (IPC), a nonpartisan organization, estimated that "households headed by undocumented immigrants paid a combined $11.2 billion in state and local taxes during 2010" (Unauthorized Immigrants Pay, 2011, p. 1). Based on this and other findings, the IPC concludes that the value unauthorized immigrants add to the economy not only as taxpayers but also as consumers and workers should be kept in mind when making policy decisions. Research by Hinojosa-Ojeda & Fitz (2011) found that in California alone, the removal of unauthorized immigrants would result in the loss of $301.6 billion in economic activity. Hinojosa-Ojeda (2010) set forth that on top of the cost of detention and deportation, "mass deportation would reduce U.S. GDP by 1.46 percent, amounting to a cumulative loss of $2.6 trillion in cumulative loss GDP over 10 years, not including the actual cost of deportation" (para. 11). The Perryman Group's 2008 research indicates that, without undocumented workers, the United States would experience in the short run $1.757 trillion in annual lost spending and $651.511 billion in annual lost output. Added to these research findings is experience from states that have passed strict anti-immigration measures indicating that "the impact of the laws can hinder prospects for economic

[handwritten margin note: America would lose Trillions of dollars if unauthorized or undocumented immigrants are deported.]

growth, and the costs of implementing, defending, and enforcing these laws can force taxpayers to pay millions of dollars" (Immigration Policy Center, 2012).

The Congressional Budget Office (CBO), which provides nonpartisan analysis of the federal budget, reported that

> over the past two decades, most efforts to estimate the fiscal impact of immigration in the United States have concluded that, in the aggregate and over the long term, tax revenues of all types generated by immigrants—both legal and unauthorized—exceed the cost of the services they use. Generally, such estimates include revenues and spending at the federal, state and local level. (2007, p. 1)

On the other hand, the 2007 CBO report also indicated that at the state and local level taxes paid do not totally offset the cost of services undocumented immigrants receive. The CBO analysis refers to that impact as modest; their analysis indicates that, in most cases, state and local spending was less than 5% of total spending in the three major areas where costs are incurred. These areas include education (all children regardless of legal status are entitled by federal law to a free education), emergency medical care (also mandated by law), and law enforcement. Undocumented immigrants are ineligible for the majority of other social welfare programs available to U.S. citizens.

Although the costs in the three areas may be a small percentage in terms of overall expenditures, the actual dollars required are not insignificant. California, with the largest population of undocumented immigrants, faces the largest burden in terms of dollars spent on services. It is not the only state where the costs of educating the children of undocumented immigrants puts a significant strain on already extremely tight state and local budgets. Nadadur (2009), pointing out the burden of the fiscal costs borne by states and local governments, raises the question of the allocation of resources between federal and state governments. Among others, Standard & Poor's[3] has suggested that the federal government should play a role (e.g., using undocumented workers' contributions to social security) to offset the disproportionate cost burden states experience due to undocumented immigrants (McNatt & Benassi, 2006).

Two other debated issues regarding the impact that undocumented workers have on the U.S. economy is to what degree they take jobs that U.S. citizens would otherwise fill and whether their presence in the labor force depresses wages. There are some who argue that illegal immigration reduces employment opportunities for U.S. citizens along with depressing wages (Briggs, 2010). On the other hand, Pia Orrenius, the senior economist for the Federal Reserve Bank of Dallas, states that the major question at stake among economists is why undocumented immigrants

---

[3] Standard & Poor's is a well-known financial services company that provides analysis on credit ratings, stocks, and bonds and provides investors with financial information.

actually have such a small impact on the labor market (Fastenberg, 2011). Camatora and Zeigler (2009), discussing their analysis of U.S. Census Bureau American Community Survey data, set forth that there are many factors that impact employment and wages and that not every job an immigrant takes is a job lost to a native. At the same time, they say that if immigration policy results in a dramatic increase in workers in certain occupations, there will be an impact on employment opportunities and wages of natives.

Legislative Overview

Immigration policy, which the federal government has primary authority over, has gone through periods of welcoming immigrants and eras when we want to push them out and put strict limits on who is legally allowed into the United States. For the first 100 years after declaring independence, immigration was encouraged. In 1875, the first exclusionary legislation was passed targeting criminals, prostitutes, and Chinese contract laborers. The 1882 Chinese Exclusion Act went a step further and barred all Chinese workers. "Lunatics" were also barred under other legislation passed that same year (Ewing, 2012).

The Immigration Act of 1924 put in place a national quota system limiting the number of those who could emigrate from certain countries. It also extended who was barred to include all Asians (Ewing, 2012). The quota system, which sought to keep out those nationalities deemed undesirable, was in place until the passage of the 1965 Immigration and Naturalization Act. Numerical limits were not applied to immigrants from Latin America until 1965. In fact, Mexican farm laborers were in demand following the entrance of the United States into World War II. The severe shortage of farm laborers led to the birth of the *bracero program,* which, between 1942 and 1964, brought between 4 million and 5 million Mexicans into the United States to work in the fields. They were issued temporary visas (Rural Migration News, 2006). The program was eliminated when it became clear the demand for farm workers from outside the United States had diminished, although it does still exist. For example, state agricultural officials in Alabama noted that a labor shortage led to crops rotting in fields after their 2011 crackdown on undocumented workers (Reeves, 2012).

As noted above, the 1965 Immigration and Naturalization Act (Hart-Cellar Act) put an end to the national origin quota system that was very discriminatory and had been in place for over 4 decades. It was replaced with a system that, in large part, is still in place today. This system gives preference to those who either possess specific skill sets or have family members who are citizens or residents of the United States. Numerical restrictions remain but with different criteria (U.S. Immigration Legislation, n.d.). One outcome of the 1965 legislation has been large demographic changes in America (Ludden, 2006).

Two decades later, the Immigration Reform and Control Act (IRCA) of 1986 was passed in hopes of curtailing illegal immigration. This two-pronged approach included sanctions against employers who knowingly hired or retained undocumented immigrants, and it increased Border Patrol. At the same time, it granted "amnesty" for undocumented immigrants in certain types of seasonal jobs and those who could verify they had entered the United States prior to 1982 and remained here consistently. Approximately 2.7 million individuals became lawful residents of the United States as a result of IRCA. Research as to the impact of IRCA on dissuading illegal immigration suggests that the amnesty program under IRCA did not appear to either encourage or discourage illegal immigration in the long run (Orrenius & Zavodny, 2003).

Four years after IRCA was passed, the Immigration Act of 1990 did something IRCA had not—it raised the annual caps on the number of immigrants who would be allowed into the states. Some of the other federal legislation passed in the 1990s did the following: increased Border Patrol, instituted a 3- and 10-year reentry ban of undocumented immigrants who reside in the United States, and barred undocumented immigrants, and legal ones, for 5 years from receiving means-tested[4] welfare services.

Immigration remained a hot button issue, and a few years after the turn of the century, President George W. Bush called for an overhaul of immigration policy:

As a nation that values immigrants and depends on immigrants, we should have immigration laws that work and make us proud. Yet today we do not. Instead we see many employers turning to the illegal labor market. We see millions of hard-working men and women condemned to fear and insecurity in a massive undocumented economy. (Bush Calls for Overhaul, 2004, para. 7)

President Bush proposed a temporary work program allowing undocumented workers to stay in the states, or come to the United States, if an employer confirmed they had a job. His plan was met with a great deal of resistance and went nowhere.

What did pass during the Bush era was the 2006 Secure Fence Act, which authorized the building of a fence approximately 700 miles wide along the U.S.-Mexico border, as well as more checkpoints and technological surveillance equipment. Much controversy has continued to surround the wisdom of building the border fence outlined in the 2006 act, as well as whether the fence that has been built is adequate. Those in favor of the Secure Fence Act claimed that, while it was only one part of the solution, it was a very necessary step in securing the border, as it

---

[4] Means-tested programs are those in which one's income falls below a certain level in order to be eligible to receive benefits, for example, food stamps, cash assistance, child care subsidy, and Medicaid.

will serve to impede those who want to cross the border illegally. Opponents of the act pointed out that on top of the literally billions of dollars in costs to build the fence, which would serve to shift those crossing to more dangerous routes into the United States, there were environmental and cultural costs. In fact, environmental regulations were waived to build the fence.

In 2011, the Department of Homeland Security reported completion of about 99% of the fence, built to meet the requirements of the amended version of the 2006 Fence Act. The amended version allowed for border security to determine the type of fencing needed, resulting in only 36.3 miles of double-layer fencing called for in the original act and only 4.3 miles of double-layer fencing built during the Obama era. Critics say that President Obama has not lived up to taking the necessary step of building a 700-mile double fence and thus has not taken an important step to secure our borders (DeMint, 2011). Nor do some critics believe the Obama administration is spending enough on border security, citing that the $573 million dollars spent in 2011 is significantly less than that spent during President Bush's last year in office (Mora, 2011). While whether or not Obama has taken the necessary steps is debated, the fact that the Obama administration has fared no better than the previous administration about comprehensive reform is not up for debate. That does not mean no efforts have been made.

President Obama supports a pathway to citizenship for undocumented workers with stipulations, including that they pay a penalty for entering the country illegally. While not comprehensive reform, he supported the Development, Relief, and Education for Alien Minors Act (Dream Act), which would have provided certain immigrant students who grew up in the United States the opportunity to apply for temporary legal status and to become eligible for citizenship if they went to college or served in the military. Due to Republican opposition, this legislation failed to gain enough votes to pass in 2011. This led to President Obama using his executive powers to make a policy change that gives young undocumented immigrants the right to apply for 2-year work permits that can be renewed indefinitely if they can verify that they entered the United States before the age of 16; lived in the United States for a least 5 years; do not have a criminal record; are under the age of 31; and are in school, graduated high school, or are veterans in good standing. It is believed that approximately 800,000 undocumented immigrants meet these criteria (Preston & Cushman, 2012).

The failure of Congress to act on immigration reform led President Obama to again, in November 2014, use executive power to put in place an order that he says will help people "come out of the shadows." At the same time, the order includes increasing border security to reduce the chances of unauthorized individuals crossing the border. Stating he is not granting a path to citizenship, as only Congress has the authority to do that, the order eliminates the risk of deportation for undocumented immigrant parents of U.S. citizens or legal permanent residents who have been in the United States for more than 5 years and can pass a criminal background check.

The enforcement side of President Obama can also be seen by the Immigration and Customs Enforcement (ICE) greatly increasing its focus on investigating employers suspected of hiring undocumented immigrants. "Since January 2009, the Obama administration has audited at least 7,533 employers suspected of hiring illegal labor and imposed about $100 million in administrative and criminal fines" (Jordon, 2012, p. 1). Another focus has been on preventing overstays. For example, in 2009 nearly 2 million out of 7.7 million visa applicants were refused, most because the consular officer suspected they would overstay their visa (Alden, 2010). Since President Obama took office in 2009, there has also been a significant number of undocumented immigrants who have been deported. The emphasis has been on those with criminal records. In 2011, approximately 400,000 undocumented immigrants were deported, half of whom had felony or misdemeanor convictions (Vargas, 2012). During the first 6 months of 2012, ICE reports that they have deported 45,000 individuals who are parents of U.S. citizen children (Caldwell & Medina, 2012). Using federal statistics, a Center for American Progress report estimated that the cost of mass deportation over 5 years would be anywhere from $206 billion to $230 billion (Fitz, Martinez, & Wijewardena, 2010).

The detainment of undocumented immigrants has increased significantly at the same time as the number of undocumented immigrants in the United States has stabilized. In 2014, 425,000 individuals were detained, including many women and children. They are mainly housed at county jails and private prisons. While some argue detainment is necessary and justified, there is much controversy over the need for this type of detainment and the conditions many of those detained are subjected too. Advocates report lack of medical care, lack of legal counsel, being denied access to contact with family, harsh living conditions marked by poor quality food (e.g., infested with maggots), and incidents of child sexual abuse (Karaim, 2015).

Failure at the federal level to pass comprehensive immigration legislation led to many states taking action. In 2010, Arizona passed a very restrictive immigration law and five other states have since passed similar bills. In June of 2012, the U.S. Supreme Court delivered a split decision on the Arizona legislation; it upheld the provision that requires that police check the immigration status of anyone they stop or arrest if they determine there is "reasonable suspicion" that those in the car do not have legal papers. On the other hand, the Court did not uphold provisions of the law that were determined to interfere with the federal government's role in setting policy. One measure struck down would have allowed the state to charge undocumented immigrants with criminal penalties for such things as trying to secure employment (Liptak, 2012).

Without a national policy, laws will continue to vary greatly between states when it comes to barriers to obtaining higher education for undocumented individuals. Still, more and more states are passing what are called "tuition equity" laws. As of 2016, 21 states allowed undocumented individuals seeking to attend college to pay in-state tuition rates. This is a difference of thousands of dollars and often makes the difference in whether many can afford higher education. Six states go further and offer state financial college aid to some undocumented individuals. Counter to these states are examples such as Georgia, which does not allow undocumented individuals to enroll at its top five campuses and at the other campuses charges them higher out-of-state tuition regardless of how long they have lived in the state (Gordon, 2016).

Public Opinion

Considering public opinion does not necessarily indicate what the best solution is, but it does provide some insight into an important factor that influences public policy. In the recent past, we have seen a softening of views about immigrants in general and undocumented immigrants specifically. A June 2012 Gallup Poll found that 66% of Americans believe that immigration is a good thing for the United States, and for the first time in 40 years, more Americans (42%) were in favor of keeping levels the same rather than in decreasing them (35%) (Jones, 2012, p. 1).

As indicated previously, the public's, as well as policy makers', perceptions are of course not always based on empirical evidence. Despite a significant increase in the number of Border Patrol agents from 1990 to 2010 (from less than 3,000 to more than 20,700), more border fence, and surveillance systems, a 2011 Rasmussen public opinion poll found that two thirds of Americans did not think the border is more secure, and some thought it was less secure than it had been 5 years before (Alden & Roberts, 2011, p. 1).

Next Steps?

Although the federal government has failed at passing comprehensive legislation, there have been continuous efforts to address illegal immigration. Where we go in the future is still up in the air. Following the 2012 election there was hope on both sides of the aisle that a comprehensive bill would pass, but it did not happen, leading President Obama to put in place an executive order. The drop in the number of those entering the country illegally, and a decrease of 58% from 2006 to 2010 in the number of arrests (despite beefed-up security) of people trying to cross the U.S.-Mexico border, suggest that at least on one measure the problem is not as significant as it once was (Romo, 2011). Shannon O'Neil (2012), from the Council of Foreign Relations, notes that the new trend in far fewer people coming illegally to the United States changes the nature of the issue, which has not yet been discussed in political debates. With this issue, as with others, there is a need for informed citizens to state their opinion in order to better inform those in office, so that they can represent the public's views and use a fact-based approach to policy.

TOUGH DECISIONS

The girls had dinner almost prepared when they heard Mr. Torrez at the door. "Hola, Papa," shouted Adrianna from the kitchen. "Hi, Mr. Torrez," Santana said as she went into the hallway to greet him. When she saw him she could not contain her laughter. The laughter brought Adrianna running and left Mr. Torrez looking puzzled. "I'm sorry," Santana blurted out, trying to control her giggles. "Papa, what happened?" Adrianna exclaimed. "It looks like they had you working in a grime pit today." Mr. Torrez took a few more steps so he could look at himself in the hall mirror, and a big grin crossed his face. "Boy, I hardly recognize myself," he chuckled, as he noticed his hair was caked with mud, and splotches of grimy mud were splattered on his face and arms.

"Just a little dirty work, for a little extra pay," Mr. Torrez responded, after he quit staring at the mirror. The smile left Adrianna's face. She knew her father sometimes volunteered for work that was dangerous if he could earn extra and then blew it off like it was nothing. Rather than confront him before dinner, and possibly start an argument, Adrianna decided she would bring it up later—letting it drop was not an option she considered. She left it at "Papa, you have time for a quick shower to get at least one layer of grime off before dinner."

The food was delicious. Mr. Torrez got a little choked up expressing his gratitude to both girls for the special meal and telling Adrianna her cooking skills definitely matched those of her mom. "Papa, compared to your cooking, anything tastes good," was her only verbal response, but her beaming face gave away how much it meant to hear that from her dad.

They had all helped themselves to seconds when out of the blue Mr. Torrez calmly stated, "By next month, I will have saved enough money for the twins to be safely escorted to the United States to live with us." Adrianna felt such a rush of emotions, she was not sure whether to hug her father, cry, or yell at him for keeping his plan from her. "Papa, why didn't you tell me you were saving money, and that's why you were working all those long hours, and sometimes taking on jobs that could have gotten you injured or worse?" was what came out. "I thought you were sending every dollar we could spare back home because Granddad needed more medical care."

"The medical bills did take a big chunk of my earnings, Adrianna. That's why it took so long to save enough to pay for the twins' passage. I swore to myself I was going to make good on the promise I made to your mother that we would either all return to Mexico to live, or I would bring the twins here. It has taken almost

4 years, but I can make it happen." Santana felt a bit awkward and thought it would be better to leave Adrianna and her dad alone to talk, so she excused herself and went to the kitchen to start to clean up. While she was happy for the possibility of the Torrez family being together, she was also frightened for them, and the fears for her mom she had been holding at bay were suddenly greatly intensified. It had been dangerous crossing the border back when her dad was young, and the danger had increased exponentially. She had read about too many instances of people being robbed, sexually assaulted, or abandoned by their coyote and left to die of dehydration. To believe there was such a thing as "safe escort" for undocumented immigrants who were attempting to sneak across the border was ridiculous.[5]

In addition to physical safety, the other risk, of course, was that with more border security, the chance of getting caught and being detained at the border increased. If that were to happen, what would Mr. Torrez do? If he made it back into the United States without incident, but authorities discovered he had left the United States and returned with his daughters, who also lacked appropriate papers, he and the girls could be in jeopardy of deportation.

Even if all went well with the crossing, and they stayed under the radar of authorities, life would not necessarily be easy for them in the United States. What if the twins felt greater resentment toward Mr. Torrez than Adrianna did? They had much more of a bond with their grandparents than with Mr. Torrez. She knew that young children often perceived a parent's absence as choosing not to be with them versus sacrificing for them. They barely knew their father, and Adrianna had been gone for over half of their lives. They might all adapt quickly, but based on the difficult experiences of some families who had been separated for years, Santana knew there were certainly no guarantees.

Adrianna burst into the kitchen clearly excited about the news, and Santana was not about to dampen her spirits. She knew in the next day or so, after Adrianna really started to think about all that was involved, the excitement would diminish as concerns about the risks involved were considered. And, she knew then Adriana would seek her out and want to discuss all the pros and cons of bringing her siblings to the United States. Then, regardless of what Adriana concluded was the best course of action, she would want input on figuring out how to talk to her dad about some of the realities that he was in denial about. Santana sure did not have the answers, but, as always, she would be there for her friend.

---

[5] The border fence and increased surveillance has resulted in crossings in more remote and treacherous areas under a scorching sun and brutally high temperatures. Samaritan groups leave water jugs along some routes, and this has helped prevent deaths, but still too often those crossing do not have adequate amounts of water. One Samaritan group, No More Deaths, estimated that they had found at least 214 human remains of children and adults in the desert in southern Arizona alone in the first 8 months of 2010 (Cohen, 2010). The Border Patrol reported finding 368 bodies of suspected undocumented immigrants who had died trying to cross the border in 2011 (Moreno, 2012).

QUESTIONS FOR DISCUSSION

1. Present some of the key statistics surrounding the issue of undocumented immigrants in the United States, and discuss the value of these statistics in determining effective policy.

2. Respond to the following: Why don't "they" just get a green card and enter the country legally?

3. Discuss the reasons that we have historically gone through eras where we welcome immigrants to the United States and eras when we push them out.

4. Discuss what research indicates regarding the economic costs and benefits associated with undocumented immigrants.

5. Discuss the social costs to families and communities of treating undocumented workers as criminals.

6. Discuss key reasons that the Dream Act did not pass, but yet we have seen increased funding for approaches such as more Border Patrol, surveillance equipment, and the fence.

7. Discuss the two executive orders President Obama has issued relating to undocumented immigrants. Are these sufficient, or is more needed?

8. Critique the effectiveness of federal and state legislation, in the last 15 years, in addressing "illegal" immigration. If we are to create a more effective immigration system, what key features must it include? Draw from the case to provide policy suggestions.

9. What do Adrianna and Mr. Torrez need to consider in making a decision on whether or not to bring her siblings (his other children) to the United States?

CASE ANALYSIS WRITING ASSIGNMENT

Option A

1. Read the assigned case study thoroughly prior to class in order to be fully prepared to join in the discussion.

2. Write an analysis in which you set forth four recommendations that should be part of a comprehensive immigration policy. Use content from the case study, as well as social work values and ethics, to provide support for your recommendations. You may set forth a recommendation that is not directly touched on in the case, but that is not the expectation.

3. The analysis should be an approximately two-and-a-half- to three-page, typed, double-spaced essay. Your essay should reflect the standards and expectations of college-level writing: spelling, grammar, and appropriate use of paragraphs all matter. If you quote directly from the case study, use quotation marks, and at the end of the quote, indicate the page number the quote appeared on. For example, "There is a marked divide in public reaction toward immigrants who are here legally versus those who are here without legal documentation" (Lewis, 2015, p. 8).

4. Your case analysis is due _____ and worth a maximum of _____ points.

Option B

Substitute the following for Option A above: *Tough Decisions* is a narrative about immigration. We come to our understanding of social problems based on the narrative that best resonates with us, that is, the one we believe presents the most convincing evidence or fits with our idea of what is fair and just.

Regardless of your personal position—in your two- to two-and-a-half-page analysis you are to *set forth and defend one* of the following summaries about the author of *Tough Decisions:*

A. The author is largely neutral on the issue of immigration and presents a balanced background section and story line.

B. The author constructs a narrative that suggests the United States should back off its current immigration policies (other than the executive orders) and allow for more open borders.

C. The author constructs a narrative that suggests U.S. immigration policy needs to do a better job of securing borders and reducing the number of undocumented workers and children in the United States as they are a drain on our economy.

You can draw from the story about Santana and Adrianna for some evidence, but for the most part, your evidence needs to draw *heavily from the background information in the middle section of the case.*

*Note—Option B calls for a shorter essay than Option A

INTERNET SOURCES

Immigration Policy Center (IPC) (www.immigrationpolicy.org)

Center for American Progress (https://www.americanprogress.org/issues/immigration/view)

Department of Homeland Security Office of Immigration Statistics (www.dhs .gov/xlibrary/assets/statistics/publications/ois_ill_pe_2010.pdf)

Heritage Foundation (www.heritage.org)

National Immigration Law Center (www.nilc.org)

Urban Institute (www.urban.org)

Vargas, Jose: TED Talk (http://tedxtalks.ted.com/video/Jose-Vargas-at-TEDx MidAtlantic)

REFERENCES

Alden, E. (2010, May 25). *Visa overstay tracking: Progress, prospects and pitfalls. Council on Foreign Relations.* Prepared testimony for the House Committee on Homeland Security. Retrieved from http://www.cfr.org/immigration/visa-overstay-tracking—progress-pitfalls/p21734

Alden, E., & Roberts, B. (2011, August). Are U.S. borders secure? *Foreign Affairs.* Retrieved from http:// www.foreignaffairs.com/articles/67901/edward-alden-and-bryan-roberts/are-us-borders-secure#

BBC. (2014, September 30). Why are so many children trying to cross the border? *BBC.* Retrieved from http://www.bbc.com/news/world-us-canada-28203923

Bergeron, C. (2013, March). Going to the back of the line: A primer on lines, visa categories and wait times. *Migration Policy Institute.* Retrieved from http://www.migrationpolicy.org/research/ going-back-line-primer-lines-visa-categories-and-wait-times

Briggs, V. (2010, April). Illegal immigration and immigration reform: Protecting the employment rights of the American labor force (native-born and foreign-born) who are eligible to be employed. *Center for Immigration Studies.* Retrieved from http://www.cis.org/employment-rights

Bush calls for overhaul of U.S. immigration system. (2004, January 7). *FoxNews.* Retrieved from http://www.foxnews.com/story/0,2933,107644,00.html

Caldwell, B., & Medina, J. (2012, November 27). Family forced to abandon the US in order to be together. *New America Media.* Retrieved from http://newamericamedia.org/2012/11/family-forced-to-abandon-the-us-in-order-to-be-together.php

Camatora, S., & Zeigler, K. (2009, August). Jobs Americans won't do? A detailed look at immigrant employment by occupation. *Center for Immigration Studies.* Retrieved from http://www.cis.org/ illegalImmigration-employment

Cohen, A. (2010, September 8). Why a ruling on leaving water in a desert is troubling. *Time Magazine.* Retrieved from http://www.time.com/time/nation/article/0,8599,2016513,00.html

Congressional Budget Office. (2007, December). *The impact of unauthorized immigrants on the budget of state and local governments.* Retrieved from http://www.cbo.gov/sites/default/files/ cbofiles/ftpdocs/87xx/doc8711/12–6-immigration.pdf

DeMint, J. (2011, May 10). Speeches and summits won't secure the border. *The Corner—National Review Online.* Retrieved from http://www.nationalreview.com/corner/266899/ speeches-and-summits-wont-secure-border-jim-demint

Ewing, W. (2012, June). Opportunity and exclusion: A brief history of U.S. immigration policy. *Immigration Policy Center: American Immigration Council.* Retrieved from https://www

.americanimmigrationcouncil.org/research/opportunity-and-exclusion-brief-history-us-immigration-policy

Fastenberg, D. (2011, June 6). Are illegal immigrants really taking jobs away from American workers? *Careers Articles.* Retrieved from http://jobs.aol.com/articles/2011/06/06/could-hiring-immigrants-actually-help-the-american-worker

Fitz, M., Martinez, G., & Wijewardena, M. (2010). The costs of mass deportation: Impractical, expensive, ineffective. *The Center for American Progress.* Retrieved from http://www.americanprogress.org/wp-ontent/uploads/issues/2010/03/pdf/cost_of_deportation.pdf

Gordon, L. (2016). Some states bypass Congress, create their own versions of the DREAM Act. *PBS Newshour.* Retrieved from http://www.pbs.org/newshour/rundown/some-states-bypass-congress-create-their-own-versions-of-the-dream-act

Grayson, G. (2012, June 24). Immigration order will hurt unemployed Americans. *Center for Immigration Studies.* Retrieved from http://cis.org/OpedsandArticles/George-Grayson-DREAMAct-%20mmigration-Hurts-Workers

Hinojosa-Ojeda, R. (2010). Raising the floor for American workers: The economic benefits of comprehensive immigration reform. *The Center for American Progress.* Retrieved from http://www.americanprogress.org/issues/2010/01/raising_the_floor.html

Hinojosa-Ojeda, R., & Fitz, M. (2011). Revitalizing the golden state: What legalization over deportations could mean to California and Los Angeles County. *The Center for American Progress.* Retrieved from http://www.dhs.gov/xlibrary/assets/statistics/publications/ois_ill_pe_2010.pdf

Hoefer, M., Rytina, N., & Baker, B. (2011). Estimates of unauthorized immigrant population residing in the United States: January 2010. *Department of Homeland Security Office of Immigration Statistics.* Retrieved from www.dhs.gov/xlibrary/assets/statistics/publications/ois_ill_pe_2010.pdf

Immigration Policy Center: American Immigration Center. (2012). *Bad for business: How anti-immigration legislation drains budgets and damages: Fact Sheet.* Retrieved from https://www.americanimmigrationcouncil.org/topics/state-and-local

Jones, J. (2012, June 16). Americans more positive about immigration. *Gallop Poll.* Retrieved from http://www.gallup.com/poll/155210/americans-positive-immigration.aspx

Jordon, M. (2012, May 2). Fresh raids target illegal hiring. *Free Republic.* Retrieved from http://www.freerepublic.com/focus/f-news/2879220/posts

Karaim, R. (2015, October 23). Immigrant detention. *CQ Researcher, 25,* 889–912. Retrieved from http://library.cqpress.com/cqresearcher/document.php?id=cqresrre2015102300

Krogstad, J., & Passel, J. (2015, November 19). 5 facts about illegal immigration in the U.S. *The Pew Research Center.* Retrieved from http://www.pewresearch.org/fact-tank/2015/11/19/5-facts-about-illegal-immigration-in-the-us

Liana, S. (2012). Home again in Mexico: Illegal immigration hits net zero. *Christian Science Monitor.* Retrieved from http://www.csmonitor.com/World/Americas/2012/0408/Home-again-in-Mexico-Illegal-immigration-hits-net-zero

Liptak, A. (2012, June 25). Blocking parts of Arizona law, justices allow its centerpiece. *New York Times.* Retrieved from http://www.nytimes.com/2012/06/26/us/supreme-court-rejects-part-of-arizona-immigration-law.html

Ludden, J. (2006). 1965 immigration law changed face of America. *National Public Radio.* Retrieved from http://www.npr.org/templates/story/story.php?storyId=5391395

Martin, J., & Ruark, E. (2011, February). The fiscal burden of immigration on U.S. taxpayers. *The Federation of American Immigration Reform.* Retrieved from http://www.fairus.org/site/DocServer/USCostStudy_2010.pdf?docID=4921

McNatt, R., & Benassi, F. (2006, April 7). *Econ 101 on illegal immigrants.* Retrieved from http://www.bloomberg.com/news/articles/2006-04-06/econ-101-on-illegal-immigrantsbusinessweek-business-news-stock-market-and-financial-advice

Mora, E. (2011). Obama has halved spending on border fencing, infrastructure, technology: Leaving 1,300 miles of Mexico border unfenced. *CNS News.* Retrieved from http://cnsnews.com/news/article/obama-has-halved-spending-border-fencing-infrastructure-technology-leaving-1300-miles

Moreno, C. (2012, August 18). Border crossing deaths more common as illegal immigration declines. *Huffington Post.* Retrieved from http://www.huffingtonpost.com/2012/08/17/border-crossing-deaths-illegal-immigration_n_1783912.html

Nadadur, R. (2009). Illegal immigration: A positive economic contribution to the United States. *Journal of Ethnic and Migration Studies, 35(6).* Retrieved from http://www.tandfonline.com/doi/abs/10.1080/13691830902957775

O'Neil, S. (2012, February 16). Illegal immigration and the 2012 campaign. *CNN World.* Retrieved from http://globalpublicsquare.blogs.cnn.com/2012/02/16/illegal-immigration-and-the-2012-campaign

Orrenius, P., & Zavodny, M. (2003, August). Do amnesty programs reduce undocumented immigration? Evidence from IRCA. *Demography.* Retrieved from http://ecademy.agnesscott.edu/~mzavodny/documents/Demography_amnesty.pdf

Passel, J., & Cohn, D. (2015). Unauthorized immigrant population stable for half a decade. *Pew Research Organization.* Retrieved from http://www.pewresearch.org/fact-tank/2015/07/22/unauthorized-immigrant-population-stable-for-half-a-decade

The Perryman Group. (2008). *Impact of the undocumented workforce.* Retrieved from http://americansforimmigrationreform.com/files/Impact_of_the_Undocumented_Workforce.pdf#page=69

Preston, J., & John Cushman, Jr. (2012, June 15). U.S. to stop deporting some immigrants. *New York Times.* Retrieved from http://www.nytimes.com/2012/06/16/us/us-to-stop-deporting-some-illegal-immigrants.html?emc=eta1

Reeves, J. (2012). Alabama farmers cut back crops, citing crackdown. *USA Today.* Retrieved from http://www.usatoday.com/USCP/PNI/Nation/World/2012-05-14-BCUSAlabama-Immigration-LawFarmers1st-LdWritethru_ST_U.htm

Romo, R. (2011, May 11). Border arrests of undocumented immigrants down 58% in 5 years. *CNN.* Retrieved from http://articles.cnn.com/2011-05-11/us/immigration.arrests.decline_1_border-arrests-illegal-immigration-arrests-of-undocumented-immigrants?_s=PM:US

Rural Migration News. (2006, April). *Braceros: History, compensation.* Retrieved from http://migration.ucdavis.edu/rmn/more.php?id=1112_0_4_0

Semple, K. (2012, June 18). In a shift, biggest wave of migrants is now Asian. *New York Times.* Retrieved from http://www.nytimes.com/2012/06/19/us/asians-surpass-hispanics-as-biggest-immigrant-wave.html?_r=0

Unauthorized Immigrants Pay Taxes, Too. (2011, April 18). *Immigration Policy.* Retrieved from http://www.immigrationpolicy.org/just-facts/unauthorized-immigrants-pay-taxes-too

U.S. Immigration Legislation Online. (n.d.). *1965 Immigration and Nationality Act (Hart-Cellar Act).* Retrieved from http://library.uwb.edu/guides/usimmigration/1965_immigration_and_nationality_act.html

Uwimana, S. (2010, March 10). O'Reilly, Dobbs wrong that undocumented immigrants don't pay taxes. *Research Media Matters for America.* Retrieved from http://mediamatters.org/research/2010/03/10/oreilly-dobbs-wrong-that-undocumented-immigrant/161434

Vargas, J. (2012, June 25). Shadow Americans. *Time Magazine.*

Walser, R., McNeill, J., & Zuckerman, J. (2011). The human tragedy of illegal immigration: Greater efforts needed to combat smuggling and violence. *Heritage Foundation.* Retrieved from http://www.heritage.org/research/reports/2011/06/the-human-tragedy-of-illegal-immigration-greater-efforts-needed-to-combat-smuggling-and-violence

Chapter 2

Community Organizing Concepts and Principles

Rebuilding Holyoke From the Ground Up

Gina Travor was beaming when she hung up the phone. "Isaac, you're not going to believe it," she hollered to her roommate, who was just headed to bed after working a double shift.

"The president of the Rosebaum Apartment Tenant's Council offered me a job—a real job in my field. I've been hired as the primary consultant and director of the newly established 'Rejuvenate Holyoke' community organization."

Before he could stop himself, Isaac responded, "Holyoke? Seriously, Gina, why would you want to return to one of the worst neighborhoods in the city?" As soon as the words were out, he regretted it.

"Isaac, have you ever considered thinking before you speak so you don't end up coming across like such a jerk? A simple 'Congratulations, I'm excited for you,' would have been a nice response."

"Ah Gina, I didn't mean it like it came out. It's not that you won't be great for the position, and I know you were really hoping to get it, but well, I am concerned about the toll it might take on you."

Gina wanted to be angry with Isaac, but even as she was expressing her excitement to him, even before he spouted off, she could feel a slight sense of dread creeping in as she contemplated the assignment she had just accepted. Of course, she didn't need Isaac's instant negativity, but she knew his concern was valid. Her exuberance was short lived, and she really couldn't blame Isaac for killing it. He was still trying to apologize and wanted to talk more, but she decided to wait until he got some sleep to share with him the question she was already asking herself: *What did I just agree to do?*

GINA AND THE SCHOOL OF HARD KNOCKS

[Handwritten margin notes: Analyis of Community. Civil unrest, Drug deals, Schools need repair, abandoned buildings, unkept landscape, & garbage. Building Condemed!]

Holyoke is an urban neighborhood with very high poverty rates and no shortage of problems. It sits in the southwest corner of Middleton, a city of approximately 824,000 residents. Rosebaum Apartments in Holyoke was Gina's childhood home. She "escaped" at age 16 from an environment where drug deals on the corner were the norm, schools were in ill repair with leaking ceilings and holes in the walls, too many teens got a kick out of intimidating people on the streets, dilapidated buildings were a great hangout for troublemakers, vacant lots were overgrown with weeds, and garbage of all kinds added to the eyesore. Gina has been afforded the opportunity to try to make a difference in this troubled neighborhood she had told herself she would never return to. She wonders if she is up to it.

Gina's earliest memories include watching her mother, Alice, do whatever it took to get her next fix, with different men parading in and out of their small apartment that should have been condemned. Often Gina was left alone with little food in a filthy, drafty, apartment, but at least she was never left alone with any of her mother's "boyfriends." From 1992 to 1995, during the first few years of Gina's life, Alice only used drugs occasionally. She was determined to provide a better childhood for her daughter than the one she had with an alcoholic mother and abusive father. A high school dropout with no marketable skills, Alice found herself in dead-end, low-wage jobs and felt weighed down by the inability to pay for child care costs on top of all her other expenses. Days with little to eat were not uncommon, nor was having the electricity shut off.

[Handwritten margin note: Gina's history]

Gina remembers, when she was very young, finding her mom alone in her bedroom on many occasions distraught over her circumstances, which she felt she had no control over. She would tell Gina, "All I want is to be able to provide you with a good home, enough food and nice clothes, and the love that I never experienced." It was during those early years that Gina recalls feeling her mom cared deeply about her and wanted the best for her. But, as time went on, and the struggle to survive intensified, so did Alice's drug abuse.

During the years Gina was in Head Start and first grade, Alice would stay clean for 1, 2, or 3 months and then start using again. Then in second grade, Gina watched through a child's eyes as her mom's drug use began to spin totally out of control. Warnings by Child Protective Services that Gina would be placed in foster care fell on deaf ears, and caseworkers, with high caseloads, were hard pressed to follow up. Gina so clearly remembers the empty promises her mom made to her that "this time I will quit for good." She had her hopes dashed so many times that, by age 8, she knew better than to believe her mother's talk about the two of them escaping the Rosebaum Apartments.

While the odds were that drugs would destroy Alice, a beating, by someone she owed money to, put her in the hospital and changed the course of her life. Alice says the beating, which nearly killed her, was her wake-up call. Thanks to some strings pulled by a hospital social worker, Alice was able to get into a treatment facility. Then, it was back to the Rosebaum Apartments but with a new attitude and outlook on life and links to the supports she knew were essential to her being able to stay clean. The road was rocky; Alice did have one relapse, and making ends meet continued to be a struggle. However, she had social supports, including a social worker who helped her find her inner strength, set goals, and address some of her guilt. It took a long time for Gina to start to trust her mom. Gina recalls telling her mom more than once that she would never trust her after the lies Alice had told her.

[handwritten margin note: Stress was causing Relapse. -Counseling to help w/ stress]

In recalling the turbulent times, Gina says, "I loved and hated my mom. For too long I knew I couldn't count on her and often felt totally alone and so afraid." Gina is quick to follow with "but from the age of twelve on, my mom became a different person, or maybe she just became the mom I remember before all she cared about was her next high. All I know for sure is that she got clean, and the parade of 'boyfriends' ended. Of course, I was skeptical that the change would last. My mom seemed to accept that she had to prove herself to me, and she did." By the time Gina was sixteen, her mother was, with a government subsidy, able to afford an apartment in a better section of Middleton, and they said good-bye to Rosebaum Apartments and Holyoke.

[handwritten margin note: The root of "skepticism" is fear.]

[handwritten note: using her social supports & links she got out.]

HOLYOKE AND ROSEBAUM APARTMENTS

[handwritten note: Issues!]

Today, Rosebaum Apartments provide housing to 410 residents in the Holyoke neighborhood. Like most urban areas, Middleton includes very wealthy neighborhoods, where the value of the average home is $500,000, and very poor neighborhoods like Holyoke, where the majority of families live below the poverty level. While the school facilities and resources in Holyoke are subpar to those in wealthier neighborhoods of Middleton, some of the teachers are known for their commitment to the students. Still, very few extracurricular activities are available to students of any age, and Holyoke has little to offer to keep teens out of trouble. Fighting and turf wars between teenage groups is such a common occurrence that many parents are afraid to let their young children play outside. Taking them to the park is also not an option. The city put in new playground equipment and cleaned up the park about 10 years ago. It stayed nice for a few years but then became a prime hangout spot for a local gang. Today the equipment has fallen into disrepair, and trash litters the area.

[handwritten margin note: NO activities for students to keep them out of trouble]

[handwritten margin note: Park unkept! NO police presence!]

[handwritten note: Gangs at Parks.]

REJUVENATE HOLYOKE

[handwritten margin note: Defeated]

Rejuvenate Holyoke was created in early 2013 when a small group of residents, including two members of Rosebaum's tenant council, came together as a result of a rash of burglaries committed by teens and an increase in vandalism in some of the empty houses and other buildings. The lack of activities for youth, lack of job opportunities for all ages, and an increase in drug deals also served as impetus for the creation of the group.

[handwritten margin note: "No assets" Ignored by "Constituents"]

Holyoke residents felt the city was ignoring their concerns, as it had done so often in the past. Other neighborhoods in the city, including some with a high percentage of poverty, had a community center, at least one useable park, and an accessible free health clinic. Holyoke had none of these assets. Nor did many residents believe public transportation met their needs in regard to accessing shopping, social services, and employment opportunities. Holyoke had plenty of taverns but was a food desert with only a couple of convenience stores that carried mainly processed food and very little in the way of fresh produce.

[handwritten margin note: Transportation problems/issues]

[handwritten margin note: "Lack of grocery" stores that sell produce]

In late 2014, the Middleton Community Foundation (MCF) promised up to $400,000 of their 2015 neighborhood revitalization dollars to help Rejuvenate Holyoke if they gained 501(c)(3) status (the tax status required to be considered a legitimate nonprofit organization) or worked through an existing organization and came up with a solid community-driven plan. MCF let it be known that they believed funding grassroots efforts that have gained a lot of community support was much more likely to be fruitful, compared to organizations with a few elites at the top making all the decisions. MCF provided the Rejuvenate Holyoke group with a small sum of money to hire a consultant to help them get started with the plan. The understanding was that the consultant would be brought on full time, as their community organizer, if a solid plan was developed. It was also clear that MCF's funding would not be long term, so alternative funding sources would need to be secured after 2018.

A member of the group from the Rosebaum tenants' council suggested that they contact Gina for the position. The council was aware of Gina's education, a master's in social work with an emphasis in community development, which was a credential they found desirable. Gina and five other candidates were interviewed, and Gina was by far the top choice for the position—not only due to her qualifications, but also because the committee felt that as a former resident Gina would be more committed and would understand their situation better.

SECOND THOUGHTS

[handwritten margin note: Doubting her gifts capabilities, education]

Gina grew more disconcerted as Isaac slept and impatiently waited for him to wake. While Isaac had no filter, which was maddening at times, he also was the person Gina felt understood her best and would give her honest feedback.

"Finally," Gina said when Isaac rolled out of bed.

"Hey, take it easy on me," Isaac mumbled. "These double shifts are killing me. Anyway, it took me a while to get to sleep as I felt bad I wasn't more positive about your job offer."

"Well," Gina responded, "I'm not saying your first response didn't irritate me, but to be honest, I am really nervous about the job. I have been gone from Holyoke for almost 8 years, and despite what I was told at the interview, I am not at all sure some of the residents will trust a former resident who left and returned with an education. Also, during the interview, I got the feeling there were things the committee was not being fully open about.

"Isaac, what if I'm not up to the demands of the position? What if I take the position and nothing improves?"

"Gina," Isaac said in his calming tone, "I'm not going to pretend I'm not concerned about your taking this job, but I have no doubt the committee made the right decision. You've got what it takes to make a difference, if anyone can. Your knowledge and interpersonal skills topped with your work ethic and killer determination—they are lucky to have you."

Gina cut in, "Isaac, enough building me up. What about your concerns?"

"Well, let me finish," retorted Isaac. "I just don't want you to go into this with unrealistic expectations and beat yourself up if things don't go according to plan. Progress will be too slow for you, and although you understand that's the way it is, knowing it and not letting it bother you are two different things. Also, and this is my biggest concern, you see the best in people, and there are people who will try to take advantage of you and have unrealistic expectations of you."

Gina totally got Isaac's concerns as they paralleled some of her own. Still, while bailing on the job was tempting, it was not an option she seriously considered. She had endured a lot of adversity in her life, and while very nervous about what lay ahead, she had never been one to shy away from a challenge.

BACKGROUND INFORMATION

Organizing for change to achieve greater social, political, and economic justice and to move closer to the ideals our country was founded upon is the norm in our society. Women's suffrage, child labor laws, civil rights, environmental protections, gay rights, worker safety, 8-hour workdays, child abuse laws, protection from domestic violence, and improved treatment of individuals with intellectual disabilities are examples that illustrate the power that ordinary citizens have when they join together and demand change. At the local level, organizing has resulted in outcomes such as living wage ordinances, afterschool tutoring and youth activities, improvements in public transportation, removal of toxic waste, recycling initiatives, bike paths, community gardens, and refurbished houses. While so much of what we have today is taken for granted, we are actually reaping the benefits of the long, hard-fought struggles of people who organized and demanded change. Great progress has been made, but we are not done. Organizing efforts are still vital in continuing to improve circumstances at the neighborhood, local, state, federal, and international levels.

Why Neighborhoods Matter

The relationship between neighborhood conditions and well-being is nuanced, and there is variation in outcomes for residents not just between but also within orderly and disorderly neighborhoods. Still, research provides evidence that living in neighborhoods marked by crime, violence, and environmental health hazards puts children at significant risk for poor outcomes (Shonkoff & Phillips, 2000). Effectively organized neighborhoods promote the well-being of residents by providing functions such as health, safety, socialization and raising children, provision of jobs, local food, and caregiving (McKnight & Block, 2010). Harvard professor Robert Sampson coined the term *collective efficacy*, which refers to how willing neighbors are to act for each other's benefit. In broken neighborhoods where there is no sense of trust, and cynicism and alienation prevail, collective efficacy is likely to be low. The consequence is the persistence of violence and a detrimental impact on child well-being (Hurley, 2013). Clearly, neighborhood communities matter. And community organizing can lead to improved neighborhoods.

Forms of Organizing

There are many models and forms of organizing. This section focuses largely on community organizing that builds long-term citizen organizations to address issues that most significantly impact those with lower incomes. Before moving on to define *community organizing* (often referred to as grassroots organizing), it is important to differentiate between organizing and other approaches that are used to assist people living in low-income areas. Social services, advocacy, and mobilizing are all approaches used to address problems, and all three are valuable, but they do not entail organizing for the long haul, nor do the first two necessarily try to engage those most directly affected by current conditions. Social service organizations provide needed resources such as food and shelter, which is necessary, but does not require those who need the services to work together for systemic change. Advocacy often entails people speaking on behalf of those who need assistance in meeting basic needs. For example, many people advocated for free school breakfast and lunch programs, but that did not change the power relationship between those who have power and those who do not. Mobilizing is another approach that has resulted in positive changes, and it often has involved those with low incomes working with others to bring about change. For example, a group of citizens may come together to pressure city officials to tear down vacant and dilapidated houses in their neighborhood. Once they achieve this goal, they disband. Organizing encompasses mobilizing and is about winning issues, but more important, the focus is not just on an issue or problem, it is on building the organization for the long haul (Kahn, 1991, pp. 50–51). The belief is that by building the organization and building power, more wins can be had over the long term.

mobilizing

Defining Grassroots Community Organizing = For the long haul = generation

As alluded to previously, the underlying premise that drives community organizing is that bringing people together can result in collective action to achieve the community's desired goals. People joined together create a power base that is capable of challenging and holding accountable traditional power bases in society. Together, members of community organizations "identify common problems, look for solutions and craft strategies to reach, educate and mobilize others, so we can all join together to make the changes we need and deserve" (Hightower as cited in Kahn, 2010, p. x). Although the problems may have existed for years and appear intractable, time and again community organizations have developed effective strategies (and have power through people) to chip away at common problems. Effective community organizing requires crossing ethnic, racial, political affiliation, and socioeconomic divisions that often exist and building new relationships. At its heart, community organizing is a grassroots democratic approach to bringing about social and economic justice.

Identify = look for solutions = craft strategies = educate & mobilize others

Oftentimes professional community organizers are hired to help build the organization and help members deal with organizational challenges as well as develop strategies and tactics needed to be successful in winning on issues. Their role is to build leaders within the community and encourage members to find their voice, their power, and to speak for themselves (Chambers, 2004). Saul Alinsky, referred to as the father of modern community organizing, stressed what became known as the Iron Law of organizing: "Never do for others what they can do for themselves" (Chambers, 2004, front matter). Both Alinsky and Chambers worked with populations who were from low-income areas and did not feel empowered to bring about change. Chambers, a modern-day organizer, learned from and built upon Alinsky's style of organizing. His approach is less combative and more focused on relationship building than his predecessor. Chambers is not well known in the general public, but he is within the field of community organizing. President Obama is a very well-known public figure who spent time as a community organizer in Chicago after college. He worked to organize residents who lived in a public housing project to pressure the city to improve the poor conditions in the complex.

Community organizers: Build leaders, encourage members to find their voice, their power, and speak for themselves.

Community organizers work to change people's passive mindsets and help them feel empowered.

History of Community Organizing

An overview of the history of community organizing provides lessons for organizing today. The roots of community organizing in the United States can be found in the settlement house movement and the labor union movement.

In the late 1800s and early 1900s, the settlement house movement, started by Jane Addams, grew out of the desire of some middle- and upper-class individuals to address the needs of people living in poor and very crowded immigrant neighborhoods of industrial cities. Settlement houses used two approaches to addressing people's needs: providing direct services and organizing. They directly provided services for neighbors such as English classes, daycare, kindergartens, summer camps, sewing, dance, and art classes. Settlement house workers also organized; they lived in the immigrant neighborhoods to build relationships and trust and worked with their neighbors to lobby for legislation addressing the severe economic hardships encountered by the immigrants. Many in the immigrant neighborhoods were barely making enough to survive—hunger and inadequate shelter were common. Jane Addams and others in the settlement house movement collaborated with other reform groups to bring about legislation that addressed social ills. Their organizing efforts brought significant changes, a few examples being child labor laws, laws to improve factory safety, factory inspections, kindergartens in Chicago, and tenement house regulations (Library of Congress, n.d.).

The labor movement is given credit by Saul Alinsky, who began his life as an organizer in the 1930s, for demonstrating how organizing can bring about positive change. What the labor unions were doing in factories is what Alinsky took to poor neighborhoods; he was driven by his belief that social justice could be achieved through American democracy. Hailed by *Time Magazine* in 1970 as "a prophet of power to the people," he is still viewed by many as having been the most influential community organizer in the United States (Radical Saul Alinsky, 1970, p. 60).

Alinsky's method was to show the "have-nots" how to organize their communities, target the power brokers, and politically outmaneuver them. In other words, he led residents of poor communities to engage in effective political activity. One of his often-used sayings in referencing the challenge of winning on issues was, "It becomes a contest of power: those who have money and those who have people, we have nothing but people" (Berman, 2010, p. 120).

The living conditions in the neighborhoods Alinsky organized in during the 1950s and 1960s were atrocious. Workers would toil in nasty factories all day for low pay and still hardly be able to feed their families, who lived in unhealthy, crowded quarters often infested with rats and lice. As a skilled organizer, he was able to mobilize residents in poor communities and get them to believe that through acting together they had power. Part of this empowerment included building indigenous leadership and having them take the lead in building the organization and working for change. Recall his Iron Law: "Never do for others what they can do for themselves." The organizer's job is to help educate citizens on how to build an organization and develop effective strategies and tactics, to build indigenous leaders, and then to stand aside.

Two brief examples provide a flavor of the bold tactics promoted by Alinsky to pressure city officials. There was lack of adequate garbage pickup in one Chicago neighborhood that Alinsky was organizing in. The residents were told this was due to a lack of city funding. In response, residents secured trucks, loaded them with garbage that had not been picked up, and dumped it on the front lawn of the area alderman (city official). Miraculously, the city found funds to resume regular garbage pickup in the neighborhood. In another example, in the Woodlawn area of Chicago, there were building violations that posed serious health hazards for people living in them. The community organization in the area threatened to unload a thousand rats on the steps of city hall. The outcome was that Mayor Daley took action and had the residential building problems addressed (Horwitt, 1989).

The Industrial Areas Foundation as Evidence of "Power of the People"

The legacy of Saul Alinsky, who passed away over 40 years ago, lives on in the Industrial Areas Foundation (IAF), which he founded in 1940.

[The IAF] partners with religious congregations and civic organizations at the local level to build broad-based organizing projects, which create new capacity in a community for leadership development, citizen-led action and relationships across the lines that often divide our communities. (Industrial Areas Foundation, 2013a, p. 1)

The training and consultation the IAF has provided to faith-based and other community organizations has led to significant improvements for millions of citizens. The following are just a smattering of examples of the wins in 2011 and 2012 by organizations associated with the IAF. BUILD, an IAF member organization in Baltimore, was successful in garnering enough support for the passage of a bottle tax in 2012 that will generate an estimated $10 million a year to be used to secure $155 million in bond funding. The funds will be used to build and modernize 10 elementary schools. This endeavor will also be a job creator. Valley Interfaith, an IAF affiliate in Phoenix, used community pressure to get officials to reinstate afterschool programs for youth. In Texas, leaders from 35 IAF member organizations worked with San Antonio Mayor Castro to get the public to vote for a one-eighth cent increase in the sales tax. This increase is expected to generate $248 million over 8 years and will be used to expand pre-K centers in the city. In New York City, after documenting safety hazards in public housing, an IAF affiliate used the evidence to convince Mayor Bloomberg and the director of public housing to invest $10 million for cameras and other measures to increase safety.

Another IAF member, Northern Louisiana Interfaith, lobbied the governor and a ranking congressman to support $208,000 for job training that would lead to higher wages in the delta region. In El Paso, Texas, Border Interfaith was able to get the city to put in a new water distribution system that supplied clean water to about 300 residents after many years of hard, persistent work. Until late 2012, when the system was completed, these 300 residents were living with high levels of contaminants (such as arsenic) in the water, making it unsafe to drink and often foul smelling. Some residents would also not always have water in their homes.

In addition, in New Jersey, the Interfaith Community Organization (in 2011) made strides in their 20-year campaign to have industrial waste, known to cause cancer, removed from Jersey City. They partnered with the National Resources Defense Council and filed a lawsuit against PPG Industries, whose Jersey City factories, long ago, created tons of toxic waste that they failed to remove. The court decision called for PPG Industries to remove 600,000 tons of toxic waste (Industrial Areas Foundation, 2013b).

These examples from IAF members, or affiliate organizations, leave no doubt that, while it may require long, concentrated efforts, citizen organizations have a great deal of capacity and power in creating change and instilling hope. There are hundreds more examples that could be provided not only by IAF but also by community organizations not associated with IAF.

Principles of Community Organizing

Many of the basic principles of effective community organizations were touched upon in the discussion of the history of community organizing and the IAF. The need to build the organization and establish a solid foundation cannot be over-emphasized.[1] This requires tapping into the self-interest of potential members, as self-interest is a key motivator of people. People get involved because there is something in it for them or those they care about. Bobo, Kendall, and Max (2010,

---

[1] The purpose of the organization needs to be clearly articulated and understood. The funding base needs to be determined. Also, the structure of the organization must be decided. For example, is there going to be staff, an advisory committee or a board, what will the makeup of the board be, and so on.

p. 6) warn us to be careful about how we define self-interest and not to limit our-selves to a narrow definition. We should not consider self-interest to be only about acquiring material needs, for example, safe streets, adequate nutrition, access to health care, clean water, or shelter, although it certainly includes the acquisition of basic material needs. Self-interest also entails the desire to help meet the needs of others and the community. It encompasses the need to feel respected, appreci-ated, and worthwhile. And it goes beyond that: "The word interest comes from the Latin *inner esse,* which means to be among. So, self-interest has to do with self among others. That is, where do my needs fit into those of the larger society" (Bobo, Kendall, & Max, 2010, p. 6). A final caution from Bobo, Kendall, and Max (2010) is that the self-interest of a potential member should never be assumed. It requires a relationship with individuals and applying the skills of listening to make this assessment.

A sense of belonging to your community. Along with respected, appreciated.

✗ A community organization cannot be built, grown, and sustained by itself with-out the organizers understanding and heeding the significance of relationships. Good organizing is based on establishing good relationships.[2] It is the key to suc-cess (Bobo, Kendall, & Max, 2010; Chambers, 2004; Kahn, 1991). People are the most vital resource organizations have. Therefore, organizers and leaders need to take the time to find out not only the interests and concerns of potential members ✗ but also their skills, energy, and what they can bring to the organization.

A primary way some organizers begin to build relationships is through face-to face-meetings (person-to-person). While friendly, these meetings are very intentional and aimed at serving a purpose. It creates a group of organizers who increase their interpersonal communication skills, listen and gain awareness to the perspectives and viewpoints of others and in doing so increases awareness of their own needs and interests. These meetings serve as the foundation for trans-forming communities and bringing about social change (East Brooklyn Congre-gations, 2015).

The relationships that current members have with each other are also critical. Social capital building is ongoing. Social capital is the "features of social organ-ization such as networks, norms, and social trust that facilitate coordination and cooperation for mutual benefit" (Putnam, 1995, para. 3). In other words, as members get to know each other, they are more likely to develop feelings of mutual responsi-bility for each other and the organization. They are more likely to want to help each

---

[2] Although not a focus in this background section, it is important to mention the critical role of social media and the Internet in mobilizing people who may not have personal relationships with one another. As mentioned, there are many models and forms of organizing, and the use of technology has undoubtedly enabled significant social change efforts to make headway.

Creating an atmosphere where relationships can form. Strong bond created.

other out and look out for one another. If there are strong bonds among members, some tensions may be avoided, and there is a greater chance of effectively dealing with conflict that may arise. Strong bonds are created through repeated interactions and through getting to know the stories of members.

In addition to the importance of relationships, building social capital, and choosing issues based on the shared self-interest of members, there are many other basic principles of community organizing. Even though they were referred to earlier, it is worth examining them more closely. The organization should be inclusive of all who share the same interests, and it must be driven and controlled by members through a democratic process. Members must have input from the beginning and not after a plan is developed by a few leaders or a few members and a community organizer. Organizers should not present as if they know the best way to approach matters. Relying on past approaches that worked may not be the most effective way to go today. Moreover, a key premise of community organizing is that citizens have the ability to make decisions and bring about change. If members are included in the thinking, planning, and decision making, and know their input matters, they are more likely to feel a sense of ownership and be more committed (Kahn, 1991).

Empower community leaders by including them in the planning & decision-making

Working together often means forming partnerships and collaborations with other groups focused on the same issues. People equal power, and more people equal more power if effectively organized. Organizations will not remain effective if they do not continually focus on the development of leaders. In this endeavor it is important not to rule out quiet or reserved citizens, as leadership skills can be learned. At times, the most unlikely people can emerge as leaders, if given the opportunity. Whether members emerge as a leaders or not, "every single person has capacities, abilities, and gifts that make the community stronger" so it is important to focus on the strengths rather than the deficits (Kretzmann & McKnight, 1993, p. 13).

Strategies and Tactics

Developing strategy and choosing tactics are essential to effective organizing. A lot of questions must be asked and research done to develop a good strategy. The organization must consider its starting point, for example, what are the strengths and weaknesses of the organization, what are its financial resources, how much time can people invest, how challenging will it be to get to where they want to go, what might the roadblocks be, and how will they be addressed. A well-developed strategy does not guarantee success, but it will improve the chances of getting the hoped-for end goal. Organizations must be flexible in regard to adjusting strategy, but if they do not have a detailed plan of where they want to go, it is unlikely they will get there.

A young organization that wants significant wins quickly, without building the organization and power, is less likely to be successful than if the organization starts with small, quick winnable goals and then progressively moves on to more difficult ones. Quick wins are important to keep members motivated, but taking on too much too soon and experiencing early failure will not build power or hope in the organization. Kahn (1991) points out that good strategy builds on people's experiences, involves people, plans for the possible and the improbable happenings, includes the steps needed to carry out the strategy, is rooted in what the organization's members have the skills to do, and enables the members to learn about the organization, politics, and power (pp. 138–139).

The Midwest Academy Manual for Activists (Bobo, Kendall, & Max, 2010) provides a valuable template to use as a guide when developing strategy. The template requires attention to the following: landing on short, intermediate, and long term goals; determining organizational resources such as finances, staff, members, and reputation; assessing who the allies and opponents are and what resources they both possess; figuring out the target—those who have the power to make a decision relative to the issue; and deciding what tactics might prove to be most beneficial. Tactics are the actions such as letter writing, educational meetings, marches, public hearings, petitions, and accountability sessions needed for the strategy to be successful.[3] They are the actions necessary to pressure those with power to concede (Bobo, Kendall, & Max, 2010.)

Kahn (1991) points out that, while choosing a tactic may appear simple, the impact of different potential tactics must be carefully weighed. They need to fit with the overall strategy. Relying too heavily on confrontational tactics may not serve an organization well. Today, many organizations rely on both cooperation and confrontation. Whatever type of tactic is used, whether it is confrontational or relies on cooperation, it should demonstrate the strength of the organization and influence decision makers. Tactics should also help build the organization and impact public opinion.

Building strong community organizations that result in positive neighborhood change is both art and science. It takes leadership and a lot of time and energy. Community organizers need to help members of the organization celebrate small victories along the way to keep members motivated for the long haul. Gina has the knowledge and philosophy needed to bring residents together, foster indigenous leadership, and assist those involved in establishing an organization to better their

---

[3] "An accountability session is a meeting between citizens and public officials. The purpose of an accountability session is to hold a decision maker—someone with the power and authority to give you something you want—accountable for the decisions he or she makes" (Western Organization of Resource Councils, 2006, para. 1).

neighborhood. She is very aware that what awaits her will seem overwhelming at times, and it won't be all smooth sailing.

THE CHALLENGES KEEP MOUNTING

A text came in from Isaac at 6:30 p.m. at the end of Gina's first week on the job. It read, "What's up? We're waiting for you to head to the beach for the weekend."

Oh, no, thought Gina. *I don't want to go. I have so much to do to be ready for Monday's meetings. But, Isaac will be so disappointed, and while he won't say it, he will probably be thinking he told me I would let this job consume me. Ugh, I'll just try to take some work along.*

"Be there in 15 minutes. My clothes are packed," was the response Gina sent in text. She added, "Can we drive together so I can talk to you about some things that have come up at work this week?" With their work schedules they had only seen each other in passing all week.

"Done," was the response Isaac sent back.

As soon as they were on I80, Gina started in, "You know the feeling I had that I wasn't getting the whole scoop? Well, I'm getting a bit more of the picture each day. It's not like I wasn't expecting underlying issues to emerge, but there are so many that just further complicate the process of coming up with a community-driven plan. For starters, the tensions within the organization, while not insurmountable, pose a significant challenge. There are conflicting ideas about how to go forward and where to focus. And there are a few members who are vying for power. Terrell Jackson, officially the vice president of Rejuvenate Holyoke, has a reputation as a rather pushy and self-interested know-it-all. He has some credibility as a former civil rights activist during the 1960s (although he was very young, and his actual contribution to America's civil rights struggle has always been a bit hazy). Then there's Sonia Hernandez, who is not afraid to voice her opinion that the board should reflect the ethnic makeup of the neighborhood, which it does not. Getting board members to get past personal agendas and egos and be able to work together is critical and won't be an easy feat. Added to that, something I definitely wasn't told is that having a board with the power to make decisions was questioned by some residents who believe every participating resident ought to have a direct vote rather than giving that power to a board. Moreover, there are hard feelings since the board members were not elected by residents." Gina paused to take a breath, then added, "Here's the thing, Isaac, I'm just getting started telling you all I learned about the challenges this week."

"Go ahead, tell me the rest. We have 50 more miles to the beach house," Isaac responded, pretty sure that Gina was not asking him to try to problem solve at this point but just wanted him to hear what she was dealing with.

Gina!
↓
Tension
within the
*organization
*Conflicting ideas
*Power struggles

Fighting for
Cohesiveness

"Most residents in Holyoke don't even know about the newly formed Rejuvenate Holyoke," continued Gina anxiously. "And their input hasn't been sought. One resident, Mavis Johnson, told a local reporter covering the announcement by the Middleton Foundation, 'I've been working my tail off for nearly 20 years trying to rejuvenate this neighborhood, and now some group comes along and wants to take charge. I wasn't even invited to participate.' I have to quickly make sure residents get the message that their input is valued. Holyoke is, after all, their community."

Isaac interrupted, "You know, Gina, you are sounding more enthusiastic than scared."

"Yeah, you're right, I am nervous, but this is definitely the type of challenge I was looking for. And there are others in the area I have met who will be a great help. There are a couple of private social service agencies within Holyoke, as well as an ecumenical group of ministers who meet regularly and have begun to talk about the need for more collaboration. Pastor Bemis, a gentle spirit, who chooses to live in Holyoke although he could afford not to, appears to have the respect of not only the ministerial group but also the current board members. Reverend Rita, whose congregation is known for reaching out to help area residents, also appears to be trusted and known to be good for her word. They seem genuinely committed to change, and both are skilled communicators. Both know that face-to-face communication is critical, but they also will take advantage of social media to reach out to people in the neighborhood."

"That's great," Isaac exclaimed. "You have allies to support you and work with you."

"Yes, hooray for the good news because there is one more huge factor I want to share with you that complicates matters. Waste Begone, a new company, is in the process of obtaining the necessary permits to build a hazardous waste incinerator in the commercial area just bordering Holyoke. Industries have long used (and abused) this commercial area, enticed by tax exemptions and an abundance of low-wage workers in the neighborhood. Plants have come and gone (once their tax relief period expires), leaving behind toxins and unemployed workers. Residents of Holyoke are split on the decision of whether the city should bring in another plant that provides some employment but also further damages the environment and could negatively impact the health of residents. Waste Begone has spent a good deal of money on their public relations campaign aimed at convincing the community of the economic benefits that will result from locating in Middleton while arguing that the emissions of any pollutants will meet clean air standards. Groups against the plant claim the costs far outweigh the short-term gains. They note that air quality is already poor, asthma rates are high, and air standards are not sufficient to protect the residents of Holyoke (especially the young, the old, and those with respiratory problems). Many of the critics argue that if Waste Begone locates in Middleton it will make it more difficult to recruit other businesses to the area." Before Isaac could respond, Gina continued, "I know we won't solve these issues before we get to the beach house, but I just needed to share with you what I'm dealing with. Now that I have, I think I'll be able to enjoy the weekend."

"Glad I could be of assistance. Now let's have some fun," Isaac cheerfully responded.

MONDAY MORNING

On her way to work Monday, Gina continued with a mental list she had started of what needed to be done and what should be a priority. She knew a major task was to have a community plan, not a plan driven by a few. Making that happen when the existing Rejuvenate Holyoke organization is not seen as representing the community will be no easy feat. Also, there are other internal challenges that need quick attention and immediate problems to address such as Waste Begone. Gina pulled into the parking lot in front of the building that housed her office to find Terrell Jackson and Pastor Bemis waiting to talk to her. *Here we go*, she said to herself, as she took a deep breath and stepped out of her car to greet them.

QUESTIONS FOR DISCUSSION

1. How does the author of the case distinguish between mobilizing, advocacy, and community organizing? Discuss whether or not this distinction is helpful to your overall understanding of the case.

2. Discuss Alinsky's approach to organizing. What are the strengths and weaknesses of his approach? How does context matter when determining overall approach as well as strategies and tactics to use? *Never do for others, what others can do for themselves*

3. Discuss key lessons provided by the Industrial Area Foundation.

4. Discuss the concept of self-interest based the information in the case from Bobo, Kendall, and Max.

5. If you were giving advice to someone new to organizing, what would you want to make sure to tell that person regarding key principles, strategies, and tactics? (You have likely touched on them in the above questions).

6. What do you think should be included on Gina's list of the issues to be addressed, and how should they be prioritized? How should she go about ensuring that a community-driven plan is established? What should Gina be cautious about as she proceeds?

[Handwritten margin notes: Mobilization seeks to "build social relationships in pursuit of common interest, the foundation of the community development process, empower groups & individuals by providing skills they need to make changes. Explore common issues & set priorities, select strategy, implement through people, Assess results]

7. What does Gina have working in her favor? *Passion, motivated, Respected as a leader (her voice) history/residents*

8. Discuss the importance of involving community members in the organizing process. How would you reach out to involve community members to (1) engage them, (2) help them feel ownership of the organization, and (3) build the capacity of community leaders?

9. Discuss how Gina might negotiate conflict that arises to increase the likelihood that all community members will get and stay involved.

10. What might Gina do to ensure she is not seen as an outsider coming in to tell "the poor" what they need to do? *Let them know she's an allie.*

CASE ANALYSIS WRITING ASSIGNMENT

1. Read the assigned case study thoroughly prior to class in order to be fully prepared to join in our discussion.

2. Gina decides it would be good to get her thoughts down on paper to make sure she is gleaning lessons from her education (especially in regard to organizing principles, strategies, and tactics), critically thinking through how to prioritize the tasks at hand, and putting in place a process to develop a community-driven plan. For this essay, put yourself in the role of Gina and address each of the above topics.

3. The analysis should be an approximately two-and-a-half- to three-page, typed double-spaced essay. Your essay should reflect the standards and expectations of college-level writing: spelling, grammar, and appropriate use of paragraphs all matter. If you quote directly from the case study, use quotation marks, and at the end of the quote, indicate the page number the quote appeared on. For example, "Building strong community organizations is both art and science" (Lewis, 2015, p. 109).

4. Your case analysis is due _____ and worth a maximum of _____ points.

INTERNET SOURCES

The Asset-Based Community Development Institute (http://www.abcdinstitute.org)

Community Development Institute (https://www.cditeam.org)

Community Development Works (http://www.communitydevelopmentworks.org)

Grassroots Leadership: Helping People Gain Power (http://grassrootsleadership
.org/tags/si-kahn)

How Painting Can Transform Neighborhoods (https://www.ted.com/talks/
haas_hahn_how_painting_can_transform_communities)

Industrial Areas Foundation (IAF) (http://www.industrialareasfoundation.org)

Midwest Community Development Institute (http://www.midwestcdi.org)

REFERENCES

Berman, A. (2010). *Herding donkeys: The fight to rebuild the Democratic party and reshape American politics.* Canada: D & M.

Bobo, K., Kendall, J., & Max, S. (2010). *Organizing for change: Midwest Academy manual for activists.* Santa Ana, CA: The Forum Press.

Chambers, E. (2004). Roots for radicals. New York, NY: Continuum International.

East Brooklyn Congregations. (2015). *About metro IAF.* Retrieved from http://metro-iaf.org

Horwitt, S. (1989). *Let them call me rebel: Saul Alinsky: His life and legacy.* New York, NY: Vintage Books.

Hurley, D. (2013). The enduring importance of neighborhoods. *Discover Magazine.* Retrieved from http://discovermagazine.com/2013/april/9-getting-personal-with-robert-sampson

Industrial Areas Foundation. (2013a). *Who we are.* Retrieved from http://www.industrialareas-foundation.org

Industrial Areas Foundation. (2013b). *Issues and victories.* Retrieved from http://www.industrial areasfoundation.org/issuesvictories/8

Kahn, S. (1991). *Organizing: A guide for grassroots leaders.* Washington, DC: National Association of Social Workers Press.

Kahn, S. (2010). *Creative community organizing: A guide for rabble rousers, activists & quiet lovers of justice.* San Francisco, CA: Berrett-Koehler.

Kretzmann, J., & McKnight, J. (1993). *Building communities from the inside out: A path toward finding and mobilizing a community's assets.* Chicago, IL: ACTA.

Library of Congress, America's Story. (n.d.). *The good work of Jane Addams.* Retrieved from http://www.americaslibrary.gov/aa/addams/aa_addams_work_2.html

McKnight, J., & Block, P. (2010). *The abundant community: Awakening the power of families and neighborhoods.* San Francisco, CA: Berrett-Koehler.

Putnam, R. (1995). *Bowling alone: America's declining social capital.* Retrieved from http://xroads.virginia.edu/~HYPER/DETOC/putnam1/putnam.html

Radical Saul Alinsky: Prophet of power to the people. (1970, March 2). *Time.* Retrieved from http://search.time.com/?site=time&q=alinsky

Shonkoff, J., & Phillips, D. (2000). *From neurons to neighborhoods: The science of early childhood development.* National Academies Press. Retrieved from http://www.nap.edu/read/9824/chapter/16

Western Organization of Resource Councils. (2006). *How to hold an accountability session.* Retrieved from http://www.worc.org/userfiles/Accountability-Session.pdf

Chapter 3

Achieving Racial Equality

Education, Housing, Health, and Justice . . . A Long Way to Go

"James," yelled the lifeguard at the municipal pool, "you push her into the pool and you're out for the rest of the day." Thinking the lifeguard was distracted by James, Louis climbed onto the lifeguard chair and made as if he was going to jump into the shallow end. "Out of here now, Louis, and don't come back tomorrow either," shouted the lifeguard. "What is up with you two anyway?"

Nothing was really up—they were just looking for some fun. James, Louis, and Trevor, the mighty trio, were getting ready to leave the pool for the day anyway, so Louis's getting kicked out just sped up the process a bit. The three of them spent most waking hours together, and in the summer that typically included a couple of hours a day fooling around at the city pool, but they never caused any serious trouble.

They came from families without a lot of extra money for entertainment, so they took advantage of whatever low-cost activities the neighborhood had to offer, which included the pool plus summer baseball and basketball leagues. These activities, along with the close rein Trevor and Louis's grandma and mom kept on the brothers, had helped them, thus far at least, avoid hanging out with a couple of groups of youth in their neighborhood who did get into serious trouble.

At 14 years old, Trevor was a year older than Louis and James, but he was slight of build and looked younger and more vulnerable than they did. Louis took it upon himself to look out for his older brother. For the last 5 years, he also saw himself as James's protector. James was athletic and usually didn't need protecting, but Louis had come to his rescue when, back in third grade, a bunch of Louis's friends started teasing James. James, one of the few White students at Halverson School, was new to the area at the time, having moved with his mom, who was escaping an abusive relationship. He wore clothes that looked to be a size or two too small for him, which, coupled with his "Spock ears," made him a target.

It took James by surprise that someone was standing up for him. At a very early age, he decided he was pretty much on his own and had to take care of himself. Susan, his mom, was in and out of bad relationships. Trying to keep whichever boyfriend she had at the time happy, and sometimes working two part-time jobs, left little time to spend with James, who was left to fend for himself. Except for Ben, two boyfriends ago, the guys his mom got into relationships with mostly ignored him. James buried himself in books and spent many solitary hours lost in the world of science fiction. He had a couple of friends before his move to Halverson but none that impressed him like Louis did.

Louis was well liked by many in the neighborhood for his quick wit and friendly nature. He somehow had figured out how to gain the respect of the known "troublemakers" without joining them. Coming out the victor in the few fights he had been in helped. He was wicked fast, and his dad had taught him some effective kajukenbo moves. While James thought he could stand up for himself, the fact that someone, for once, seemed to be looking out for him drew James to Louis like a magnet. Louis was tough but softhearted, and he had big plans for his life, which was not something James was used to seeing exhibited by many of the adults he had been around.

Jewell Norby, Trevor and Louis's mom, had high expectations for her boys, as did their maternal grandmother, Jocelyn (Nana Jo) Nickels. Nana Jo moved in with them the year the boys turned 10 and 9—the same year the boys lost both their father and grandfather. Their grandpa worked construction and fell to his death when a platform he was standing on gave way. It was a fluke accident that left Jocelyn with home mortgage payments that she couldn't keep up with as he had no life insurance, and the company only paid his funeral and burial expenses as compensation. Three months later, the boys' father was hit by a drunk driver and didn't pull through. Beyond devastated, somehow Jewell and Jocelyn kept it together enough to be there for the boys. They decided that what would be best for all of them was for Jocelyn to sell her home and move in with her daughter, Jewell. Nana Jo could help out with the boys, especially by being home in the evenings when Jewell worked swing shift as a licensed practical nurse.

It was not only Jewell's children who benefitted from Jocelyn's move. Jocelyn's job as an attendant at a Springdale Nursing Home came to an end due to health issues that prevented her from being on her feet for long hours, so she began volunteering 2 days a week as a tutor at the afterschool program that the boys attended. The children there gravitated to her. She was no-nonsense and didn't put up with bad manners or inappropriate behavior, but she was also full of joy and warmth, always laughing and joking with the children. Trevor and Louis didn't mind sharing their grandma with the kids in their mostly African American neighborhood and liked that other kids thought she was a "cool grandma." Some of them even started calling her Nana Jo, too.

Jocelyn brought that same cheer and a sense of stability to Jewell's home. Many evenings when Jewell was at work, Nana Jo would share stories with the boys, often including James, about her own childhood as well as the lives lived by their ancestors. After Louis befriended James, Nana Jo also took James under her wing and gave him the love and support she sensed he wasn't getting at home. He spent many evenings at the Norby/Nickels's home, and on weekends and in the summer he often spent the night.

Trevor and Louis never tired of listening to Nana Jo tell and retell what to them were fascinating stories. "Please, Nana Jo, tell us more," the boys would say in unison, when she ended their evening ritual.

"One more, then lights out. Did I ever tell you about the swimming hole I went to as a young girl?" she said with a smile, knowing they had heard this story at least a dozen times. Without waiting for an answer, she went on. "As you know, Blacks were not allowed to go to the municipal swimming pool in Wilcox, South Carolina, where we lived until the year I turned 10, so my brothers, some friends, and I would sneak down to a swimming hole on the river. Our parents didn't want us going there, as sometimes the current was fairly strong. We always approached the area carefully and would leave quickly if we saw a group of White kids already there, but if the coast was clear, we would take turns swinging on a strong tree vine and dropping into the water. To hit the water on hot days was like a taste of heaven. One of us always stood guard in case some White kids came along. We didn't want trouble so would hightail it out of there if we needed to, which was the case on several occasions."

"One time when we took off we didn't go far from the water but to our favorite tree, a giant weeping willow that concealed us and provided shade as we quietly lay relaxing and drying off. We heard a scream coming from the direction of the swimming hole and knew something was wrong. Without thinking, two of my brothers, Thomas and Jacob, ran in the direction of the scream and saw a White boy being swept downstream by a current. My brothers were not the best swimmers, and the current was pretty fast there, but the two of them got to a place along the river a little ways down from the boy and made a two-person human chain. Thomas hung onto a bunch of saplings from a tree for support and waded waist deep into the water. Jacob grabbed Thomas's hand and waded further out into the water and was able to reach out and grab the boy. I don't know how they did it. They had no time to plan—they just acted, working in unison, and saved that little boy's life. Almost immediately after they got him to shore, the other White kids made it to where the little boy and my brothers were. Rather than being grateful, a bunch of them yelled at my brothers to get away, shouting at them to not touch the White boy. My brothers left quickly and said nothing. We couldn't tell my parents, as we were not supposed to be at the swimming hole, plus that sort of treatment was so common we were used to it."

The first time James heard this story he was bewildered. "I don't understand. Why couldn't you swim in the same pool? Why couldn't you share the swimming hole? Why were those kids so mean?" Though her grandsons had heard it before, Nana Jo did her best to explain to all three boys the state-sanctioned system of segregation that existed when she was young, for example, having separate schools, places Blacks could not sit or eat, separate drinking fountains, and a pool only open to the White kids. She also made it clear that there were Whites who showed kindness and didn't agree with segregation and what was clearly "separate and unequal" treatment of Blacks.

BACKGROUND INFORMATION

Then presidential candidate Barack Obama, in a March 2008 speech quoting American writer William Faulkner, stated, "'The past isn't dead and buried. In fact, it isn't even past.'" He went on to say, "We do need to remind ourselves that so many of the disparities that exist in the African-American community today can be directly traced to inequalities passed on from an earlier generation that suffered under the brutal legacy of slavery and Jim Crow" (NPR, 2008, para. 2).

In that same vein, before discussing the extent of, and some of the reasons for, these enduring inequalities and the resulting disadvantaged position of too many African Americans, this section presents a brief historical overview of race relations in the United States, and content on the racism and discriminatory practices that persist despite the progress made (e.g., significant changes in attitudes and legislation) are covered. Finally, broad ideas about what will move the United States closer to affording opportunity and justice for all will be touched upon. The focus on Blacks is certainly not meant to ignore the biases and barriers that others—women; Lesbian, Gay, Bisexual, Transgender, Queer, and Intersex (LGBTQI) individuals; other people of color; and many low-income Whites—too often face; yet, to cover all groups in this relatively short case is not feasible. Often, issues of inequality are more advantageously addressed along lines other than race (e.g., income), especially when creating policy, but doing so can also make it harder to understand this crucial, contested, and complex issue.

The United States Before the 1964 Civil Rights Act

While there is much in the history of our country that is positive and should be applauded, there is also a great deal of ugliness and grossly unjust practices that have had a lasting impact. "[Eighty] percent of this country's four centuries have involved extreme racialized slavery and extreme Jim Crow legal segregation" (Yancey & Feagin, 2015, para.11). The system established was based on the socially constructed, not biologically based, concept of race. Blacks, like Native Americans, in this narrative, were less intelligent than Whites; in fact, they were not fully human (they were counted as three fifths of a person). This narrative was used to justify the bondage and inhumane treatment of human beings that our nation allowed, sanctioned, and enforced until 1865 with the ratification of the 13th Amendment to the U.S. Constitution. In fact, such a narrative was necessary because humans don't treat humans like that. The narrative did not die with the abolishment of slavery, nor with the passage of the 14th and 15th Amendments,[1] but can be seen in Jim Crow laws and beyond. As the Faulkner quote states, the past is still not past. Despite significant progress, it is still with us today.

A dominant narrative in the South during the Jim Crow period, which ended less than 60 years ago, can be summarized as follows:

> Many Christian ministers and theologians taught that whites were the Chosen people, blacks were cursed to be servants, and God supported racial segregation. Craniologists, eugenicists, phrenologists, and Social Darwinists, at every educational level, buttressed the belief that blacks were innately intellectually and culturally inferior to whites. Pro-segregation politicians gave eloquent speeches on the great danger of integration: the mongrelization of the white race. Newspaper and magazine writers routinely referred to blacks as niggers, coons, and darkies; and worse, their articles reinforced anti-black stereotypes. Even children's games portrayed blacks as inferior beings. (Pilgram, 2000, para. 1)

Jim Crow laws put in place, primarily in the South circa 1877 and lasting over 90 years, amounted to a racial caste system that relegated Blacks to second-class citizenship. Pilgram (2000) notes Jim Crow was more than just laws: it was a way of life that legitimized racism against Blacks. The message was loud and clear that Blacks are "less than" and needed to "stay in their place," which was not with Whites except in a subservient role. Blacks were often prevented from voting. They could not go to the same schools as Whites, sit with Whites, shake hands with Whites, drink from the same drinking fountains, use the same public restrooms, show affection to each other in public, question what a White person said, male Blacks better not have looked too closely at or spoke to White women first, and the list went on. Segregation and oppression were the norm, and the reality was far from "separate

---

[1] The 14th Amendment (adopted in 1868) ensured that "all persons born in the United States . . . excluding Indians not taxed" were citizens and were to be given "full and equal benefit of all laws" (Kelly, n.d., para. 1).

The 15th Amendment, adopted in 1970, granted Black males the right to vote.

but equal." Blacks, for the most part, remained poor and lived in fear of state sanctioned, or ignored, brutality, including lynchings.

Blacks faced hostility in the North as well but not to the same extent. Mass migration to northern cities by Blacks in hopes of obtaining gainful employment in the
1920s fueled racist attitudes of some. In the 1930s, blatant racism in government programs was not uncommon. For example, "Federal housing agencies deemed black
neighborhoods unworthy of credit, and federal officials segregated public housing.
Blacks did benefit from some of the New Deal public works programs but the New
Deal did not (and could not) eliminate the harmful discrimination that was rampant
in the areas of employment, wages and working conditions" (Woolner, 2010).

"The 1930s and 1940s also saw White riots—in cities such as Chicago, Detroit,
and Los Angeles—aimed at restricting Blacks to neighborhoods they already occupied" (Steel, 2009, para. 9). Still, the North passed many laws to end discriminatory activity in advance of the Civil Rights Act of 1964, in part due to mobilization
and demands of antidiscrimination activists. These laws opened up jobs and other
opportunities for Blacks. Another sign that the narrative of the segregationists
was up against powerful counter narratives was the landmark decision by the
U.S. Supreme Court, *Brown v. Board of Education* in 1954, which stated separate
schools for Whites and Blacks were unconstitutional.

1960s to Present

Almost 100 years after the passage of the Civil Rights Act of 1866 and the Recon-
struction Amendments (the 13th, 14th, and 15th amendments), all of which aimed
to ensure Blacks' civil rights, the broad-based Civil Rights Movement culminated in
the passage of the Civil Rights Act of 1964. That act, which outlawed discrimination
based on race, color, religion, sex, or national origin, and the Voting Rights Act of
1965, which outlawed discrimination in voting, were monumental, essentially putting an end to the reign of legal (de jure) discrimination based on race. It would have
never happened had civil rights activists not participated in actions such as marches,
boycotts, sit-ins, and protests. Great sacrifices were made by the activists including,
for some, their lives. It was their hard and steadfast efforts that put pressure on the
government to take action. A 2013 CBS poll indicated that 96% of Blacks and 95%
of Whites believe that the passage of the 1964 Civil Rights Act (CRA) was an important to very important event in U.S. history (Polling Report, 2015).

The passage of the CRA, a giant step forward in addressing discrimination, did
not bring a sudden end to the practice of racial discrimination, also referred to as de
facto discrimination. The act itself could not put a stop to racist attitudes or completely counter a racist narrative that many still clung to. And it did not include the
power to enforce the new policies, which led to other legislation being passed in

later years. For example, one common practice was *redlining,* which entails such actions as banks refusing to lend to non-Whites to buy homes in certain geographic areas, landlords not renting to non-Whites, or insurance companies refusing to sell to or drastically increasing costs for certain groups of people. Redlining, part of the legacy of racism, led not only to segregated neighborhoods and a lack of wealth to pass on to the next generation in terms of the value of a home but also to a lack of employment opportunities for Blacks in these neighborhoods, which in turn contributed to other social problems such as crime and inferior funding for neighborhood schools. Neither the Fair Housing Act of 1968 nor the Community Investment Act of 1977 put an end to redlining as they were intended to do. Until 1988, enforcement against redlining was all too often lax (Popple & Leighninger, 2011), and even today there are discriminatory practices in place.

In addition to redlining, many government housing policies and practices carried out in cities did not take into account, or did not care about, the negative consequences they would have on low-income individuals, many of whom were African Americans. Urban renewal, coined "negro removal" by novelist James Baldwin, was to rid cities of "slum" areas in order to redevelop and revitalize metropolitan areas. These "slum" areas housed communities of people who saw their homes literally demolished as bulldozers came through and leveled entire blocks. On the one hand, urban renewal did get rid of dilapidated and unsafe housing units, and it did have significant economic benefits for many. On the other hand, low-income Blacks had their social community displaced in addition to losing their housing.

Twenty years into urban renewal, a member of President Nixon's urban renewal task force pointed out the failure of the program to replace destroyed housing units with affordable units, leaving hundreds of thousands of people displaced (Anderson, 1969). High-rise public apartments—known for drugs, violence, and rat infestation; deaths due to fires; dangerous elevators; and overall neglect by city officials—were the only option available to many low-income people who were displaced. There were activists calling for building mixed-income public housing units, rather than segregating and isolating Blacks even further in the most deteriorated areas of the city, but that approach very rarely won the day. In retrospect, the high-rise apartments are seen as a public housing failure by many (Moore, 2014; Ziemba, 1986). The last of the high-rises are coming down, but, as with slavery, the impact they had on many families is still in play. Although far from meeting the need, government support for mixed-income housing took off in the early 1990s under the Clinton administration, which implemented Hope VI, a Housing and Urban Development plan to replace the worst public housing units with less dense mixed-income housing (Moore, 2014).

Eminent domain, a government policy used in the name of progress, and often part of urban renewal, gives the state authority to take private land for public use as long as there is just compensation. The use of eminent domain for federally subsidized highways to run through city centers resulted in significant upheaval of low-income Black neighborhoods. Even when there were protests against the destruction of communities for the sake of the almighty car and quick transport, activists' efforts were frequently unsuccessful.[2]

Another example of government policies inadvertently (or not) leading to harmful policy for Blacks was the subsidizing of development in the suburbs at the expense of investing in the city. As more and more Whites left the cities, taking the tax base with them to the suburbs and county governments, certain areas of cities fell further into disrepair. Trying to make up for the lost tax base by increasing tax rates just increased the *White flight,* the rapid exodus of Whites from cities to suburbs, and further impoverished those too poor to leave.

Government intervention to desegregate schools, to fulfill the 1954 Supreme Court ruling that outlawed school desegregation, did not bring about the results hoped for by reformers in support of the *Brown* ruling. Reporting on research conducted by the Civil Rights Project at Harvard, Orfield and Eaton (2003, para. 2) state that "the integration of black students . . . had improved steadily from the 1960s through the late 1980s. But, as of the 2000–01 school year, the levels have backed off to lows not seen in three decades." In their 1996 book *Dismantling Desegregation: The Quiet Reversal of* Brown v. Board of Education, Orfield and Eaton set forth that *Brown v. Board of Education* "failed to spell out, either in educational or numerical terms, what successful desegregation should look like" (Kirkus Review, 2010, para. 1). The result was "divisive strategies such as school busing programs, accompanied by white flight to the suburbs, district gerrymandering, and other attempts to get around the Court's decision" (Kirkus Review, 2010, para. 1). Moreover, Orfield, a professor of education at the University of California at Los Angeles, contends that many of the reforms put in place following *Brown v. Board of Education* in 1954 "were only seriously enforced for a few years, and that other provisions have been slowly stripped away in the years since the landmark case" (Orfield, cited in Bidwell, 2013, para. 2).

Where We Stand Currently Relative to Racial Equality–Public Opinion

Perceptions of how much progress has been made in getting rid of racial discrimination since the 1960s and how much discrimination still exists in regard to Whites and Blacks differ greatly based on whether one is Black or White. In a June 2014 CBS poll, 28% of Whites believed that Whites have a better chance of getting ahead than Blacks, and 63% believed it to be about equal (there was a +/- 3 margin of error). Additionally, 46% of Blacks believed that Whites have a better chance of getting ahead, and 46%

---

[2] Jane Jacobs led the charge to protest the Mid-Manhattan Expressway and was successful. This was not a predominantly Black neighborhood.

believed Blacks and Whites had about an equal chance of getting ahead. Given that 38% of Blacks said there hasn't been much real progress since the 1960s, and 88% believe there is some, or a lot of, racial discrimination against African Americans, it is surprising that 46% of Blacks believe that Blacks and Whites have about an equal chance of getting ahead (Polling Report, 2015). In a 2016 Pew Research poll, 88% of Blacks, 7% of Hispanics, and 53% of Whites say that more change is needed to achieve equality between White and Black in America, and 38% of Whites say equality between Whites and Blacks has already been achieved (Stepler, 2016).

A CBS/*New York Times* poll taken July 13, 2016, indicates that perceptions of race relations has plummeted a 40-point drop since 2009 and an 11-point drop since 2015. The poll, taken the week following two different incidents where men who were Black were shot by police[3] and a lone gunman then shot and killed five police officers, showed that approximately 70% of Americans believe that race relations are bad. Close to 60% of Americans said race relations are getting worse, while just 9%, versus 21% a year ago, indicated improvement (Dutto, DePinto, Backus, & Salvanta, 2016).

The last time race relations were perceived as this bad was following the Rodney King incident[4] in 1992 that sounded the alarm to police using excessive force. It is certainly likely that widely publicized incidents in 2015 and 2016, such as those in Ferguson, New York City, Baltimore, Cleveland, Charleston, Baton Rouge, and St. Paul, have increased a lot of peoples' awareness of the degree of racial tension and of realities that most middle- and upper-class Whites are far distanced from. (Most of these incidents are discussed in a later section.)

Public polls provide a barometer of peoples' perceptions, but to gain solid research-based knowledge about where we stand as a nation in regard to racism; we turn to social science research that indicates "this country's racial oppression became well institutionalized and thoroughly systemic over many generations, including how it has been rationalized and maintained for centuries" (Yancey & Feagin, 2015, para. 11). The narrative referred to earlier, in which African Americans were dehumanized and framed as the "inferior race," is what led to institutionalized and systematic racism. In other words, we put in place structures and systems that led to racial inequalities. Although some policies and practices have changed, the system as structured still results in inequalities and lack of opportunity. The narrative, *at least overtly,* may have changed, but oppressive systems remain.

---

[3] See section "Incidents of Police Misconduct" for information about the deaths of these two men, Alton Sterling and Philando Sterling, and the subsequent killing of five Dallas police officers.

[4] Rodney King's brutal beating by four Los Angeles police officers, while other officers stood by, was caught on video by a bystander and brought the issue of police treatment to people of color to national attention. There were riots in the streets after the officers were acquitted. It spurred a major overhaul in the L.A. police force to address racial profiling and police brutality (Taylor, 2012).

Yale University assistant professor Velsa Weaver informs us that civil rights era policies launched the Black middle class, and 20% of Blacks have made considerable financial gains in the last 50 years. On the other hand, the bottom 20% of Blacks have made no financial gains. Weaver goes on to say that "racial inequality persists because policies of the civil rights era were inadequate to addressing the situation of blacks in the bottom third of the income distribution" (Weaver, cited in Drew, 2014, para. 1). Weaver also makes the point that it is problematic that we "focus primarily or solely on individual discrimination by bad actors rather than on the cumulative disadvantage that has marked the lives of the segregated poor"; and "this colorblind approach robs our nation of a useful vocabulary for explaining persisting racial inequality that looks eerily similar to past systems" (Weaver, cited in Drew, 2014, para. 1). The fact that a good many Blacks are doing well financially helps to justify the bad actors narrative and calls for personal responsibility of low-income people of color rather than looking at structural issues.

Georgetown Law Professor Sheryll Cashin, who like Weaver and others says we need to dismantle institutionalized discrimination, sets forth that "we have a lot of enduring structures of Jim Crow. . . . So we have persistent racial inequality in large part because of these enduring structures, often tied to where you live" (Cashin, cited in Drew, 2014, para. 1). In making this point, she refers to the residential and interrelated educational segregation and disparities that are prevalent today:

If you are lucky you won the lottery of birth and picked the right parents and can afford to buy your way into a solid middle- or upper-middle class neighborhood—particularly if you can buy your way into a gold-standard neighborhood—you have access to quality education that sets you up very, very well in life. If you don't there's a lot of inequality. (Cashin, cited in Drew, 2014, para. 2)

WHERE WE STAND CURRENTLY RELATIVE TO RACIAL EQUALITY IN EDUCATION, HOUSING/BANK LENDING, HEALTH, CRIMINAL JUSTICE, AND INCIDENTS OF POLICE MISCONDUCT. ALSO, A WORD ABOUT CONCENTRATED POVERTY

Education

Today in our nation's school system there is a very high degree of racial and socioeconomic class segregation. While there is greater racial and ethnic diversity in some suburban communities than in the past, others remain extremely racially segregated. The same is the case with many inner-city schools. Southern schools have not returned to being as segregated as they were before *Brown,* but overall our nation's schools are again about as segregated as in the 1960s (Orfield & Frankenberg, 2014). The integration that occurred with school busing, which had its own set of problems, did lead to more integrated schools. Due to court decisions, by the end of the 1990s, busing ended, leading schools (on average) to become more segregated. Acknowledging that integration is not always feasible, nor a panacea, Orfield and Frankenberg (2014) point out that "a half century of research shows that many forms of unequal opportunity are linked to segregation. Research also finds that desegregated education has substantial benefits for educational and later life outcomes for students from all backgrounds (Executive Summary, para. 8).

> Furthermore, students in high-poverty, racially segregated schools are not exposed to high-quality curricula, highly qualified teachers, or important social networks as often as students in wealthier, predominantly White schools. . . . Schools where White students are in the majority are more than twice as likely to offer a significant number of advanced placement classes as schools where Black and Latino students are in the majority. Black and Latino students with the same test scores as White and Asian students are less likely to be placed in accelerated courses and more likely to be placed in low-track academic courses. (Annie E. Casey Foundation, 2006, paras. 5–6)

Housing and Bank Mortgage Loans

The racial and socioeconomic makeup of students in our nation's schools reflects the racial and socioeconomic makeup of neighborhoods. A study released in 2012 by the Manhattan Institute for Policy Research, "The End of the Segregated Century," had some thinking the tide had turned. It concluded that neighborhoods are "more integrated than they've been since 1910" and "all-white neighborhoods are effectively extinct" (Glaeser & Vigdor, cited in McWhorter, 2012). This study sparked a great deal of controversy from many fronts that point to ample evidence to indicate progress in regard to residential integration but high degrees of segregation that still exist in many cities across the United States. In response to the report,

> the Chicago Area Fair Housing Alliance (CAFHA), a consortium of fair housing and advocacy organizations, government agencies, and municipalities, says the report 'overstates and oversimplifies the gains made in integration over the last century' and 'does not reflect the complexities of racial segregation, particularly in housing, that arise out of multi-faceted forces including public policies, private sector investment, and public perceptions about race.' (Valbrun, n.d., para. 19)

Some critics also pointed out methodological flaws, for example, Glaeser and Vigdor had only two categories, Black and non-Blacks, so when more Blacks and Latinos are living in the same neighborhood than in the past, it appears integrated whether or not Whites live in that neighborhood (Valbrun, n.d.). Rolf Pendall (2013), director of the Metropolitan Housing & Communities Policy Center at the Urban Institute, states that "less segregated metropolitan areas still have levels of racial segregation far higher than the Fair Housing Act promised" (para. 16). Pendall also refers to Urban Institute research in claiming that

> racially exclusionary zoning practices persist. Public housing authorities per-petuated segregation well into the 1990s; such practices have not ended just because they are illegal. Illegal discrimination against black and Hispanic renters and owners goes on, as ample Urban Institute research has shown. And whites still seek out and are steered to predominantly white neighborhoods. (Pendall, 2013, para. 7)

A report submitted to the U.N. Committee on the Elimination of Racial Discrimi-nation on behalf of more than 50 civil organizations and experts supports Pendall's claim. It sets forth that "in spite of U.S. legal standards . . . U.S. policy has failed to address both societal and government discrimination, and continues to support racially and economically segregated housing patterns" (Haberle & Soto, 2014, Introduction, para. 1).

As mentioned previously, lending practices contribute to the problem. In 2009, the Center for American Progress, a nonpartisan research and educational insti-tute, released a report of their analysis to determine if racial disparities in lending occurred in 14 of the largest mortgage lending banks in the United States. An analysis of 2006 data indicated that although illegal, nonetheless "significant dis-parities exist in the prevalence of high-cost lending between minorities and whites" (Jakabovics & Chapman, 2009, Conclusion, para. 1). When borrowing from one of the large banks, 41.5% of African Americans got higher priced mortgages than Whites. Moreover, the analysis, taking income into account, found that "among high-income borrowers in 2006, African Americans were three times as likely as whites to pay higher prices for mortgages" (Jakabovics & Chapman, 2009, Intro-duction, para. 4). The question the researchers could not answer from their analysis was why this disparity occurred.

Health

The *Journal of the American Medical Association* (JAMA), the Institute of Medicine (IOM), and the *On-Line Journal of Issues in Nursing* have all published articles indicating that there is evidence that racial and ethnic disparities in health care exist (Baldwin, 2003; Egede, 2006; Fiscella, Franks, Gold, & Clancy, 2000). Moreover, the IOM and the authors indicate there is a desire to better understand reasons for lower quality care of non-Whites and rectify the problems given that, as Egede (2006) put it, "many times patients of minority ethnicity experience greater morbidity and mortality from various chronic diseases than non-minorities" (para. 1). There is acknowledgment that socioeconomic position is a stronger indicator than race/ethnicity in regard to health outcomes and, when controlled for the effect of race/ethnicity on health outcomes, decreases significantly and sometimes disappears (para. 6).

Criminal Justice

The United States has the highest incarceration rate in the world, and those behind bars are disproportionately people of color. African Americans make up approximately 13% of the U.S. population but account for 40% of the prison population (Tonn, 2014). African Americans are six times more likely to be incarcerated than Whites according to a 2010 report by the Pew Research Center (Drake, 2013). Although drug offenders do not differ considerably by race, the Human Rights Watch reported in 2000 that "African Americans constitute 80–90 percent of all drug offenders sent to prison" (Alexander, 2012, p. 98).[5]

Stop-and-frisk policies in New York City during the first decade of the 21st century resulted in literally millions of people in the city being stopped, in theory based on probable cause. Research though showed that 87% to 89% of these stops did not produce any evidence of criminal activity and disproportionately affected minorities. Over 50% of the stops were of African Americans (Sharp, 2012).

Palumbo-Liu (2015) reported the findings of researcher Sam Sinyangwe, who found that Black people are three times[6] more likely to be killed by police in the United States than White people. More unarmed Black people were killed by police than unarmed White people last year. And that's taking into account the fact that Black people are only 14% of the population (para. 32).

These statistics and many others leave no doubt that gross disparities still exist within our criminal justice system. What they do not tell us is why they exist or the interrelationship between the role of race and socioeconomic class. Mauer and Ghandnoosh (2014), research analysts for The Sentencing Project, present four key contributing factors for the disparities. The first is socioeconomic (SES)

---

[5] Alexander draws from surveys that frequently indicated that White youth sell and use cocaine, crack, and heroin at a much higher rate than Blacks (2012, p. 99). The same is true for marijuana use (Matthews, 2013).

[6] The *Washington Post* findings indicate Black people are 2.5 times more likely to be killed by police in the United States than White people (Lowery, 2016).

inequalities. They contend that "economic disadvantage that is compounded by racial inequality . . . erode economic and social buffers against crime making people of color more likely to commit more serious property and violent offenses, but not drug offenses" (Mauer & Ghandnoosh, 2014, "Causes of Racial . . ." para. 1).

Second, they point to underfunding in the criminal justice system that results in disadvantages for low-income people. For example, the limited financial resources of low-income people of color make them less able to post bail. Research shows that those who are detained at the time of trial have higher conviction rates, are more likely to accept less favorable plea deals, and are more likely to be given longer sentences. Also, too often those with low incomes, who cannot afford a lawyer, end up with public defenders who have high caseloads or limited experience (Mauer & Ghandnoosh, 2014, "Resource Allocation Decisions . . ." paras. 2 & 3).

Third, there are policies and practices that on the surface are race neutral but due to how they combine with SES patterns result in disparities. For example, stop-and-frisk tactics and other heavy policing that occurs in certain neighborhoods where more low-income people of color reside will lead to more arrests of people of color. Sentencing laws that are harsher for certain classes of offenders often impact people of color more than Whites (Mauer & Ghandnoosh, 2014).

Finally, "studies of criminal justice outcomes also reveal widespread implicit bias among criminal justice professionals, people of color fare differently than whites even when accounting for other relevant factors including class, offense type, and criminal history" (Mauer & Ghandnoosh, 2014, "Implicit Bias Among . . ." para. 1). Implicit bias is unconscious and unintentional cognitions about a group. A person may be an ardent supporter of antidiscrimination efforts and strongly believe they do not hold any negative stereotypes about Blacks (or other groups), but unconsciously they do—they are just not aware of it. Roberts (2011) reports that while over 85% of people in the United States don't consider themselves to be prejudiced, "researchers have concluded that the majority of people in the United States hold some degree of implicit racial bias" (Mauer & Ghandnoosh, 2014, "Implicit Bias Among . . ." para. 2). Mooney (2014) reports that the majority of White online takers of Harvard's Implicit Attitude Test[7] demonstrate a bias toward Blacks that they are often unaware of. Implicit bias stems from a narrative about African Americans that includes many negative stereotypes that people are exposed to and have passed down through generations.

There is no shortage of studies that point to implicit bias across the criminal justice system. Roberts (2011) points to a study in which judges granted sentences to dark-skinned defendants that were 8 months longer than sentences for light-skinned

---

[7] The Implicit Attitudes Test is a popular online tool that researchers use to understand prejudice and racism. It can be found at UnderstandingPrejudice.org

defendants for identical offenses. Mauer and Ghandnoosh (2014) point to numerous studies, one being of juvenile probation officers in Washington, who in narrative reports "attributed the problems of white youth to their social environment but those of black youth to their attitude and personality" ("Implicit Racial Bias . . ." para. 6). Another study Mauer and Ghandnoosh reference shows that Blacks are three times more likely than Whites to be searched after being pulled over for a traffic stop and twice as likely to be arrested during a traffic stop as Whites.

There are efforts under way in the criminal justice arena in many cities to help officers identify their implicit biases. For example, Charles Ramsey, Commissioner of Philadelphia police and chair of the president's task force on 21st century policing, has a program in place where new officers are trained to identify their biases. Furthermore, his new officers also spend a week learning about the history of policing in America.

> 'If you were in the South, you might have been tracking down slaves,' Ramsey says. 'Who enforced Jim Crow Laws? Police. So just as our democracy has evolved, so have we. But what about those people who were on the other side? That baggage is still there. It ain't gone away. So why is there more tension in one community vs. another community? A lot of it has to do with the history of policing. Now I'm not saying you spend your life looking in the rearview mirror, but I am saying you can't move forward until you understand where you have been.' (Vick, 2015, p. 39)

Referring to the current situation with police as a crisis, Ramsey is optimistic regarding what the end result can be. "Because it's in crisis that you can implement the kind of change that you need. . . . You wish you didn't have to go through it, but we'll come out better tuned to the community as a result" (Vick, 2015, p. 39).

Incidents of Police Misconduct

Most police officers carry out their responsibilities with respect and civility.[8] Still, there have been far too many incidents in which police officers have seriously violated the rights of people. In contrast to the Sam Sinyangwe study noted above, a 2015 study by the *Washington Post* found that an unarmed Black man is seven times more likely to be shot at than an unarmed White man (Kindy & Elliot, 2015). Regardless of the discrepancies over the exact level of increased danger Blacks face in encounters with the police, it is clear that this is a critical issue. In 2014, there

---

[8] "Thousands of police officers in this country are committed to public safety, and that commitment has to be honored by changing the culture in a way that we can trust one another. Good police officers want to be held accountable, and we need to hold ourselves accountable as a nation for segregation, lynching and terrorism, slavery, and for the police misconduct that we've tolerated" (Stevenson, 2016, para. 6).

were numerous high-profile cases in which Black males died as the result of a police officer's actions. Michael Brown was shot and killed in Ferguson, Missouri, and Eric Garner was put in an illegal choke hold by a New York police officer and died. John Crawford had picked up an unpackaged BB gun and was said to be waving it around and pointing it at people in a Walmart store. He was shot and killed by police who arrived at the store after a 911 call. Akai Gurley was in the stairwell of a housing project when a police officer on what is called a "vertical patrol" fired down the stairwell and killed Gurley, who was not the suspect but rather an innocent bystander. And 12-year-old Tamir Rice was shot and killed by Cleveland police at a playground. He was holding a toy gun (Childress, 2015). These are just a few examples from one year. In 2015, Walter Scott was shot seven times in the back as he tried to flee police on foot after being pulled over for a traffic stop. The highest profile case in 2015 that led to mass riots in Baltimore and other cities was the death of Freddie Gray. Gray was not shot but died of spinal injuries after an arrest in which he cried out in pain and a ride in a police van in which he was placed on his stomach, not seat-belted in, and not given medical attention when he fell unconscious (Gunter, 2015).

The Scott, Gurley, and Gray cases resulted in indictments. The others in 2014 and 2015 did not. Although no indictment occurred in the Michael Brown case, the Justice Department did investigate the Ferguson police department and found a culture of bias against Blacks. Specifically, they found regular discriminatory action such as arrests for petty offenses, illegal traffic stops, and excessive force. Reforms have been mandated. Ferguson was one of 20 police departments in the last 5 years that the Justice Department has investigated for discrimination and police brutality (Childress, 2015).

As of 2015, 14 of 20 police departments investigated were found to have a culture in which systematic civil rights violations had taken place. Among the 14 are New Orleans, Detroit, Cleveland, Chicago, Ferguson, Miami, Newark, and Portland, Oregon. They and others are under forced agreements with the Justice Department to overhaul their departments to address the injustices. For example, in Cleveland, the police department was expected to eliminate pistol whippings and the use of neck holds, stop using Tasers if a suspect is fleeing, create a system of layered oversight, implement problem-oriented policing, and improve investigation of civilian complaints. While the Justice Department is more aggressively attempting to ensure that changes are made in departments in violation of appropriate policing, there have been concerns raised about the outcomes and whether or not the changes will be lasting (Weichselbaum, 2015).

The latest high-profile deaths by police, before this book went to press, occurred in the first week of July, 2016. In Baton Rouge, Louisiana, Alton Sterling, who was Black, was shot and killed by police while being held face down on the ground by two police officers (Lowery, Andrews, & Miller, 2016). A few days later, Philandro

Castile was stopped for a taillight that was not working properly and because the officer, citing his "wide nose," stated to dispatch that he and his girlfriend looked like robbery suspects. Castile's girlfriend, with her 4-year-old daughter in the back-seat, recorded part of the incident immediately after Castile was shot. The video went viral as did video taken of the Sterling incident. The governor of Minnesota questioned if the shooting would have occurred if Castile had been White. He stated, "I'm forced to confront, and I think all of us in Minnesota are forced to confront, that this kind of racism exists" (Domonoske & Chapell, 2016, para. 9). The head of the National Association of Police Organizations responded that the governor's comments "exploited what was already a horrible and tragic situation" (Shapiro, Bever, Lowery, Miller, & Sharp, 2016, para. 6). These two incidents set off what began as peaceful gathering in cities throughout the United States. The gatherings in Dallas turned violent when one individual, believed to be acting alone, shot and killed five police officers (Karimi, Shoichet, & Ellis (2016).

A week after the tragedies reported in the above paragraph, Tim Scott, a Republican senator who is Black, shared on the Senate floor that he had been pulled over by police seven times in the past year, and that the majority of the times he was "driving a new car in the wrong neighborhood or something else just as trivial" (Kelly, 2016, para. 3). Noting that while many police officers do good, some do not, he spoke of encounters his brother and staff member had experienced. His staffer, after getting tired of being pulled over for having a nice car, finally just got rid of the car. Senator Scott expressed concern about the divide between law enforcement and communities, stating that "I do not know many African American men who do not have a very similar story to tell, no matter their profession, no matter their income, no matter their disposition in life. . . . There is absolutely nothing more frustrating, more damaging to your soul than when you know you're following the rules and being treated like you are not" (Kelly, 2016, paras. 6 & 8). He ended his speech telling his colleagues to "recognize that just because you do not feel the pain, the anguish of another, does not mean it does not exist" (Kelly, 2016, para. 10).

Concentrated Poverty (Areas of High Poverty)

Numerous university researchers have shown the negative effects of living in a neighborhood with high rates of poverty. That is a census tract area in which over 40% of the population lives below the federal poverty level. Before the turn of the 21st century, neighborhoods with concentrated poverty were on the decrease, but in the last 15 years, we have witnessed an increase. Today, one in four Black Americans live in high-poverty neighborhoods. One in 13 Whites lives in high-poverty areas. Living in these areas has a significant effect on opportunity and outcomes, such as social mobility, of those in the neighborhood (Florida, 2015).

WHERE TO FROM HERE?

In an interview about the murder of eight African Americans attending their church in Charleston, Bryan Stevenson, founder and executive director of the Equal Justice Initiative, argues the narrative in the United States regarding race is still that there is a difference between Blacks and Whites. Policies and practices discussed above that lead to inequities and the Implicit Association Test provide concrete support for Stevenson's belief that people have not fully embraced, accepted, internalized, and acted on or believe the narrative that there is no real difference between races (Johnson, 2015). The majority of Americans react strongly against overt racism against Black citizens and want all to have equal opportunities, but to move toward racial equality we must do what Stevenson says we have not yet done.

We must examine and change the narrative that allowed us to enslave people and then legally discriminate against people, as it still lives on and can be seen in our culture and how African-Americans are characterized. We must educate ourselves and gain an informed understanding of the existing policies and practices that perpetuate racial inequities. In doing this, we will see that too often race-neutral policies are not race neutral in practice, suggesting strongly that race-conscious practices must be considered and confirming the need for the often uncomfortable yet necessary direct and open dialog about race.

Part of the challenge in moving forward is addressing implicit bias, which a plethora of research says exists. It is promising that there is more acknowledgment of implicit bias, and within many professions there are efforts to address it. The horrifying events in, for example, Charleston, Ferguson, Baltimore, New York City, and Cleveland[9] put the issue of racism on the radar of many citizens. Now the question is if our nation is willing to change the narrative that drives those biases. Charles Ramsey provides an example of the type of action needed to improve society by discussing and addressing prejudice and discrimination.

A LONG WAY TO GO

During one evening of Nana Jo's storytelling, Trevor jumped in with "Was it my great-grandpa or great-great-grandpa who was a slave and tried to escape but was

---

[9] June 2015, Charleston, South Carolina: Dylann Roof, who is White and whose writings indicate he adhered to White supremacist ideology, opened fire in the AME Church killing nine African Americans attending a Bible study.

August 2014, Ferguson, Missouri: Michael Brown, a Black 18-year-old, was fatally shot by a White police officer. The case was controversial and sparked a great deal of civil unrest.

caught and beaten?" He had a hard time keeping straight which generation in his family was the last one enslaved.

"That was your great-great-great-grandpa, Trevor, so a very long time ago, but, yes, he almost made it to the North and to freedom but was caught. Your great-great grandparents and great-grandparents were sharecroppers."

"Oh yeah, I know about sharecroppers," said Trevor, and he went on to explain the hardships experienced by most sharecroppers. The next time James was over and story time started, he said with pride, "I have something in common with you guys. My mom told me that her great-grandparents and grandparents were share-croppers and went hungry a lot. It sounds like some Whites had it hard, too." Nana Jo gave James a hug, agreed, and left it at that.

"Enough about sharecropping for tonight. This old body is heading to bed."

Nana Jo heard Jewell come in as she headed for her room. *Uh-oh,* she thought, *what is my daughter doing home at this time?* "Jewell?" Nana Jo said softly when she saw that Jewell had been crying.

"I have taken enough of their rude comments. I should not have to put up with that crap," said Jewell, on the verge of tears. "It is one thing when older residents make racist comments like 'I don't want a Black girl helping me into my chair' or whatever it is. I can typically just joke with them, and if I make light of it, most often those few residents seem to change their attitude toward me. What I am sick and tired of is when I overhear ignorant comments made by staff members. I know other White workers don't like it either, as some have told me so, but I don't know that any of them have ever said anything to the offenders. Both the subtle and overt comments and actions are becoming more frequent. Last week Sandra was the target. She opened her locker, and to her horror saw "nigger go back to Africa" scrawled on a piece of paper on the inside of the door. I think administration has a good idea who left it, but there were no fingerprints or witnesses, so no one has been held accountable yet.

"I'm still rattled by that incident, and then tonight I walk into the break room unnoticed to hear a derogatory comment being made about Sandra. I figured the two talking were maybe the same ones who taped the hateful message on her locker door. Then I realized they are talking about me, too, not knowing I had entered the room. I hear that for a 'lazy, fat, Black bitch she at least has a sense of humor.' I cough, and they turned to see me. With an embarrassed look on their faces, they had the gall to greet me and ask how Carla, one of my residents who they know has been really sick, was doing. I just turned around, walked out, and went to talk to the shift supervisor, who helped write up a complaint. The supervisor, who is White, was so irate that I actually ended up calming her down.

"We decided that confronting the two tonight might not be best in the long run, so she was going to put the complaint on the director's desk and also call first thing in the morning. I took her up on the offer to take off early as I felt I might say something I would regret if I had to encounter those two again tonight. She guaranteed me that I would be paid for the full shift. Mom, I know you dealt with this kind of bullshit, and much worse, all the time, but when is it going to end? Are we ever going to move past being discriminated against and seen as less than?

"I have always appreciated that you aren't bitter and have made it clear to the boys that despite the conditions, there was laughter, fun, love, and joy in the lives of their ancestors just as was the case today. I don't want to be bitter either, but right now that's how I feel."

Jewell was more worked up than Jocelyn had seen her for years. When she got a chance to break in, she said, "Jewell, you know I have had feelings of bitterness on and off. I have just chosen not to get stuck there. Let's keeping talking, but, if you are ready, why don't you go say goodnight to the boys first. I think they may have overheard us."

Jewell gave her mom (who was also her best friend) a quick hug, then headed to the boys' room to find them giggling about something. She was relieved that they hadn't been trying to eavesdrop on her conversation with her mom. It's not that she wouldn't share what happened, but she wanted to put some thought into how best to word it and needed to calm down first.

Jewell entered the room and was greeted with, "Hi Mom," from her sons, and "Hi, Ms. Jewell," from James. Jewell's spirits were lifted as the boys told her about their baseball game. They chose to leave out that earlier in the day Louis had been kicked out of the pool. Jewell hated missing so many of their games but had no choice. Knowing that Nana Jo was there cheering for them helped reduce the guilt. After about 10 minutes of listening to the boys talk about the upcoming school year, which was soon to begin, Jewell kissed them goodnight and went to find her mom.

As she walked slowly down the hallway, her mind was racing. Uncle Charlie, who had spent time in prison, came to mind. True, he had done something wrong, but the 15-year prison sentence he received for possession of some crack cocaine was, according to Nana Jo, excessive given that "if it had been cocaine rather than crack the mandatory sentence would have been for far fewer years."[10] The boys were well aware of the high percentage of African American males who end up spending time behind bars. Besides their uncle, they had friends with family members in prison and knew of gang members in the area who had already been to prison. They had heard their grandma go on about how time in prison too often becomes a life sentence that puts up hurdles to reentry into society and can even

---

[10] Legislation has passed since Charles was charged to help alleviate the disparity in sentencing for cocaine (historically, more often used by Whites) versus crack cocaine (historically, more often used by African Americans).

cost you the right to vote. Ex-felons have strikes against them, for example, having to indicate they have been convicted of a crime when applying for most jobs and when applying for certain kinds of public housing.[11] Nana Jo typically prefaced her point about the cost savings of assisting ex-felons who want to change their lives secure gainful employment with her strong belief that more must be done to ensure equal educational opportunity for all, regardless of race and socioeconomic class.

Her frustration level continued to rise as she thought of the three precious boys, who she could still hear laughing, being robbed of their innocence by the frightening realities that were brought home by the tragedies of Ferguson, New York, Baltimore, Cleveland, Charleston, Baton Rouge, St. Paul, and other places. Jewell and Nana Jo had many conversations about these and other incidents with the boys, sadly telling them there were different rules for them when it came to things like interacting with the police that were dangerous to ignore even if a majority of police officers were not consciously racist. The need for a #BlackLivesMatter movement in the 21st century further saddened Jewell.

A cup of chamomile tea was waiting at the kitchen table for Jewell. Jocelyn finished folding a batch of laundry and joined her. "Feel better?" she asked. Jewell smiled, then turned more serious. "I really do feel like Fannie Lou Hamer. I'm just sick and tired of this uphill battle we have to keep fighting against racist attitudes, actions, and policies. Life has enough challenges. I don't want the boys to encounter differential treatment just because they're Black. I didn't mention to you that Sylvia just told me that her 14-year-old son, Jay, and another friend, who is also Black, were recently stopped and frisked by a police officer on their way home from football practice. Jay has no idea why he was stopped. Two of their White friends walked by the same officer about 90 seconds before they did and weren't stopped. I am not demonizing all cops, nor supporting protestors who break the law, but I am thankful for the peaceful rallies as we better admit and make clear to politicians that we have a serious systemic problem that needs to be addressed."

"Jewell," Jocelyn finally interrupted, as she knew Jewell would go on and on, "we are not going to solve this problem tonight, and you look exhausted. Do you think you can get some sleep?"

Jewell nodded and started to clear their teacups. She felt drained and helpless. As she got ready for bed, she wondered how others seemed to let racist jokes and derogatory comments roll off their shoulders. Or maybe they didn't. Maybe some people just kept the anger and frustration bottled up. She was well aware that even the incident at work that night was not like the discrimination her mom, grandparents,

---

[11] Some communities have gotten rid of the criminal record box on job applications, and President Obama has made the suggestion to do away with it as well. That doesn't mean a potential employer is kept from knowing if an applicant has a criminal history. It just means that it is not one of the first things the employer sees.

and earlier ancestors had faced. One example came to mind when she remembered a story her mom had told her when, as a result of an application he mailed in, her paternal grandpa was asked to come in for an interview for a job at a bank. When they saw he was Black, they told him there was no way they would consider hiring a Black, and it was a mistake that he was asked to the interview in the first place.

I need to get my mind on something else or I'll never get to sleep, Jewell thought, and picked up a science fiction book on her bed stand that she was about halfway through. In less than 5 minutes, she couldn't keep her eyes open. She was awakened by Louis hollering that she had a phone call.

"Good morning, Jewell," came the barely audible voice at the other end of the phone, who Jewell recognized as the nursing home director. "I am sorry to call so early, but I came in and saw the incident report on my desk and wanted to follow up on it. The protocol, which last night's supervisor did not realize, is that the report should go to the agency ombudsman. I am sure you will be hearing from Mr. Franklin, the ombudsman for Springdale, very soon. As you know, the mission of Springdale includes having a welcoming environment for all who enter our doors. If we are falling short, we need to address it."

QUESTIONS FOR DISCUSSION

1. Discuss the practice of Jim Crow laws and their consequences. Does understanding the Jim Crow laws have relevance to understanding the circumstances regarding race (Blacks and Whites) relations today?

2. The Civil Rights Act of 1964 and the Voting Rights Act of 1965 outlawed discrimination. How effective were these major laws in ending de facto discrimination in the 20th century? Provide a rationale for your answer, including examples.

3. What was the stated intent of urban renewal, and how did it impact people from low-income areas?

4. What key examples in the case indicate that discrimination against Blacks has continued into the 21st century?

5. Discuss the research findings on implicit bias and the implications of implicit bias for things such as hiring and interactions with police officers. Where else might it affect outcomes?

6. Take the Harvard Implicit Association Test on race at https://implicit.harvard .edu/implicit/takeatest.html. Provide your reaction to the test.

7. Respond to the belief some hold that people have not fully embraced, accepted, internalized, and acted on, or believe the narrative that there is no difference between races.

8. Where do we go from here? Jot down some ideas about how we might move forward toward a more just society in regard to race.

CASE ANALYSIS WRITING ASSIGNMENT

1. Read the assigned case study thoroughly prior to class in order to be fully prepared to join in the discussion.

2. Using what you have read, write an analysis in which you discuss whether or not you think *A Long Way to Go* is a fitting title for this case. Provide evidence from the case to support your position.

3. The analysis should be an approximately two-and-a-half-page, typed, double-spaced essay. Your essay should reflect the standards and expectations of college-level writing: spelling, grammar, and appropriate use of paragraphs all matter. If you quote directly from the case study, use quotation marks, and at the end of the quote, indicate the page number the quote appeared on. For example, "When borrowing from one of the large banks 41.5% of African Americans got higher-priced mortgages than whites" (Jakabovics & Chapman, 2009, as cited in Lewis, 2016, p. 58).

4. Your case analysis is due _____ and worth a maximum of ____ points.

INTERNET SOURCES

Black Lives Matter (http://blacklivesmatter.com)

Civil Rights Project at UCLA (www.civilrightsproject.ucla.edu)

Equal Justice Initiative (http://www.eji.org)

Foreign Affairs: Racial Inequality After Racism (https://www.foreignaffairs.com/articles/united-states/2015–03–01/racial-inequality-after-racism)

Harvard's Implicit Bias Test (https://implicit.harvard.edu/implicit/takeatest.html)

Inequality.org (http://inequality.org/racial-inequality)

NAACP (www.naacp.org)

REFERENCES

Alexander, M. (2012). *The new Jim Crow.* New York, NY: New Press.

Anderson, M. (1969, December 4). *Memorandum for the President.* [Urban Renewal]. Retrieved from http://www.nixonlibrary.gov/virtuallibrary/releases/ju110/35.pdf

Annie E. Casey Foundation (2006). *Unequal opportunities in education.* Retrieved from http://www.aecf.org/m/resourcedoc/aecf-racemattersEDUCATION-2006.pdf

Baldwin, D. (2003, January 31). Disparities in health and health care: Focusing efforts to eliminate unequal burdens. *Online Journal of Issues in Nursing, 8*(1). Retrieved from http://www.nursingworld.org/MainMenuCategories/ANAMarketplace/ANAPeriodicals/OJIN/TableofContents/Volume82003/N01Jan2003/DisparitiesinHealthandHealthCare.html

Bidwell, A. (2013, October 29). Education reformers say it's time for a new civil rights era. *US News.* Retrieved from http://www.usnews.com/news/articles/2013/10/29/education-reformers-say-its-time-for-a-new-civil-rights-era

Childress, S. (2015, March 4). How the DOJ reforms a police department like Ferguson. *Public Broadcasting System.* Retrieved from http://www.pbs.org/wgbh/frontline/article/how-the-doj-reforms-a-police-department-like-ferguson

Domonoske, C., & Chapell, B. (2016, July 7). Traffic stop shooting 'absolutely appalling at all levels.' *National Public Radio.* Retrieved from http://www.npr.org/sections/thetwo-way/2016/07/07/485066807/police-stop-ends-in-black-mans-death-aftermath-is-livestreamed-online-video

Drake, B. (2013, September 6). Incarceration gap widens between whites and blacks. *Pew Research Foundation.* Retrieved from http://www.pewresearch.org/fact-tank/2013/09/06/incarceration-gap-between-whites-and-blacks-widens

Drew, F. (2014, October 9). Why does racial inequality persist long after Jim Crow? *Brookings Institute.* Retrieved from http://www.brookings.edu/blogs/brookings-now/posts/2014/10/why-does-racial-inequality-persist-long-after-jim-crow

Dutto, S., DePinto, J., Backus, F., & Salvanta, A. (2016, July 13). Negative views of race relations at all-time high. *CBS News.* Retrieved from http://www.cbsnews.com/news/negative-views-of-race-relations-reach-all-time-high-cbsnyt-poll

Egede, L. E. (2006, June). Race, ethnicity, culture, and disparities in health care. *Journal of General Internal Medicine, 21*(6), 667–669. http://doi.org/10.1111/j.1525-1497.2006.0512.x

Fiscella, K., Franks, P., Gold, M. R., & Clancy, C. M. (2000, May 17). Inequality in quality: Addressing socioeconomic, racial, and ethnic disparities in health care. *JAMA, 283*(19), 2579–2584. http://doi.org/10.1001/jama.283.19.2579

Florida, R. (2015, August 10). *America's biggest problem is concentrated poverty, not inequality.* Retrieved from http://www.citylab.com/housing/2015/08/americas-biggest-problem-is-concentrated-poverty-not-inequality/400892

Gunter, J. (2015, May 1). Baltimore police death: How did Freddie Gray die? *BBC News.* Retrieved from http://www.bbc.com/news/world-us-canada-32546204

Haberle, M., & Soto, J. (2014, July). *Discrimination and segregation in housing: Continuing lack of progress in United States compliance with the international convention on the elimination of all forms of racial discrimination.* Retrieved from http://www.prrac.org/pdf/CERD_Shadow_Report_Housing_Segregation_July_2014.pdf

Jakabovics, A., & Chapman, J. (2009, September). Unequal opportunity lenders? Analyzing racial disparities in big banks' higher-priced lending. *American Progress.* Retrieved from https://www.americanprogress.org/wp-content/uploads/issues/2009/09/pdf/tarp_report.pdf

Johnson, C. (2015, June 24). Bryan Stevenson on Charleston and our real problem with race. *The Marshall Project.* Retrieved from https://www.themarshallproject.org/2015/06/24/bryan-stevenson-on-charleston-and-our-real-problem-with-race

Karimi, F., Shoichet, C., & Ellis, R. (2016, July 9). Dallas sniper attack: 5 officers killed, suspect identified. *CNN.* Retrieved from http://www.cnn.com/2016/07/08/us/philando-castile-alton-sterling-protests

Kelly, A. (2016, July 14). Watch: Black GOP says he has been stopped by police 7 times in a year. *NPR.* Retrieved from http://www.npr.org/2016/07/14/485995136/watch-black-gop-senator-says-hes-been-stopped-7-times-by-police-in-a-year

Kelly, M. (n.d.). 14th Amendment summary: What is the Fourteenth Amendment and what does it mean? *About Education.* Retrieved from http://americanhistory.about.com/od/usconstitution/a/14th-Amendment-Summary.htm

Kindy, K., & Elliot, K. (2015, December 28). 990 people shot and killed by police this year: What we learned. *Washington Post.* Retrieved from https://www.washingtonpost.com/graphics/national/police-shootings-year-end/?tid=a_inl

Kirkus Review. (2010, May 20). Retrieved from https://www.kirkusreviews.com/book-reviews/gary-orfield/dismantling-desegregation

Lowery, W. (2016, July 11). More whites killed by police but blacks 2.5 times more likely. *Washington Post.* Retrieved from http://www.mcall.com/news/nationworld/ct-police-shootings-race-20160711-story.html

Lowery, W., Andrews, T., & Miller, M. (2016, July 6). Outrage after videos white Baton Rouge police officer fatally shooting a black man. *Washington Post.* Retrieved from https://www.washingtonpost.com/news/morning-mix/wp/2016/07/06/video-captures-white-baton-rouge-police-officer-fatally-shooting-black-man-sparking-outrage

Matthews, D. (2013, June 4). The black/white marijuana arrest gap, in 9 charts. *Washington Post.* Retrieved from https://www.washingtonpost.com/news/wonk/wp/2013/06/04/the-blackwhite-marijuana-arrest-gap-in-nine-charts

Mauer, M., & Ghandnoosh, N. (2014, October). Incorporating racial equity into criminal justice reform. *Sentencing Project.* Retrieved from http://sentencingproject.org/doc/rd_Incorporating_Racial_Equity_into_Criminal_Justice_Reform.pdf

McWhorter, J. (2012, January 30). Segregation is down. Great news, right? *Manhattan-Institute.* Retrieved from http://www.manhattan-institute.org/html/miarticle.htm?id=7852#.VbkwhfnGrLM

Mooney, C. (2014, December 14). Across America whites are biased and don't even know it. *Washington Post.* Retrieved from https://www.washingtonpost.com/news/wonk/wp/2014/12/08/across-america-whites-are-biased-and-they-dont-even-know-it

Moore, D. (2014, March 22). Public housing high-rises to become part of the past in St. Louis. *St. Louis Today.* Retrieved from http://www.stltoday.com/news/local/metro/public-housing-high-rises-to-become-part-of-the-past/article_bec3d841-0991-54cb-92ec-f63d3c28926d.html

NPR. (2008, March 18). Barack Obama's "a more perfect union" speech. *Public Broadcasting System.* Retrieved from http://newshour-tc.pbs.org/newshour/extra/wp-content/uploads/sites/2/2013/11/A-more-perfect-union-highlight-activity.pdf

Orfield, G., & Eaton, S. (1996). *Dismantling desegregation: The quiet reversal of* Brown v. Board of Education. New York, NY: W. W. Norton.

Orfield, G., & Eaton, S. (2003, February 3). Back to segregation. *The Nation.* Retrieved from http://www.thenation.com/article/back-segregation

Orfield, G., & Frankenberg, E. (2014, May 25). Brown at 60. *Civil Rights Project.* Retrieved from http://civilrightsproject.ucla.edu/research/k-12-education/integration-and-diversity/brown-at-60-great-progress-a-long-retreat-and-an-uncertain-future/Brown-at-60-051814.pdf

Palumbo-Liu, D. (2015, August 4). The casual killing of blacks: When everyday activities trigger lethal force by the police. *Salon.* Retrieved from http://www.salon.com/2015/08/04/the_casual_killing_of_blacks_when_everyday_activities_trigger_lethal_force_by_the_police

Pendall, J. (2013). Racial segregation: It's not history. *Fair Housing Council of Oregon.* Retrieved from http://www.fhco.org/pdfs/published%20articles/read_on%20articles/RacialSegNotHistory.pdf

Pilgram, D. (2000, September). What was Jim Crow? *Ferris University.* Retrieved from http://www.ferris.edu/jimcrow/what.htm

Polling Report.com. (2015). Race and ethnicity. *CNN/ORC.* Retrieved from http://www.pollingreport.com/race.htm

Popple, P. R., & Leighninger, L. (2011). *Social work, social welfare, and American society* (8th ed.). New York, NY: Pearson.

Roberts, H. (2011, December 18). Implicit bias and social justice. *Open Society Foundation.* Retrieved from http://www.opensocietyfoundations.org/voices/implicit-bias-and-social-justice

Shapiro, R., Bever, B., Lowery, W., Miller, M., & Sharp, G. (2016, July 9). Police group. Minn. governor 'exploited what was already a tragic situation.' *Washington Post.* Retrieved from https://www.washingtonpost.com/news/morning-mix/wp/2016/07/07/minn-cop-fatally-shoots-man-during-traffic-stop-aftermath-broadcast-on-facebook

Sharp, G. (2012, October 15). NYPD's stop and frisk policy. *The Society Pages.* Retrieved from http://thesocietypages.org/socimages/2012/10/15/nypds-stop-and-frisk-policy

Steel, L. M. (2009, January 8). Jim Crow in the north. *In These Times.* Retrieved from http://inthesetimes.com/article/4124/jim_crow_in_the_north

Stepler, R. (2016, June 26). Five key take aways about views of race and inequality in the United States. *PEW Research Center.* Retrieved from http://www.pewresearch.org/fact-tank/2016/06/27/key-takeaways-race-and-inequality

Stevenson, B. (2016, July 11). The presumption of dangerousness behind police abuse of black people. *Equal Justice Initiative.* Retrieved from http://www.eji.org/presumption-of-dangerousness-behind-police-abuse-of-black-people-cbs-this-morning

Taylor, M. (2012, June 17). Rodney King case changed perceptions of police brutality. *ABC News.* Retrieved from http://abcnews.go.com/US/rodney-king-case-changed-perceptions-police-brutality/story?id=16589385

Tonn, S. (2014, August 6). Stanford research suggests support for incarceration mirrors whites' perception of black prison populations. *Stanford News.* Retrieved from http://news.stanford.edu/news/2014/august/prison-black-laws-080614.html

Valbrun, M. (n.d.). Experts attack Manhattan institute study claiming end to segregation in U.S. cities. *Americas Wire.* Retrieved from http://americaswire.org/drupa17/?q=content/experts-attack-manhattan-institute-study-claiming-end-segregation-us-cities-0

Vick, K. (2015, August 24). What it's like to be a cop in America. *Time Magazine.* Retrieved from http://time.com/3995798/what-its-like-being-a-cop-now

Weichselbaum, S. (2015, May 26). The problems with policing the police. *The Marshall Project.* Retrieved from http://time.com/police-shootings-justice-department-civil-rights-investigations

Woolner, D. (2010, February 5). African Americans and the New Deal: A look back in history. *Roosevelt Institute.* Retrieved from http://rooseveltinstitute.org/african-americans-and-new-deal-look-back-history

Yancey, G., & Feagin, J. (2015, July 27). *American racism in the "white frame."* Retrieved from http://opinionator.blogs.nytimes.com/2015/07/27/american-racism-in-the-white-frame

Ziemba, S. (1986, December 2). How projects rose to failure. *Chicago Tribune.* Retrieved from http://articles.chicagotribune.com/1986-12-02/news/8603310330_1_chicago-housing-authority-high-rise-projects-public-housing

Chapter 4

End-of-Life Care, Costs, Concerns, and Conflict

Too Much of the Wrong Kind of Care?

I so desperately need to get on my bike and hit the trails, Katie thought on the bus ride home from work. *Either that, or open up a pint of Ben and Jerry's double fudge. Not that I won't end up doing both.*

Until very recently, if asked, Katie would have without hesitation declared that she loved her position as a medical social worker at Regis Memorial Hospital. She had landed a job at Regis after completing her internship there while pursuing her undergraduate degree. In the 10 years since she was first hired, she obtained her master's in social work, left the hospital to work at a mental health facility for older adults, and then returned to the hospital setting. She enjoyed her position at the mental health clinic, but despite some policies at the hospital that she believed were not necessarily in all patients' best interests, she felt Regis was where she belonged.

At the hospital, Katie thrived on the fast pace, meeting people from diverse backgrounds, and the constant problem solving required. And she knew no matter where she worked, she would encounter individuals struggling with mental health issues, and the hospital setting provided lots of chances to work with older adults. Moreover, she had many interests outside of work, and the schedule she worked at the hospital afforded her more time, and a bit more money, to engage in those activities.

Recently when the opportunity to move to the intensive care unit (ICU) arose, Katie decided to go for it. She thought it would allow her to spend more time with families than was the case in the emergency room where she currently worked or the other units that she had previously been assigned to. One frustration she had at the hospital is that it seemed that discharge planning started the second someone entered the hospital, with too little time to assess the nonmedical needs of the patients. Katie believed a more holistic approach to patient care would reduce the number of readmits, increase patient satisfaction, and improve patients' overall well-being.

What Katie had not realized was that work in the ICU would take more of an emotional toll on her than had been the case in other units she had worked in. Now, if asked, she would still say she loved her job, but although she didn't admit it to many others, she was worried that the stress was already starting to get to her.

Katie often felt conflicted about choices that doctors or family members made regarding end-of-life interventions that she believed were merely prolonging suffering. There were also the cases where, for the elderly in particular, symptoms were addressed by different specialists, yet there was no one trying to determine the underlying cause of the symptoms. Katie understood that doctors were too busy to take all the time it would require to figure out the puzzle, and understood their going the extra mile for children, but it galled her that it seemed our society could so easily just write off the elderly. Another major stressor for Katie was what the health care system did, and did not, provide funding for. This too often meant older people died in an institution rather than at home.

As the bus neared her apartment, Katie was mulling over a couple of the cases she had dealt with earlier that day that were unsettling. She had met with Mr. Panthian previously when he had been transferred from the nursing home to the ICU, then back to the nursing home. Katie heard that this time, once his infection was under control, the doctor wanted to insert a feeding tube. Mr. Panthian was having trouble swallowing and was even frailer than when he was admitted 3 weeks ago with a raging infection.

"I am done with hospitals and endless treatments," were Mr. Panthian's first words to Katie when she entered his room. His voice was weak, and Katie had a hard time making out what he was saying. "All I want is to die in peace at home, not hooked up to machines with tubes sticking out of me, and sure as hell not in this hospital, or in that damn nursing home. I should've gone with my intuition and never started the chemotherapy treatments. All they did was poison my system, make me violently sick, and weaken me." Just making his case wore Mr. Panthian out, and as Katie started to respond, she could see he had drifted off to sleep, so she slipped out of the room to call Jason, Mr. Panthian's only living child.

Prior to being diagnosed with lung cancer 3 years prior, Mr. Panthian, then 79, had lived by himself in the home he had built shortly after he married. Once the side effects from the chemotherapy started, his son, Jason, moved in with him. The two had always been close, and the arrangement worked well for both of them. Mr. Panthian had lost his wife to ovarian cancer in 2005, and Jason, who experienced a few heartbreaking relationships over the years, was single. He had told Katie, "I am swearing off romantic relationships." He had added with a chuckle, "At least for the foreseeable future." In a more serious tone he added, "I want to be there for Dad as much as possible."

"Jason here," Katie heard in the receiver. "Hi Jason, this is Katie Francis. I know you are on the road and already got a call letting you know your dad is in the hospital."

"Yes, another infection I was told, and the docs thought it might take him. I figure Dad is wishing that it had. I know he is pretty out of it most of the time, but I will try to call later and at least let him know I will stop in at the hospital tomorrow to see him. That is, if they haven't shipped him off to the nursing home again. This back and forth between facilities is ridiculous. Why can't they just treat an infection at the nursing home? Anyway, Katie, what did you call about?"

"I didn't know you were back in town tonight," Katie responded. "It will lift your dad's spirits to see you. How about if we meet tomorrow after you see your dad? Well actually, I would like to meet with both of you together if he has the energy to do so. I want to talk to the both of you to clarify his wishes. I hope I am not the one informing you that one of the ICU doctors wants to put in a feeding tube. Also, we can talk about your concern regarding the frequent transfers."

"Sounds like a plan. And yes, I heard about a feeding tube but have some questions about it, and I am doubtful it is something my dad will be interested in. Oh, heavy traffic. Gotta go. Thanks, Katie. Talk to you tomorrow."

Katie had chosen not to mention the possibility of hospice[1] care for Mr. Panthian at the nursing home. She knew it was better to wait and talk in person, not on the phone, especially since she was not sure what Jason knew about hospice. Jason had tried to sound cheerful on the phone, but Katie could hear the sadness in his voice as he talked, and she assumed, based on past conversations, he was likely still feeling guilty that he couldn't stay home and care for his dad. It was just not financially feasible, nor was hiring the care needed to be able to keep Mr. Panthian at home. While less than ideal, Katie figured that hospice care in an institutional setting was better than no hospice care. Mr. Panthian was competent and therefore able to make his own decisions, so for legal reasons, Jason's input was not required, but Mr. Panthian had made it clear that he wanted Jason there when care decisions were made.

---

[1] Hospice is a program of care and support for people who are terminally ill and who are determined to have 6 months or less to live. It may be paid for through Medicare or Medicaid. The purpose of hospice is helping the person live comfortably but not on trying to cure the illness. Care can be provided in the home or in a hospice facility. Hospice focuses on addressing the needs of the whole family (close loved ones). "A specially trained team of professionals and caregivers provide care for the 'whole person,' including physical, emotional, social, and spiritual needs. Services typically include physical care, counseling, drugs, equipment, and supplies for the terminal illness and related conditions" (Centers for Medicare and Medicaid, n.d., p. 4).

After her call to Jason, Katie made some other calls to set up arrangements for patients, then went to meet with three of Vivian McCallister's four adult children. All three of them had been up most of the night hanging out at the hospital, and Katie figured they must be exhausted. Mrs. McCallister had been admitted to the hospital the previous evening when Christy, her oldest daughter and who Mrs. McCallister had been residing with for the past 5 years since the death of her husband, called the paramedics. Although Christy believed her mom would want to die peacefully at home rather than be rushed to the hospital, and Christy wanted to respect that wish, she panicked when she noticed that her mom didn't seem to be breathing normally.

Before meeting with them, Katie checked Mrs. McCallister's file and found that there were no advance directives in her file, despite the fact that she had been admitted to the hospital two other times in the past 4 months. Katie figured this was likely due to the fact that Mrs. McCallister had advanced dementia and had not established advance directives when she was still cognitively able to, nor unfortunately had she given anyone the durable power of attorney. In her review of the file, Katie was surprised to see that Mrs. McCallister was getting no services outside of the hospital. The social worker who had met briefly with them was no longer at Regis, so Katie did not have that person as a possible source for more information. At the very least, she would have thought a visiting nurse would have been assigned to see Vivian in her home and that there would have been more interaction with a licensed social worker.

The first thing Katie heard when she entered the meeting room, just down the hall from Vivian's room, was Christy's distressed voice: "Enough is enough. Let's just let Mom die in peace instead of prolonging her suffering. You don't see her every day like I do. She is miserable. I only brought her to the hospital because I knew you two would never forgive me if I didn't."

"Christy, you're too dramatic. It's not like Mom is brain dead and has been on a ventilator for months to keep her alive. Dr. Phinney says that she's not in distress, so what is your hurry in depriving her of medical treatment that may help her to live longer?" responded Catalina, Christy's youngest sister, almost sounding accusatory.

Their brother James chimed in, "Christy, we know you want what's best for Mom, but I have to agree with Catalina. You can see that Mom appears to be resting comfortably, and the fact that she has periods when she is alert is promising. None of us want her to suffer, but I don't think it is accurate to assume that she is."

He started to say more, but Christy cut him off, "Oh James, please, don't give me that crap, and Catalina, if you get on your moral high horse again I'm going to scream. You have no idea what it is like to care for her day in and day out. She can't do anything for herself, she doesn't sleep much of the night, and I hear her moaning and muttering but making no sense. And she has no control of her bladder or bowels. That is not living; it's existing in a state of frustration. I have no doubt she's suffering. How many times should she be brought to the hospital and put on a machine that may help her for a short time but doesn't in any way improve her life?"

"Sorry to interrupt the three of you," Katie quietly said, knowing she had walked in at a tough moment. But, there was no good time to interrupt, and given what little she had heard of the conversation, she was pretty sure the conversation was going nowhere positive. This thought was confirmed when Katie heard an audible sigh of relief from each of them, followed by James saying they were thankful for the interruption. Her entry may have stopped the arguing, but it didn't put them at ease. Katie suddenly understood that old cliché and felt that she could have almost physically cut the tension in the room with a knife. She also worried that she was seen by the sisters as more of an intruder than someone who could help.

"Hi, I am Katie Francis, the social worker for the ICU. Dr. Phinney, of course, is the primary person who will provide you with information about your mom's medical condition and medical treatment options. If you are willing, though, I would be glad to help you think through some of the decisions that have to be made and can also discuss resources that may be helpful to you."

Christy's defensiveness was strong, and she was the first to speak. "I really don't want some social worker butting into our family affairs."

"Oh, for Pete's sake, Christy, give us all a break, and let's move on," James shot back. "Let's see what Katie has to say. What are you afraid of anyway? We don't have to hide our family secret anymore. Dad is dead, and he is not coming back to hurt us or Mom. We are adults now. We don't have to live in fear of reaching out for a little help." Christy shot James a look of anger, but it was clear she was on the verge of tears. Catalina, who had been quiet, went over and gave Christy a hug, and the floodgates opened. They wept.

Christy said nothing as Katie spent the next 20 minutes listening to James and Catalina tell her how the three of them had promised each other they would take care of their mom, who had spent their childhood protecting them from their dad, who had been emotionally and physically abusive to all of them. They had hoped she would leave him, but that did not happen. It was Dave, the second oldest, who had gotten heavily involved in drugs, likely as a way to escape the reality of their home life, and had left the family. They rarely heard from him, and right now they had no way of contacting him.

Christy had gained control of her emotions and interjected, "Yes, Dad was a jerk, but that doesn't help us figure out what to do for Mom. I don't think the two of you get how exhausting it has been for me these last few months. When Mom could take care of herself and was just losing it slowly, I could deal, but now I just can't take much more of this. And don't start thinking I want to let her die to get rid of her since it is more than I can handle."

"Christy, if you didn't try to play the martyr and had simply told us how hard it was, we could have tried to help out more," James responded, without much sensitivity to how upset she was. Catalina, seeing Christy was about to cry again, came to her defense. "James, Christy did try to ask for help in her own way, which I will give you wasn't very direct. Still, I knew she was struggling, and I think we both just figured she would handle it like she always has everything else."

A million thoughts were going through Katie's mind. She could have spent hours with the McCallisters talking about issues that went well beyond the immediate situation but that still impacted how they were dealing with it. Katie, always aware that she had other patients to meet with but never wanting to appear rushed, attempted to get to the task at hand. "Just to make sure we heard the same message from Dr. Phinney, please tell me what your understanding is as far as the medical status of your mother and what he is recommending or the options he provided." Katie did not share with them that Dr. Phinney, the primary doctor in the ICU who had been involved with Mrs. McCallister's care, was one who didn't want a patient to die on his watch. He believed that it was his responsibility to do what he could to extend life and not give up on keeping the patient alive. Though partially admirable, the consequences were often harmful and counter to what families and patients wanted—and she wished he would be more up front about how his beliefs affected his recommendations.

Katie looked up just as the bus drove by her stop. This wasn't the first time she was thinking about work and missed her stop. Thank goodness this time, unlike some of the others, she didn't have far to backtrack. Despite her headache, she would be home, on her bike, and out on the trails that were only a couple of miles from her house in no time.

BACKGROUND INFORMATION

Discussing families who want ever more tests and medical treatments conducted on their chronically ill loved ones, instead of accepting that more treatment is futile, hospitalist Dr. Bowron (2012) writes, "We want our loved ones to live as long as possible, but our culture has come to view death as a medical failure rather than life's natural conclusion" (p. 1). Although many deny it, avoid thinking about it very much or at all, or look to the promising advances in science and medicine that suggest we may be able to delay death to a much greater extent than ever before, there is no doubt that our death is inevitable. Moreover, there is a very strong likelihood that at the end-of-life, many difficult medical decisions, along with other end-of-life decisions, must be made.

For those who live into old age, simply passing away peacefully during sleep after a long life with no complex health issues is rare, not the norm. Thus, it is crucial that, as a society, we figure out how to ensure that the dying process is marked by compassion, comfort, dignity, and as much choice as possible. In other words, what is needed to foster a good death,[2] not merely extending life regardless of quality. What does the current reality mean for a dedicated medical social worker such as Katie Francis?

To address these overarching questions, it is necessary to first provide foundational information and context. Therefore, this section includes some information on demographics of the aging population;[3] research on medical treatments at end of life; costs of treatments; public opinion regarding end-of-life care; progress made and key challenges still faced; and recommendations for end-of-life health care that doesn't prolong life at all costs and that is holistic in approach. This chapter is intentionally and necessarily limited in scope and not intended to address all issues relevant to end-of-life care. For example, whether physician-assisted suicide ought to be considered part of a good death is a necessary discussion. However, it is outside the scope of this chapter even though some of the most visible and wrenching cases involve younger people such as Brittany Maynard,[4] whose situation and YouTube video about her choice moved many people. Another critical issue that merits more attention than given here is that of caregiver stress.

The 2010 Census Bureau report indicates that adults in the United States who are 65 or older make up 13% of the population (40.3 million people). That number has jumped 15.1% between 2000 and 2010 and will continue to climb as the baby boomers age (Brandon, 2012). By 2050, the number of those 65 and older is projected to be 88 million (Vincent & Velkoff, 2010). This demographic change will have a profound impact on society. At the same time that there will be more elderly, with end-of-life needs, there will be fewer younger people available to provide care. A huge impact will be the significant costs. Currently "one out of every four Medicare

---

[2] The Institute of Medicine defines a good death as "one that is free from avoidable suffering for patients, families and caregivers in general accordance with the patients' and families' wishes" (Gustafson, 2007, para. 4). Kehl (2006) reviewed relevant articles and came up with the following as what people considered a good death: "Being in control, being comfortable, having a sense of closure, having one's values affirmed, trusting in care providers, and recognizing impending death, beliefs and values honored, burden minimized, relationships optimized, leaving a legacy, and family care" (Abstract, para. 1).

[3] While end-of-life care decisions must be made by, and for, people of all age groups, the focus of this background information is on older adults.

[4] Maynard, a 29-year-old woman diagnosed with terminal brain cancer, gained national attention as a death with dignity advocate. Following her diagnosis and her decision that she wanted to end her life with dignity, she moved to the State of Oregon, which allows for terminally ill patients, who met specified criteria, to end their lives with lethal medication that is prescribed by a physician. Brittany shared her situation and reasoning for her decision with millions of people through social media. She did not take the lethal medication immediately but is said to have waited until she was having continual seizures and significant neck and head pain (Bever, 2014).

dollars, more than $125 billion, is spent on services for the 5% of beneficiaries in their last year of life" (Wang, 2012, p. 1). That does not include out-of-pocket expenses for Medicare recipients that, for 40% of households, exceed their financial assets. Of critical importance is that, without a continued shift away from futile treatments, the elderly will be getting care that does not necessarily result in improved quality of life and, in fact, can cause more discomfort or pain (Adamopoulos, 2013; Allen, Beres, Herring, & Seller, 2011; Bakalar, 2013; Bowron, 2012; Hsieh, 2014; Wang, 2012).

There are a few signs that suggest America is undergoing a paradigm shift in our medical approach to end-of-life care, yet there is strong evidence, based on research, indicating the state of affairs is nuanced, and that an overhaul is badly needed (Adamopoulos, 2013; Bakalar, 2013; Callahan & Lawler, 2012; Teno et al., 2013). On the upside, there has been progress made. More people are dying at home, more people are using hospice[5] services, more people are using advance directives to inform doctors of their wishes for end-of-life care, and more discussions between doctors, patients, and their family members are occurring (Adamopoulos, 2013). Unfortunately, the positive signs are only a small part of the overall story.

Where One Dies

In their trend study assessing data from 2000, 2005, and 2009, Teno et al. (2013) concur with Centers for Disease Control and Prevention (CDC) reports that decedents age 65 years and older are more likely to die at home today than in the past. In comparing the end-of-life care of Belgium, Canada, England, Germany, the Netherlands, Norway and the United States, a study found that the percentage of people who died in the hospital was lowest in the United States (Vora, 2016). Still, even though most Americans express an interest in dying at home, between 2000 and 2009 there was only a 10% increase in Medicare beneficiaries who did. It rose from approximately 24% to 33.5% (Gleckman, 2013). As Bernstein (2014, para. 13) puts it, "In their last days, older patients are increasingly likely to be shuttled among hospitals, nursing homes and hospices in pursuit of Medicare and Medicaid coverage. Ultimately, most die in an institution, rather than at home."

Just how much shuttling occurs was well captured in a study by Teno and colleagues (2013). In 2009 they found that "nearly one-half of decedents experienced

---

[5] There has been a slow but steady climb in the percentage of people in the United States using hospice services in the past 15 years. Just in the last five years the increase was from approximately 1.38 million to 1.66 million. This is over 45%. Hospice is often accessed only very close to the end of life. In 2014, for 50% of individuals, hospice was accessed in the last 2 weeks of life, and 35% were on hospice for 7 days or less. The median for the length of time on hospice was 17 days (National Hospice and Palliative Care Organization, 2015).

a transition in the last 2 weeks of life" (Teno et al., 2013, "Health Care Transitions," para. 4), and "there was a slight increase in the number of people who were moved from one facility to another in the last 3 days of life" (para. 2). Getting moved around at the end of life is stressful, and the average number of moves was three times in the last 90 days of life. Some of the transfers were to a hospice facility. While hospice care overall is viewed very positively, 31% of the transitions occurred in the last few weeks of life, with 28% of hospice transfers entering hospice care only for the final 3 days of their life (Gleckman, 2013). "We have these frail older people moving about in the medical-industrial complex that we've constructed," Dr. Teno said in an interview. "It's all about profit margins. It's not about caring for people" (Bernstein, 2014, "On Dying in America," para. 3).

Too Much of the Wrong Type of Care at End of Life?

Surely, litigation concerns also play into this situation. Cleveland Clinic's Department of Bioethics states in their policy guidelines on foregoing life-sustaining or death-prolonging therapy that health care providers have a legitimate moral and legal presumption in favor of preserving life and providing beneficial medical care with the patient's informed consent. Clearly, however, avoiding death should not always be the preeminent goal. Not all technologically possible means of prolonging life need be or should be used in every case. For the gravely ill patient and for his or her family, friends, and health care providers, decisions about the use of life-sustaining treatment have profound consequences (Cleveland Clinic, 2005).

While it is likely that most hospitals across the nation share a similar philosophy, there is empirical research and a plethora of people who have witnessed the care and death of a loved one who claim that, too often, aggressive or futile[6] care is provided at the end of life.[7]

Of course there are cases when one party believes that not enough aggressive care is provided. A 2007 study conducted by Barnato et al. sets forth that there is a "marked geographic variation in Medicare end-of-life spending [that] is well documented, and this variation is believed to be driven by physician practice style rather than by differences in patients' preferences for aggressiveness of treatment at the end-of-life" (cited in Nicholas, Langa, Iwashyna, & Weir, 2011, "Conclusion," para. 2). But, the concern most prominent in the literature and in this chapter is the overuse of medical interventions at the end of life that have no physiological

---

[6] Futile medical care is treatment that serves no useful purpose and there is no physiological benefit to the patient. There are cases where there is not universal agreement regarding what is futile care.

[7] Dr. Erik Fromme, a palliative care specialist, points out that "emergency medical service protocol is to provide full treatment including resuscitation and transport to a hospital" (Oregon Health and Science University, 2014, para. 3).

benefit. Dr. Ezekiel Emanual, in a study published in the *Journal of the American Medical Association,* found that patients in the United States were twice as likely to spend time in the intensive care unit in the last 6 months of their life as in Belgium, Canada, England, Germany, the Netherlands, or Norway. And almost 40% of patients with cancer were administered at least one round of chemotherapy in their last 6 months of life (Vora, 2016).

Geriatric health care expert Dr. Joanne Lynn, director of the Center for Elder Care and Advanced Illness at the Altarum Institute, is among the many advocating for major changes to end-of-life practices, which she refers to as "wasteful and misdirected." She discusses the tests, surgeries, and medical procedures encountered by Medicare beneficiaries that don't lead to improved health but that beneficiaries "endure" during their last days. Terry Berthelot, senior attorney with the Center for Medicare Advocacy, states that "currently folks are getting all types of end-of-life care that's very, very expensive that doesn't in any way save lives. It only prolongs life at a huge cost with very, very little real benefit because of all of the misery at the end-of-life when somebody's dying in a hospital" (Adamopoulos, 2013, "Too much care," para. 7).

Dr. Teno et al.'s (2013) study provides evidence showing that in the first decade of the 21st century, there has not been a trend toward less aggressive care at the end of life. In fact, between 2000 and 2009, the use of ICUs in hospitals actually increased for people in the end-of-life situation. In the last month of life, almost 30% of Medicare beneficiaries spent time in the ICU. Nicholas et al. (2011) state their finding, in a *Journal of the American Medical Association* article, that end-of-life hospital treatment is a major driver of end-of-life expense and a setting in which many aggressive procedures to sustain life are performed.

In their study of intensive care units in the UCLA Health System from December 15, 2011, to March 15, 2012, Huynh et al. (2013) found that "treatment that is perceived by physicians to be futile is common: more than 1 in 10 patients received such treatment during their ICU stay. The outcomes of these patients were uniformly poor; two-thirds died during the hospitalization and 85% died within 6 months" ("Discussion," para. 1). The researchers do note that a limitation of their study is that the University of California, Los Angeles Health System is known for its resource intensive treatment and so is not necessarily generalizable. Still, Huynh et al.'s study, along with the other studies discussed above and innumerable anecdotes and their own experiences with loved ones, certainly provides evidence that aggressive care that prolongs life but does not improve one's health occurs on a regular basis.

Dr. Ken Murray (2012), a clinical assistant professor of family medicine at the University of Southern California, arguing we need to rethink futile care, sets forth with brutal honesty the harm he believes comes from futile care. "The patient will get cut open, perforated with tubes, hooked up to machines, and assaulted with drugs. All of this occurs in the Intensive Care Unit at a cost of tens of thousands of dollars a day. What it buys is misery we would not inflict on a terrorist" (para. 4). In further making his point, Murray powerfully speaks of the countless physicians he knows that choose not to get the aggressive treatment they provide for others (Murray, 2012).

Key Challenges to Progress

Keeping in mind there are some signs of a paradigm shift, moving in that direction takes us on a path laden with large obstacles that will not be easily overcome. Key challenges to a good death include what patients want, or very often what their loved ones want for them when they cannot make the choice, the role doctors play, and the structure of our current health care system. Research published in the *American Journal of Critical Care* adds to and expands on these challenges. The study assessed the views of over 1,400 critical care nurses on how to improve end-of-life care. The nurses expressed challenges that relate to some of those just stated. Lack of appropriate education of physicians on end-of-life care; communication problems, including doctors not wanting to be forthcoming with patients and family members regarding the patient's condition; and family members having unrealistic expectations were all seen as standing in the way of increasing the number of good deaths. Many nurses in the study believed that a key obstacle is that many doctors see death as a personal failure and make treatment decisions based on their needs rather than the patients' needs. Staffing patterns and staff shortages were also mentioned as problems (Beckstrand, Callister, & Kirchhoff, 2006).

In addition to doctors having varying views on treatment at the time of death, a PEW Foundation (2013) poll indicates variability among expectations of doctors for end-of-life care:

Fifty-seven percent [of participants] say they would tell their doctors to stop treatment if they had a disease with no hope of improvement and were suffering a great deal of pain. And about half (52%) say they would ask their doctors to stop treatment if they had an incurable disease and were totally dependent on someone else for their care. But about a third of adults (35%) say they would tell their doctors to do everything possible to keep them alive—even in dire circumstances, such as having a disease with no hope of improvement and experiencing a great deal of pain. In 1990, by comparison, 28% expressed this view. (p. 1)

Moreover, a national study by Barnato et al. (cited in Nicholas et al., 2011) found that 42% of White Medicare beneficiaries worried about receiving too much care at the end of life, whereas an equal proportion worried about receiving too little.

Doctors often are not aware of the wishes of the patient (because they are not documented or the document is not in the chart) and fear not doing what the family asks, if the patient can't communicate. Speaking about family members who are in a position of making end-of-life care decisions for loved ones, Dr. Ken Murray (2012), writing from his experience as a hospital physician, states that "poor knowledge and misguided expectations leads to a lot of bad decisions" (para. 8).

Doctors often find themselves in an uncomfortable and ethically challenging position regarding this issue of what care to provide or not provide. It is particularly complex, according to Kasman (2004), "when physicians have less experience with these discussions, when families and providers disagree about benefits from treatment, and when cultural disparities are involved in misunderstandings" ("Abstract," para. 1). There are circumstances, as suggested by the Barnato et al. 2007 study, when the disagreement may have more to do with philosophy about end of life rather than the benefit(s) of a specific medical treatment (cited in Nicholas et al., 2011).

The health care system is viewed as being a huge part of the problem preventing good deaths. Wilensky (cited in Riley & Lubitz, 2010) points out that while medical technology has changed significantly in the last 3 decades, Medicare's basic payment approach for doctors continues to largely be a "fee-for-service system, with financial incentives to produce more services" ("Discussion," para. 1). In an interview, Dr. Teno expands on this point:

> What you pay for is what you get. There are financial incentives to provide more care in fee-for-service care. We don't get paid to talk with patients about their goals or care or probable outcomes of care. We do pay for hospitalizations, and there are financial incentives for nursing homes to transfer patients back to acute care. We need to restructure how we pay hospital systems. (Kuehn, 2013, para. 5)

Bernstein (2014), in a *New York Times* article describing how a daughter fought for months to honor her father's wishes to die at home rather than in a hospital or one of the nursing homes that he continuously was shuffled back and forth between, interviewed Dr. Jack Resnick, who has a geriatric house call practice. Resnick claims, in regard to one's wishes to die at home, "you can't believe the forces of the system that are arrayed against it. The way the reimbursement system works, these decisions are not made on the basis of what the individuals need. They're based on what the institutions need" (Bernstein, 2014, "Dying in America," para. 7). Terry Berthelot, senior attorney with the Center for Medicare Advocacy, concurs that there are problems with the system itself, which too often fails to make long-term care plans for the trajectory of a patient's illness beyond the hospital doors. Not only is this not beneficial for the patient, Berthelot notes that this kind of care is driving up health care costs. (Adamopoulos, 2013).

In *Knocking at Heaven's Door,* the author, Katy Butler (2013) recalls a conversation she had with her father's internist, Dr. Fales, who was opposed to a pacemaker for her father. A different doctor, a cardiac specialist, focused only on the fixable problem and not the whole person's condition, argued in favor of it, and surgery to insert a pacemaker was carried out. The pacemaker later prolonged her father's life beyond when he had any quality of life left. Butler writes that "Medicare reward[ed] the surgeon and the cardiologist far better for doing the procedure than it would have Dr. Fales for making a reasoned argument against it" (p. 63), Dr. Fales stated, "I spend 45 minutes thinking through the problem, and I get 75 to 100 bucks. . . . Someone spends 45 minutes putting in a pacemaker and is paid six times as much" (p. 63). The point is not whether putting in the pacemaker was the best option or not. The point is that long-term planning, taking into account the person's overall health status, not just one specific, potentially fixable problem, is critical and often overlooked.

The wasted dollars, inefficiencies, and inhumaneness of the system is echoed in Dr. Lynn's comments regarding the consequences of what she calls "perverse financial incentives" that prevent needed types of care. She points out that while other developed countries spend much less per person on medical care than the United States, they spend about twice what the United States spends on social supports. In response to the federal spending cut for meals for seniors in 2013, she asked the question, "Why can I get a $100,000 drug but I can't get supper?" (Bernstein, 2014, "Dying in America," paras. 10 & 11).

Advance Directives

Advance directives, or living wills, are legal documents that set forth a person's wishes regarding end-of-life medical care. They let doctors and loved ones know ahead of time what medical measures to take, or not take, if the person is not competent to make the decision or cannot communicate his or her wishes. Poll results released by the PEW Foundation (2013) reported that approximately 60% of adults 65 or older said they had an advance directive, leaving close to 40% with none. There are numerous reasons for not completing an advance directive such as not understanding the importance of having one, thinking it is up to the doctor to initiate, putting it off, and spiritual and cultural beliefs (Pullen, 2012).

In addition to patient self-determination, an expectation of advance directives is that they will reduce costs at the end of life. "The Centers for Medicare & Medicaid Services estimate that more than 25% of Medicare spending goes towards the five percent of beneficiaries who die each year" (Adamopoulos, 2013, para. 6).

Research indicates advance directives, if accessible, increase the likelihood that patient wishes will be honored, but there are mixed findings regarding reduced expenditures for medical costs.

Tierney et al. (2001) found that study participants, who included elderly patients with chronic illness, conveyed greater satisfaction with their primary care doctor and a significant improvement in outpatient visits when advance directives were discussed. Research by Silveira, Scott, & Langa (2010) published in the *New England Journal of Medicine* found that between

2000 and 2006, many elderly Americans needed decision making near the end-of-life at a time when most lacked the capacity to make decisions. Patients who had prepared advance directives received care that was strongly associated with their preferences. These findings support the continued use of advance directives. (Abstract, "Conclusion," para. 1)

A study by Nicholas et al. (2011) that appeared in the *Journal of the American Medical Association* led them to conclude that "advance directives specifying limitations in end-of-life care were associated with significantly lower levels of Medicare spending, lower likelihood of in-hospital death, and higher use of hospice care in regions characterized by higher levels of end-of-life spending" (Abstract, "Conclusion," para. 1). They add that advance directives appear to be most important for those who don't want aggressive treatment but live in an area where aggressive treatment is the norm.

More recently, Silveira, Wiitala & Piette (2014) published research in the *Journal of the American Geriatric Society* that indicated an increase in the percentage of decedents with advance directives from 47% in 2000 to 72% in 2010. Their sample included 6,122 people age 60 or older, who died from 2000 to 2010. They also found an increase in hospitalizations but a decrease in the number of people dying in the hospital. What they concluded was that the significant increase in rates of advance directives completion during the study period "has had little effect upon hospitalization and hospital deaths, suggesting that AD completion is unlikely to stem hospitalization before death" (Abstract, "Conclusion," para. 1).

To supplement advance directives, the Physician Orders for Life-Sustaining Treatment program (POLST) was developed in Oregon 2 decades ago. Since then, POLST programs have emerged across the United States. Today all but about five states either have POLST or are in the development stages of a program (National POLST Paradigm, 2012). The POLST program is intended for those who are critically ill or fragile and likely to be in their last year of life. In those cases, the patient, loved ones, and health care professionals have conversations regarding the care the person wishes to have. Then the person's wishes are documented on a POLST form. A study conducted at Oregon Health and Science University (OHSU) showed that of those in their study of 58,000 Oregonians who died from 2010 to 2011, 18,000 (31%) had a POLST form completed. Of those 18,000

> only 6.4 percent of patients who specified comfort measures only orders on their POLST form died in a hospital, while 22.4 percent of patients who chose limited additional interventions died in a hospital and 44.2 percent of patients who chose full treatment died in a hospital. (OHSU, 2014, para. 5)

It seems likely that if the number of people who complete advance directives continues to increase, and if there are more people, when appropriate, completing POLST forms, the number of hospital deaths and unwanted treatment will continue to decline.

Improving the End-Of-Life Experience

Throughout this background section major obstacles to providing good end-of-life care have been presented and discussed. We can do better. In 2014, a panel of experts, convened by the Institute of Medicine (IOM), drafted a report, "Dying in America: Improving Quality and Honoring Individual Preferences Near the End-of-Life." The report sets forth that "improving the quality and availability of medical and social services for patients and their families could not only enhance quality of life through the end-of-life, but may also contribute to a more sustainable care system" (National Academies of Science, 2014, para. 2).

A significant change called for in the report is clinicians paying "more attention to patients' social, emotional, and spiritual needs by collaborating closely with nurses, social workers, psychologists, pharmacists, and chaplains. . . . Death 'is not a strictly medical event' and many patients' and families' most pressing needs 'are not medical' in nature" (Graham, 2014, p. 1845). This requires improved communication, which is another needed change emphasized in the report. Conversations with patients to make sure all parties are clear regarding goals and wishes of the patient are critical to improve the quality of care.

Dr. Dzau, president of IOM, stated that doctors can't let their own discomfort prevent them from talking about end-of-life issues with patients (Graham, 2014). Without conversations between patients (or loved ones) and health care professionals, proper advance planning, which is critical, won't occur. Advance directives should be drafted not by the patient alone but after conferring with the patient's physician and should be revisited periodically with the passage of time and circumstances. More important, the panel asserts that conversations regarding medical care at end of life take physicians' time, and their value must be acknowledged by making reimbursements from government or private insurance standard practice (National Academies of Science, 2014).

Related to reimbursement, the panel stressed the need to remove the incentive for expensive medical care that is not beneficial and to move away from a fee-for-service approach. The fee-for-service, in part, leads to a mismatch between the needs of patients and the services they receive. Patients end up being transferred between medical institutions too much, and too often, and then spend too little time in hospice care. The panel recommends that what needs to be incentivized are medical and social supports, for example, training and respite for caregivers, assistance with personal care, and nutrition services, that will reduce the need for acute medical care (National Academies of Science, 2014).

The use of palliative care, including hospice, was given the strongest of endorsements by the panel members. It was emphasized that needed changes be made throughout the health care system to incentivize the use of comprehensive palliative care, which is known to improve patients' quality of life. One of the needed changes is to better educate and train health care professionals on palliative care. Also recommended are methods for educating the general public regarding palliative care and end-of-life care. We need informed and meaningful conversations about dying and suffering.

Information in this section leaves no doubt that patients, caregivers, loved ones, medical professionals, and society as a whole stand much to gain if we take the needed steps to transform the health care system. Dying in America provides a blueprint. The policy changes it calls for will require a great deal of advocacy. As social workers, we have a responsibility and will benefit greatly if we are part of the movement to put in place a more holistic, compassionate health care system that enhances quality of life at the end-of-life.

A Night's Rest and Back at It

As was often the case, Katie returned home from the ride physically spent and mentally refreshed. Although she wasn't stress-free, her headache had subsided. After making plans for the weekend with friends, she showered, grabbed a bite to eat (topped off with Ben and Jerry's ice cream she figured she had earned), and sank into her favorite chair to curl up with *The Lord of the Rings*. The next thing she knew, light was streaming through the windows. She had never slept all night in the chair before, and her back was achy. It was only 5:10 a.m. so she decided to crash for another hour in her bed, leaving herself about 20 minutes to get out the door to catch the bus. When it went off, the alarm was not a welcome sound.

As usual, Katie arrived at work about 10 minutes before the morning huddle, when the nurses from the night shift met briefly with the oncoming day nursing staff to report on any pressing patient needs. Although the information was logged in the chart, Debi, the head nurse, felt strongly that verbal communication, in addition to detailed charting, led to better patient care. She welcomed Katie joining them. Travis started out by reporting that "sadly, Joyce Oliver is back again. She needs to be receiving palliative care, not more testing and ineffective procedures." Not one to hold back on his opinion, he went on, "The surgery performed last month only made things worse, and she just can't bounce back to even the weakened state she was in presurgery. She was brought in last night with pneumonia that is causing breathing problems, with a urinary tract infection, and she is experiencing severe abdominal pain."

Debi mentioned that "Mr. Jeffrey is back again as well. He shouldn't have been sent home when he was actively bleeding internally. This may be a case where surgery is warranted and will improve Mr. Jeffery's health. Dr. Evenson will be in later this a.m. to see Mr. Jeffrey. In the meantime, we are giving him another transfusion to try to keep him stable." The reports continued for another 5 minutes. The huddles served the purposes of the nurses, and some of the therapists, allowing them to vent and support each other, as well as gather updates on patients.

Following the huddle, Katie determined her priorities for the day. She knew she must first attend to some of the paperwork she had not gotten to the day before, or a couple of patients would not have the resources they needed upon discharge. Meetings with the Panthians and McCallisters, along with three other patients, were high on her list. As always, Katie thought through her approach to each of the meetings—not that they would go as planned, but she at least needed to have end goals in mind. Planning seemed to help her keep in check her personal beliefs about what should and shouldn't happen at end of life. She also kept in mind the approach to end of life taken by the attending physician, as different doctors definitely had different philosophies. While she might not agree with a doctor's medical advice, she knew it would not be appropriate or helpful to the family to voice disagreement. Her role was to assist patients and loved ones in processing what they wanted to do after educating them about available resources. She then linked them to needed services. Katie felt like most of the doctors on the ICU appreciated her ability to address the psychosocial needs of patients and families as this was not a skill set of many of them. She also wondered if there was something she could be doing to help change public policy or at least the organizational orientation to make progress toward better outcomes.

Katie felt relieved that she would be talking to Jason before meeting with the McCallister family. He was not under any illusion regarding the limits of modern medicine or about his dad's condition. Based on past conversations, Katie thought he would fully support his dad's end-of-life wishes as far as medical treatment. She figured she would suggest that they meet privately after meeting with his dad as she wanted to give him a chance to talk, if he wanted to, about the guilt he felt for not being able to take his dad home. What they needed to accomplish first, and Katie was surprised it hadn't been dealt with at the nursing home, was crafting very specific advance directives.

Jason greeted Katie just outside his dad's room. "Katie, I really appreciate your support and assistance." He added in a quiet voice, "The doctors are good, but their primary concern seems to be keeping Dad alive, not letting him die naturally or increasing his comfort. He is semi-awake now, so let's go in."

"Good morning, Mr. Panthian," Katie said, and got a little smile but no verbal response. After a bit of small talk with Jason, which included Mr. Panthian but didn't require his input, Katie said, "Okay, ready to talk about your situation?" Mr. Panthian weakly said yes. Katie let Mr. Panthian know that she and Jason would do everything to ensure that his wishes regarding his medical care were respected. She explained that the advance directive he had signed included a Do Not Resuscitate (DNR) order but no other specific direction on what treatment to provide and what treatment he did not want. Katie knew he would be asleep before long so had prepared a draft that named certain treatments and just asked him to say yes or no to them. She included treatment that fell under palliative care (and briefly explained hospice) as well as more aggressive treatment such as a feeding tube. Panthian said weakly but firmly that "palliative care is all I want. I want to go home."

Jason responded, "Dad, I am working on that." Katie glanced at him with a look of surprise as she had no idea what he was "working on" and was pretty confident it was not something that was going to happen in the next few days. She said, "In the meantime, Mr. Panthian, there is a wing at the nursing home, away from where you were staying, that is for people who only want hospice care, which falls under palliative care. If you give the okay, I will make arrangements for you to stay there once you leave the hospital." Katie knew they wouldn't keep him at the hospital long, as his fever was already down, and his vitals were holding steady. She actually had already started making arrangements. Medicare was a stickler on who could get hospice care, so she made sure that the doctor at the nursing home would verify that Mr. Panthian's prognosis was "6 months or less to live." Katie realized that Mr. Panthian was asleep again and wasn't sure he had even heard Jason's comment. She motioned Jason to follow her, figuring they could take care of the signing of the advance directive later that day.

"Sorry, Katie, it just slipped out," Jason said sheepishly. "I may have landed a job that doesn't take me out of town so what I told Dad is not completely a lie.

I just don't know how I can afford to pay for care for him while I work, although it would cost a lot less than the state paying to keep him in a nursing home."

"No need to apologize to me, Jason. Your dad is a lucky guy to have a son who cares so much. And I agree, the way the system works doesn't make sense. How about we talk a little more after I meet with another family who is waiting for me? How soon are you leaving the hospital?"

"Other than an appointment at 1:00 for the possible job, I plan to hang out at the hospital."

"Try the rolls at the cafeteria; they're surprisingly tasty. Just page me when you get back, and I'll break away and talk to you. Good luck with the interview."

As Katie headed down the hall to Vivian McCallister's room, she thought back to the siblings' conversation she'd overheard yesterday and the one she had with them. Catalina and James were in denial that their mother's life on earth was coming to an end. Christy accepted that her mother was dying but felt guilty that she was overwhelmed, and even though she had insisted her mom live with her, she was angry at her siblings for not helping out more.

First things first, Katie told herself as she entered the room to see Christy and James nodding off in the chairs. After two nights and a day on the ventilator, Mrs. McCallister was breathing on her own again. The doctor had just written up orders to have her discharged that afternoon with an oxygen tank. "Good morning, you are here early," Katie cheerfully said.

"Where else would we be?" Christy responded. James ignored Christy's response and addressed Katie, "Hi Katie, Mom is going to be discharged today it looks like. She is tough and not ready to kick the bucket."

"Geez, James," Christy said, clearly irritated. Just then, Vivian stirred, and their attention quickly shifted to her. They spoke to her softly, and when she appeared to drift off again, Katie motioned for them to follow her to the meeting room. As they walked down the hall to the meeting room, Catalina saw them as she got off the elevator and joined them. Katie had her mental list of issues to discuss that included some respite for Christy (all three had made it clear they would fight tooth and nail against their mother being transferred to a nursing home even through Dr. Phinney had mentioned that a nursing home might be in order), home visitations by a home-health nurse, and what hospice care entailed. Katie had talked to Dr. Phinney, who said he would verify that Vivian likely had 6 months or less to live, but he had not mentioned this to her children. She expected resistance to hospice at first from James and Catalina but figured once they fully understood that it could improve the quality of their mother's life, they might change their mind. It still amazed Katie that so many misperceptions of hospice existed. *Here goes nothing,* Katie said to herself as she opened the discussion.

QUESTIONS FOR DISCUSSION

1. Discuss the demographics provided regarding the aging population, the costs of end-of-life care, and the relevance of this information to the overall challenges discussed in this case.

2. Discuss the issue of multiple transfers between hospital and nursing homes at the end of life.

3. What signs suggest that America is undergoing a paradigm shift in our medical approach to end-of-life care? Discuss the evidence that indicates otherwise.

4. Why is it so challenging to make decisions on what, and how much, medical care should be given at the end of life? Identify and discuss the reasons.

5. What are advance directives, and how much of a difference does having them make relative to care provided?

6. What changes need to be made to ensure that the dying process is marked by compassion, comfort, dignity, and as much choice as possible.

7. Be prepared to discuss the challenging position that Katie finds herself in, and provide your thoughts on how she might work effectively and with integrity in the existing system. Does the social work code of ethics provide guidance? Explain your answer.

8. Is broaching the issue of spirituality important during a person's hospital stay when the social worker is trying to connect the patient with resources and has lots of tasks to carry out. If yes, how might Katie work this issue in? If not, why not?

9. Taking care of a loved one who is at the end of life while working and taking care of children is extremely challenging. The following link provides a summary of the Family and Medical Leave Act (FMLA): https://www.dol .gov/whd/regs/compliance/whdfs28a.pdf

   (a) Based on the summary, does the FMLA appear sufficient to address these challenges? Explain.

   (b) Do we need national legislation to better address the issue, or should it be left up to individual employers to address through agency policy? Provide a rationale for your answer.

   (c) If you could change the FMLA, what changes would you make, if any? What would the impact of the changes have on employees and employers? (The point of these questions isn't to fully assess and critique the FMLA. It is to give some thought to a social welfare issue that has a significant impact on many and, as is typically the case, has far-ranging implications.)

10. What was your understanding of hospice before reading this case? Has this case impacted in any way your views regarding hospice. Explain.

CASE ANALYSIS WRITING ASSIGNMENT

1. Read the assigned case study thoroughly prior to class in order to be fully prepared to join in the discussion.

2. You have been assigned to a panel charged with improving our health care system to increase the likelihood of people experiencing a "good" death. The first step, and the goal of your analysis, is to provide the panel members with an understanding of the complexity of some of the key issues and challenges. (For this assignment, do not attempt to address physician-assisted suicide.)

3. The analysis should be an approximately two-and-a-half-page, typed, double-spaced essay. Your essay should reflect the standards and expectations of college-level writing: spelling, grammar, and appropriate use of paragraphs all matter. If you quote directly from the case study, use quotation marks, and at the end of the quote, indicate the page number the quote appeared on. For example, "By 2050 the number of those 65 and older is projected to be 88 million" (Vincent & Velkoff, 2010, as cited in Lewis, 2017, p. 55).

4. Your case analysis is due _____ and worth a maximum of _____ points.

INTERNET SOURCES

Institute of Medicine of the National Academies (www.nationalacademies.org/hmd/~/media/Files/Report Files/2014/EOL/Key Findings and Recommendations .pdf)

National Hospice and Palliative Care Organization (http://www.nhpco.org/learn-about-end-life-care)

National Institute on Aging: Health and Aging (https://www.nia.nih.gov/health/publication/end-life-helping-comfort-and-care/introduction)

National Institute of Health (http://www.ncbi.nlm.nih.gov/pubmed/19615621)

NHS Choices (http://www.nhs.uk/Planners/end-of-life-care/Pages/what-is-end-of-life-care.aspx)

NIH Senior Health (http://nihseniorhealth.gov/endoflife/preparingfortheend oflife/01.html)

Physician Orders for Life Sustaining Treatment (POLST) (www.polst.org)

U.S. Department of Health and Human Services (https://healthfinder.gov/ search/?q=Hospice+Care)

REFERENCES

Adamopoulos, H. (2013, June 3). Cost and quality conundrum of U.S. *Medicare News Group.* Retrieved from http://www.medicarenewsgroup.com/context/understanding-medicare-blog/ understanding-medicare-blog/2013/06/03/the-cost-and-quality-conundrum-of-american-end-of-life-care

Allen, S., Beres, S., Herring, R., & Seller, S. (2011, June 11). *The use of medical technology to prolong life.* Retrieved from http://www.cyberessays.com/Term-Paper-on-The-Use-Of-Medical-Technology-To/50045

Bakalar, N. (2013, September 11). Futile care at life's end. *New York Times.* Retrieved from http:// well.blogs.nytimes.com/2013/09/11/futile-care-at-lifes-end

Beckstrand, R., Callister, L., & Kirchhoff, K. (2006, January). Providing a "good death": Critical care nurses' suggestions for improving end-of-life care. *American Journal of Critical Care.* Retrieved from http://ajcc.aacnjournals.org/content/15/1/38.full

Bernstein, N. (2014, September 25). Fighting to honor a father's last wish: To die at home. *New York Times.* Retrieved from http://www.nytimes.com/2014/09/26/nyregion/family-fights-health-care-system-for-simple-request-to-die-at-home.html

Bever, L. (2014, October, 8). Cancer patient Brittany Maynard, 29, has scheduled her death for Nov. 1. *Washington Post.* Retrieved from https://www.washingtonpost.com/news/morning-mix/ wp/2014/10/08/terminally-ill-brittany-maynard-29-has-scheduled-her-death-for-nov-1

Bowron, C. (2012, February 17). Our unrealistic views of death, through a doctor's eyes. *Washington Post.* Retrieved from http://www.washingtonpost.com/opinions/our-unrealistic-views-of-death-through-a-doctors-eyes/2012/01/31/gIQAeaHpJR_story.html

Brandon, E. (2012, January 9). 65-and-older population soars. *US News.* Retrieved from http:// money.usnews.com/money/retirement/articles/2012/01/09/65-and-older-population-soars

Butler, K. (2013). *Knocking on heaven's door: The path to a better way of death.* New York, NY: Schriber

Callahan, D., & Lawler, P. (2012, July 24). End-of-life care: Role of ethics and health care. *Heritage Foundation.* Retrieved from http://www.heritage.org/research/reports/2012/07/ ethics-and-health-care-rethinking-end-of-life-care

Centers for Medicare & Medicaid Services. (n.d.). *Medicare hospice benefits.* Retrieved from https:// www.medicare.gov/Pubs/pdf/02154.pdf

Cleveland Clinic. (2005). *Policy on forgoing life-sustaining or death-prolonging therapy.* Retrieved from http://www.clevelandclinic.org/bioethics/policies/policyonlifesustaining/ccfcode.html

Gleckman, H. (2013, February 6). More people are dying at home and in hospice, but they are also getting more intense hospital care. *Forbes.* Retrieved from http://www.forbes.com/sites/howardgleckman/2013/02/06/more-people-are-dying-at-home-and-in-hospice-but-they-are-also-getting-more-intense-hospital-care

Graham, J. (2014, November 12). IOM report calls for transformation of end-of-life care. *Journal of the American Medical Association, 312*(18). Retrieved from http://jama.jamanetwork.com/article.aspx?articleid=1930814

Gustafson, D. (2007, March 14). A good death. *Journal of Medical Internet Research, 9*(1). Retrieved from http://www.jmir.org/2007/1/e6

Hsieh, P. (2014, September 29). Who decides what medical care you receive at end of life? *Forbes.* Retrieved from http://www.forbes.com/sites/paulhsieh/2014/09/29/who-decides-what-medical-care-you-receive-at-end-of-life

Huynh, T. N., Kleerup, E. C., Wiley, J. F., Savitsky T. D., Guse, D., Garber, B. J., & Wenger, N. S. (2013, November 11). The frequency and cost of treatment perceived to be futile in critical care. *JAMA Internal Medicine, 173*(20). Retrieved from http://archinte.jamanetwork.com/article.aspx?articleid=1735897

Kasman, D. (2004, October 19). When is medical treatment futile? *Journal of General Internal Medicine, 19*(10). Retrieved from http://www.ncbi.nlm.nih.gov/pmc/articles/PMC1492577

Kehl, K. A. (2006, August-September). Moving toward peace: An analysis of the concept of a good death. *American Journal of Hospital Palliative Care, 23*(4):277–86. Retrieved from http://www.ncbi.nlm.nih.gov/pubmed/17060291

Kuehn, B. (2013, February 5). Author insights: Patients face too many burdensome care transitions at the end of life. *News @ JAMA.* Retrieved from http://newsatjama.jama.com/2013/02/05/author-insights-patients-face-too-many-burdensome-care-transitions-at-the-end-of-life

Murray, K. (2012, February 8). How doctors die. *The Guardian.* Retrieved from http://www.theguardian.com/society/2012/feb/08/how-doctors-choose-die

National Academies of Science. (2014). *Dying in America: Improving quality and honoring individual preferences near the end of life.* Retrieved from http://www.nationalacademies.org/hmd/Reports/2014/Dying-In-America-Improving-Quality-and-Honoring-Individual-Preferences-Near-the-End-of-Life.aspx

National Hospice and Palliative Care Organization. (2015). *NHPCO's fact and figures: Hospice care in America.* Retrieved from nhpco.org/sites/default/files/public/Statistics_Research/2015_Facts_Figures.pdf

National POLST Paradigm. (2012). *State programs.* Retrieved from http://www.polst.org/programs-in-your-state

Nicholas, L., Langa, K., Iwashyna, T., & Weir, D. (2011, October 5). Regional variation in the association between advance directives and end-of-life Medicare expenditures. *Journal of the American Medical Association, 306*(13). Retrieved from http://jama.jamanetwork.com/article.aspx?articleid=1104465#qundefined

Oregon Health and Science University. (2014, June 9). *POLST orders successfully guide end of life medical treatment.* Retrieved from http://www.ohsu.edu/xd/about/news_events/news/2014/06-09-polst-orders-successfull.cfm

PEW Foundation. (2013, November 21). *Views on end-of-life medical treatments.* Retrieved from http://www.pewforum.org/2013/11/21/views-on-end-of-life-medical-treatments

Pullen., E. (2012, March 5). *Why don't patients have advance directives?* Retrieved from http://drpullen.com/advancedirectives

Riley, G., & Lubitz, J. (2010, April). Long-term trends in Medicare payments in the last year of life. *Health Services Research Journal 45*(2). Retrieved from http://www.ncbi.nlm.nih.gov/pmc/articles/PMC2838161

Silveira, M., Scott, K., & Langa, K. (2010, April 1). Advance directives and outcomes of surrogate decision making before death. *New England Journal of Medicine.* Retrieved from http://www.nejm.org/doi/full/10.1056/NEJMsa0907901

Silveira, M., Wiitala, W., & Piette, J. (2014, April 2). Advance directive completion by elderly Americans: A decade of change. *Journal of the American Geriatrics Society, 62*(4). Retrieved from http://onlinelibrary.wiley.com/doi/10.1111/jgs.12736/abstract

Teno, J., Gozalo, P., Bynum, J., Leland, N., Miller, S., Morden, N., . . . Mor, V. (2013, February 6). Change in end-of-life care for Medicare beneficiaries: Site of death, place of care, and health care transitions in 2000, 2005, and 2009. *Journal of the American Medical Association, 309*(5). Retrieved from http://jama.jamanetwork.com/article.aspx?articleid=1568250

Tierney, W., Dexter, P., Gramelspacher, G., Perkins, A., Zhou, X., & Wilinsky, F. (2001, January). The effect of discussions about advance directives on patients' satisfaction with primary care. *Journal of General Internal Medicine, 16*(1). Retrieved from http://www.ncbi.nlm.nih.gov/pmc/articles/PMC1495157

Vincent, G., & Velkoff, V. (2010, May). The next four decades: The older population in the United States: 2010 to 2050. *U.S. Census.* Retrieved from http://www.census.gov/prod/2010pubs/p25–1138.pdf

Vora, P. (2016, February, 2). Comparing end of life care for cancer patients in 7 developed countries. *American Journal of Managed Care.* Retrieved from http://www.ajmc.com/newsroom/comparing-end-of-life-care-for-cancer-patients-in-7-developed-countries

Wang, P. (2012, December 12). Cutting the high cost of end-of-life care. *Money Magazine.* Retrieved from http://time.com/money/2793643/cutting-the-high-cost-of-end-of-life-care

Chapter 5

Mental Illness

Community Supports and Community Dilemmas

Dr. Mandy Fauble

The crisis team arrived at the park, and the workers looked at each other with uncertainty.

"I'm just not sure what to do. This guy's living like he's homeless, but I don't think we can involuntarily commit him. We just don't have the legal grounds." Brent shook his head at Regan. "I mean, I've driven by this guy every day on my way to work. It's really sad, but I think because people keep feeding him, he's not in immediate danger, and he's not been threatening anybody. Did you know he actually has an apartment? The police info said he's so paranoid he hasn't stayed there in months. They think he's being evicted. He must have social security or some type of income, but he's in no shape to really use his resources."

Regan sighed for a minute, wondering what it would be like to be so afraid of your own home that you would leave it and find yourself on the streets. Her mind drifted to a long-haired and unkempt gentleman she had seen in her own small town. In high school, students called him "Jesus" because of his long hair and the fact that he made silent crosses and blessings in front of him as he walked through the streets, mumbling to himself and occasionally shaking imaginary hands. At the time, she'd been terrified of him, believing stereotypes about mental illness and violence. She never guessed that her job would lead her to work with so many like him, caught between worlds and living with schizophrenia.

"When I took the call the police said they've gotten quite a few calls about him from worried citizens, just people wanting to make sure he's safe, I guess." Regan explained, "His name is Simon, and they have had plenty of contact with him in the past. It was Officer Rogers who called." She paused as Brent nodded at her. They'd both worked with Officer Rogers in the past and appreciated his compassion for people with mental health needs.

"He ended up telling me that he went to high school with him and that they used to play football together. I guess he still knows some of his extended family. He said that Simon went into the army but must have gotten sick there and was discharged. I guess he's been struggling since then, which would have probably been like 20 years ago. He had a wife and son at some point, but Rogers said she wasn't from around here and moved to be with her parents during one of the times that he was in the hospital. Rogers said that there have been times, when he's feeling better, that he's been seen at the VA Behavioral Health Clinic, as well as New Hope's clinic." Regan found herself feeling sadder and sadder as she thought about the life that Simon's illness had taken from him. She continued, "So, based on what he said, it seems like Rogers and the department have a pretty good history of what's gone on with him in the past. This time's supposedly different. They said he's more escalated than they've heard about in the past, and the store owner is saying that if Simon doesn't leave, he'll press charges. Rogers told me they really don't want to take him to jail. They're worried something terrible will happen to him, and it's pretty clear he needs treatment, not to get arrested. Plus, if he's in jail, there's really no way we can figure out how to keep his apartment."

"That sucks." Brent sighed and began flipping through his paperwork. "It reminds me of this guy I worked with once who became so convinced someone else had broken into the apartment downstairs that he ended up breaking in himself to protect the landlord's property. So he got arrested. Then he was in the hospital when the hearing happened, so they issued a bench warrant. Last I knew, he'd been in and out of jail and couldn't find a place to stay. It's ridiculous to think these people can get better when they can't get adequate health care, and they aren't in one place long enough to get stable. I mean, people need a place to *belong*.

"Yeah, sometimes I wonder what good we're really doing, you know? It's the same thing, day in and day out. It's just so sad—a guy who went from playing football and starting a military career to living on the street." Regan's shoulders sank as she picked up on Brent's tone of resignation.

"We've got to do what we can." Brent looked at her pointedly. "We have some things to work with here. At least we know he has income, because he has an apartment, and we know he's been connected to services in the past, including the VA. So let's go see if we can convince this guy we're trying to help him and get him to the hospital before he goes to jail."

Regan smiled at him, and they got out of the vehicle. She loved Brent's enthusiasm for diverting people from jail, especially since he'd gone to school for criminal justice, like so many of her friends that did crisis intervention and emergency room work. What Brent found out, just as she had, is that the police spend a lot of time helping citizens with mental illness who commit petty crimes in their confusion, call attention to themselves because they're homeless, frighten people, or engage in self-harming gestures that require emergency services. There are also those rare instances where the police are called because of someone harming someone else. It turns out, most police cases are actually domestic or related to situations like this one in the sunny city park.

"There he is," Brent said, looking across the park toward a bench.

Regan followed his gaze. As they got closer, she saw a man who appeared to be in his 50s, but it was hard to tell if his situation had prematurely aged him, and he was obviously disheveled. Regan could see his matted hair, and she immediately became concerned when she noticed what he was wearing.

"Oh man," she said, "it's, like, 90 degrees today, and he's wearing that huge coat. I hope he's not all layered up under there. That could be really dangerous when it's so hot."

As they approached, Regan could hear him talking and see him gesturing to the person, or people, that only he could see. His face and features became clearer to her, and she could see dirt and grime on his face and hands. She briefly wondered when he last had a shower, if he had bed bugs, and where he was going to the bathroom. Years of working in the field made her very aware of the risks to those living outdoors. She couldn't help but wonder if anyone had ever jumped him for his precious few resources or if he ever drank himself to sleep to be more comfortable. She knew he'd been sleeping behind the pharmacy that was adjacent to the park, but that couldn't continue if he were to stay safe and out of jail.

Brent and Regan walked closer to him, each lost in their own thoughts and perfectly in tune as a team that had worked in difficult situations together many times. The teamwork and support had been vital in being able to cope with the stress and with the harsh realities their jobs forced them to confront.

Brent grew up wanting to make a difference. From the time he was a little boy, he wanted to be a police officer, and he still did. After Operation Iraqi Freedom and Operation Enduring Freedom, it was harder to find full-time work in law enforcement, as many returning military personnel filled those jobs. He knew that getting experience with crisis intervention would help with his dream to become a police officer, and he was always first in the office to go on police calls when the team responded with the police or needed the police for support. His job, however, had made him question a lot of things he'd believed about the criminal justice system. He no longer believed it was simply a fair and just system. Instead, he realized that the criminal justice system was sometimes the only place people with serious mental illness landed. He knew from his undergraduate education that people with mental illness had once been warehoused in institutions, and that couldn't have been good. He'd remembered learning about the teenagers with a range of symptoms whose parents told them they were going out for a Sunday drive, only to spend the next 25 or 30 years in a state hospital. He knew that medications changed people's options, and many of them were able to live in their communities after efforts to deinstitutionalize.

Somewhere along the line, though, something went wrong. The promise of living in the community went awry. A cycle of difficulties obtaining housing and medication, being in and out of the hospital, struggling with poverty, dealing with addictions, and being easily victimized seemed to plague a specific segment of people with mental illness. Brent found himself caught in his own conflicting values. He believed so strongly in deinstitutionalization and integration of people with mental illness. He believed in their civil right to determine their own healthcare, yet, he also couldn't help but feel a state hospital might be better than the situation in the park this hot day. He began to feel the pressure he sometimes experienced on cases—if he couldn't make something work, would this man go to jail? Would he die in the streets?

Frustrated, he grumbled to Regan, "Deinstitutionalization is great, but when you're too sick and you have no home, no job, no family, and no allies, you're institutionless. Unfortunately, our society just hasn't figured out how to handle that, so we *make you* fit in an institution. For guys like this, it's likely to be jail if we can't get him in the hospital. And then he probably won't be there long enough to get what he needs, and he'll wind up in jail anyway." He wondered how he'd be able to turn off how he felt about putting people in jail who he didn't think belonged there. Things were so much simpler when he believed jail was for bad guys. They reached the park benches, and he heard Regan's voice. He tuned out his distracted thoughts and tuned back into the work in front of them, wiping his sweaty forehead.

"Hi, I'm Regan. I'm here from the county crisis program. What's your name?"

The man regarded them hesitantly, the whites of his eyes showing. Regan picked up the malodorous clothing and a jolt of concern shot through her as she wondered how long it'd been since he'd been able to rest in a clean and comfortable environment. While she knew this man had a right to choose how he was living, she couldn't help but wonder if anyone would really choose to be on the streets, easy prey, and under constant terror induced by paranoia, or if a person could make a choice when gripped by such illness. She watched the man pace, his physical agitation and discomfort clear.

"I'm OK, I'm OK, I'm OK, I'm OK . . ." he began to chant, as if willing them to understand he didn't want their help and that this mantra could somehow quiet his paranoia.

"Hey, I'm Brent. How are you doing? Are you hot today in that coat?" Brent kept his distance but tried an introduction.

"Hot, hot, hot, hot, hot . . ."

He went on, "The fires are hot where they wait. The book, it's been written in the Book of the Lamb, Brent and Regan, Regan and Brent. Have you seen my dog? Did you poison my dog?" He looked at them wildly. Regan and Brent exchanged a quick glance, silently acknowledging that his psychosis was likely going to prevent any coherent communication.

"I'm sorry, no, we haven't seen your dog. Simon, it is Simon, right?" Regan asked hesitantly, and thought she saw a flash of clarity in his eyes at the sound of his name, but he continued to pace and mumble.

"What's your dog's name, Simon?" Regan asked, hoping to build a bridge that would help her communicate with Simon.

Brent whispered to her, "I've never seen a dog here, and the police didn't say anything about a dog."

Simon continued his agitated pace but didn't respond or look at the two workers. He looked at the sidewalk, mumbling.

Regan felt she'd lost him again. "Simon, would you come with us to the hospital? I wonder if you'd be more comfortable if you got some food in you and talked with someone who maybe could help you. Would you talk with someone in behavioral health to see what they recommend?" Regan knew she needed to make this very specific offer for behavioral health assessment, in case they had to pursue an involuntary commitment. If she failed to do so, any request for commitment would be denied by the court system. She also suspected that Simon could sense she was a safe person but probably couldn't process the information she was offering.

"No, no, no, no, no, no, no, no, no . . ." he began to repeat, exhibiting what Regan knew was echolalia, likely a symptom of his illness. She could tell he was uncomfortable with their presence, and he began to walk away.

Brent looked at her. "I don't want to spook him any further. He's clearly pretty paranoid and out of touch. Let's have a seat and figure out what on earth we're going to do. Nothing like midafternoon on Friday to encounter something like this."

BACKGROUND INFORMATION

In this case, Simon is exhibiting symptoms of schizophrenia. Schizophrenia is considered a serious mental illness, as are schizoaffective, bipolar, major depression, and borderline personality disorders. These mental illnesses are considered serious as they can contribute significantly to disability, distress, and higher use of both behavioral and physical health care, particularly emergency services. It's noteworthy that *most* people with mental illness recover and live happy and healthy lives, but It's also important to be aware of how significantly impacted some people are by their illness throughout their lifetimes. We must approach mental illness as we would with any other illness; different people experience different levels of distress, symptoms, environmental factors, and response to treatments. In this section, we review some of these illnesses, beginning with schizophrenia, as seen in Simon's situation:

The *Diagnostic and Statistical Manual of Mental Disorders*, used to diagnose mental illness, explains that "schizophrenia is characterized by delusions, hallucinations, disorganized speech and behavior, and other symptoms that cause social or occupational dysfunction. For a diagnosis, symptoms must have been present for six months and include at least one month of active symptoms" (American Psychiatric Publishing, n.d., para. 2). This means that a person living with schizophrenia symptoms may believe things that are not true (delusions) and act upon them as if they are true (as all humans act on what they believe is happening) but also experience a world different from what others do because of these beliefs. These beliefs may be reinforced by sensory experiences that the person has (hallucinations) that others aren't having. However, to the person with schizophrenia they are experienced as very real, as real as reading this page feels like a legitimate and real experience to the reader. Thus, assisting the person may be difficult as the helper and person with schizophrenia may have very different experiences of what is happening. Hallucinations and delusions are called the *positive* symptoms of schizophrenia because they are the added symptoms a person has. Based on these delusions and hallucinations, someone with the illness might come to believe that a physician offering medicine is really a government agent sent to poison him or her or that a family member who is singing is really conjuring spirits. One can imagine how frightening this may be for each party to encounter and how difficult to cross this divide. The description also states that people with schizophrenia have disorganized speech and behavior, which indicates they may seem illogical, hard to connect with or follow, or difficult to engage, and this is many times related to the way schizophrenia may impact a person's ability to think clearly, process information quickly, or recognize social cues and relate to others socially. These symptoms, when a person struggles to connect with others socially and think clearly, are called the *negative* symptoms, because they refer to a loss in experience and capacities.

According to the Centers for Disease Control and Prevention's (CDC) *Burden of Mental Illness* (2013), about 0.5% to 1.0% of people develop schizophrenia. In the United States, based on a population of 323,368,000, that is 1,616,840 to 3,233,680 people. While there is tremendous focus on the unique symptoms of schizophrenia, 1 in 10 will die by suicide, as depression and intense discomfort may be part of living with the illness. While the illness is quite serious and contributes to both the personal suffering of those diagnosed and the impact of disease in the community, this must be balanced with the body of literature on the fact that many people can (and do) recover from schizophrenia and that early treatment and intervention can prevent deterioration related to the illness. The National Empowerment Center, the Copeland Center, Recovery Innovations, and the Substance Abuse and Mental Health Services Administration (SAMHSA) provide excellence resources on recovery, and the National Institute of Mental Health's *Recovery After an Initial Schizophrenia Episode (RAISE)* project provides evidence-based intervention resources for early onset psychosis.

Serious mental illness, as stated previously, affects more people than those living with schizophrenia. Depression is another serious mental illness many are more familiar with, as it is both more common and less stigmatized. In the United States, 6.7% of all adults experience an episode of major depression during a year, and depression contributes significantly to worldwide disabilities (National Institute of Mental Health, n.d.a). Each year, about 2.6% of adults in the United States are living with an episode of bipolar disorder, which is a mental illness marked by extreme depression or a state of mania. These changes in mood, activity, thinking, and behavior are outside of the ups and downs that are experienced by everyone, and the significant highs and lows in mood and energy cause great discomfort and create serious problems in daily living, in thinking, decision making, finances, health, social and vocational situations, and a range of other areas (National Institute of Mental Health, n.d.b).

We can see in looking at just three serious mental illnesses that a large number of people are impacted. When we consider other challenges like posttraumatic stress disorder, anxiety disorders, and attention deficit disorders, we can see we have barely touched on the types of mental health concerns people have as adults and children and just how important it is to be aware of the illnesses and treatments. As these illnesses are common, and exacerbated by trauma, poverty, or other stressors, behavioral health becomes a prominent concern in a variety of helping contexts: school-based services, health care and medical settings, substance use disorder treatment, corrections, child protective services, housing and basic resource assistance, and family support.

Beyond what each of these individuals are struggling with, there might be family, friends, colleagues, fellow students in schools, church groups, and others who are impacted by the illness and its symptoms, as the person with mental illness may be changed by his or her symptoms and struggle to fulfill important life roles.

There are a few final points to reinforce the scope of these issues and the demand for helping professionals to have a basic competency in behavioral health. Consider that medications for behavioral health symptoms are some of the most prescribed medications in the United States, with one in four adult women and one in five adult men taking a mental health medication (Cassels, 2011). And 20% of all primary care visits include mental health treatment of some kind (CDC, 2014). According to the CDC, more than 41,000 citizens in the United States die by suicide each year (CDC, 2015]). Worldwide, suicide takes more lives than all armed conflicts combined (Dokoupil, 2013). Last, behavioral health concerns complicate the ability to help people in other interrelated areas. Outcomes in child welfare, substance use treatment, education, and physical health can be impacted by mental illness, as mental illness can create difficulties in these areas and impede effective assistance. This can increase the costs of helping in these areas, as well as the demands on helping resources.

It is vital for helping professionals to have knowledge of behavioral health, as so many people living in our communities might be struggling with a mental illness. However, that was not always the case. *Institutionalization* for people with serious mental illness, such as a mood disorder (depression or bipolar) or a thought disorder (schizophrenia), was at one time quite common practice. This means that the treatment for a sizable number of people was largely delivered in an institutionalized hospital setting. For instance, reports indicate that the number of individuals with severe mental illness institutionalized in state hospitals was about 559,000 in 1955 (Koyanagi, 2007). With the advent of newer medications, most notably thorazine, and programming to move people to their communities, these numbers decreased to 154,000 in 1980 (Koyangi, 2007). According to a Treatment Advocacy Center report (Torrey, Kennard, Eslinger, Lamb, & Pavle, 2010), the number further decreased as time went on, to 43,318 beds in 2010, levels below the per capita rates of the 1850s.

Aside from medications, social policy has been critical in supporting the transition from institutions to communities. After all, social policy created the state hospital systems and was necessary to provide alternatives for care, where newer medications could be used effectively. Critical movement began with the Community Mental Health Center Act passed in 1963 during the Kennedy administration. This was responsible for the creation of community-based centers all across the nation that specialize in assisting clients with serious mental illness (National Council for Behavioral Health, 2015). Many of these facilities continue to provide these services today. In another instrumental change, the Supreme Court's *Olmstead* decision has led to further efforts to deinstitutionalize and ensure psychiatric services are delivered in the least restrictive setting (ADA.Gov, n.d.). These changes have not just occurred through the efforts of policy makers and health care professionals. Advocacy efforts by people who have received mental health services and their families have also played a critical role in shaping social policy outcomes. Groups such as the National Alliance on Mental Illness (NAMI), Mental Health America

(MHA), the Copeland Center and the Schizophrenia and Related Disorders Alliance of America (SARDAA) are examples of nationally known organizations, but these efforts can also be seen in local organizations through board of director membership, peer advocacy, and efforts to combat stigma.

But these efforts to deinstitutionalize have not come without debates or complications. Dorothea Dix was the earliest crusader *for* state systems of institutionalized care for people with mental illness after she spent years observing and documenting terrible conditions in a variety of settings, including jails. It was hypothesized that a system of state psychiatric facilities, where people with mental illness could be assisted with treatments, would provide a safer alternative to jails.

By the mid-1800s, institutions for helping people with mental illness began to proliferate. In some cases, these hospital settings likely helped families who did not know how to keep their loved ones safe. They may have helped keep people with mental illness safe when their behaviors were not tolerated in their communities or their illnesses produced symptoms that led to an inability to care for themselves or that led to suicidal or injurious behaviors. While controversial, the demand for involuntary commitment, where a person is court ordered to care, continues due to extreme safety concerns sometimes caused by the symptoms of mental illness coupled with the person's lack of awareness of their illness and ability to help themselves become well.

At the same time, there have been horrific abuses in these facilities, despite being created to improve conditions for those with serious mental illness. For instance, forced sterilization in eugenics programs impacted some residents, such as the 7,000 in North Carolina between 1929 and 1976 alone (National Public Radio, 2014). About the same time, California forcibly sterilized 20,000 in various state-sponsored systems, some being state psychiatric facilities (Cohen & Bonifield, 2012). The transorbital lobotomy, legal and popularized by Dr. Walter Freeman, is another example of abuse in psychiatric institutions, as the procedure was often done without proper sedation, was performed on children, and left many permanently disabled by brain damage. A report by National Public Radio (2005) indicates that this practice was most popular between 1949 and 1952, when approximately 50,000 were done, with serious complications for many patients. Still other concerns were harsh "therapies" such as ice baths, suspending patients in wicker cages, steam baths, inducing insulin shock, overuse of early forms of shock therapy, and long-term commitments well past when patients may have needed such care. There are thousands buried in numbered and unnamed graves all across the nation, patients who died in institutions or were paupers and largely forgotten members of society. Some of their stories are told in the Willard Suitcase Exhibit, which chronicles how everyday lives were forever changed by institutionalization in New York's Willard facility (Community Consortium, 2015). There are almost 5,800 unmarked graves at Willard and 55,000 across the state of New York (Barry, 2014). While state hospital facilities have shrunk in size, there are continued concerns with their safety, as Romney (2013) identifies in California's system.

It is clear that advances in treatment, as well as a call for respect of the dignity and worth of those institutionalized, demanded a change to community-based supports. Currently, the mental health service system has a broad range of services to better meet needs, which include outpatient (office-based) services, services that go into the community to work with people, and group homes or assisted living facilities. Yet, concerns remain about how to best approach the vast array of needs for people with mental illness, especially when the current options aren't working well for a segment of the population.

CURRENT ISSUES

Our knowledge about what causes mental illness and how to intervene, which has aided in deinstitutionalization, has certainly evolved since the days of Dorothea Dix.

Why is there still a debate? Isn't it better to have people live in their communities? Haven't barbaric things been done in state psychiatric institutions? Why is this still a topic of discussion? To answer these questions, we consider four major concerns:

First, institutionalization persists. The institutionalization of people with mental illness just looks different now. According to a joint effort of the Treatment Advocacy Center and National Sheriffs Association, "There are more than three times as many people with mental illness incarcerated than in hospitals, a sharp increase that has followed deinstitutionalization from state hospitals" (Torrey et al., 2010). Three of the largest congregate living centers for people with mental illness are the Cook County Jail in Chicago, Rikers Island in New York, and the Los Angeles County Jail (Ford, 2015). A 2006 report from the Bureau of Justice Statistics indicated more than half of all inmates incarcerated were dealing with a mental health concern and that this represented more than 550,000 people (James & Glaze, 2006), a number eerily similar to those who were living in state mental hospitals during the peak of institutionalization practices. In another similarity, it is noteworthy that the Cook County system now employs a psychologist as a warden. People with mental illness are overrepresented on probation and parole, many have a co-occurring substance use disorder, and they are more likely than those without mental illness to have their community corrections supervision revoked and thus return to jail (Prins & Draper, 2009).

It is no surprise that questions have been raised about *why* so many people with mental illness are incarcerated. Torrey et al. (2010) cite the shortage in public psychiatric beds as one leading cause, with approximately one bed available for every 3,000 citizens. If it is too difficult to obtain a safe place in the hospital, incarceration may be seen as a viable option. Another cause may be that the stigma and fear created by some disorganized behaviors of mental illness contribute to public support for arrest, leading to what is sometimes called "criminalization of mental illness." Some of these behaviors violate traditional social norms and may include homelessness and loitering; sleeping outside a business or lingering around a park and talking to oneself when asked to leave; shoplifting due to confusion; appearing to be threatening due to symptoms; evading the police or having difficulty controlling oneself due to symptoms; entering a building uninvited due to symptoms; or even lesser offenses such as failing to pay fines or appear in court due to hospitalization. In addition to fear and stigma associated with these more common behaviors, there is also great misunderstanding of mental illness and psychiatry coupled with fear of violence and aggression, further conflating mental illness with criminal behavior and thinking. Metzl and MacLeish (2015) provide an excellent review of the central themes of mental illness and gun violence, the role of psychiatric diagnosis in predicting gun violence, the characterization of gun violence committed by loners with mental illness, and the role of gun control in stemming gun violence. The work deconstructs common oversimplifications of mental illness and violence, for instance, acknowledging that serious mental illness may play a role in some mass shootings but may also lead to increased risk for being victimized. In short, mental illness occurs in a social environment as do our proposed solutions to combat both terrifying social phenomenon like mass shootings and the causes we attribute to them. We must critically dissect the roles of our fear and bias in our approaches to these tragedies. Then we must employ more scientific thinking.

The treatment of incarcerated people with mental illness is an additional concern. According to Torrey et al. (2010), people with mental illness face several challenges in this system: They have higher recidivism rates, cost more to support, end up staying longer (due to rule infractions and transfer needs), are harder to manage successfully, are more likely to die by suicide while incarcerated, and may face abuse within the system. The Los Angeles County system and Rikers Island have both come under fire for abusive conditions recently, and both have faced legal consequences (Lovett, 2015). In terms of the more basic demand for treatment of their mental illnesses, inmates face a range of difficulties. In Pennsylvania, the American Civil Liberties Union has brought suit due to inmates waiting for more than a year in solitary confinement because of a shortage of psychiatric beds (Craig, 2015). Quite simply, the criminal justice system was not designed to provide intensive health care or mental health services, yet the population of those who society incarcerates is in desperate need of this care. Hertel's (2013) description of the travails of continuing on medications and finding treatment once released from incarceration indicates a problem nationwide, as people with mental illness must navigate changing (or not having) publically funded insurance, obtaining community-based mental health care with long waits for services, and potentially having to go without treatment once released due to these barriers.

While the number of people with mental illness in jail is eye-catching, a much less publicized number is those who live in nursing homes. A report in 2009 indicated that more than 125,000 people with mental illness were living in nursing homes as a result of closure of state hospitals and shortages of psychiatric beds. Furthermore, concerns have been raised about the differing ages and needs of these residents, as well as the potential for aggression in a mixed population (Johnson, 2009).

The second explanation for why we continue to debate institutionalization and deinstitutionalization is that the understanding of how to treat mental illness is evolving, imperfect, and socially bound. A good example of this is to look at the disease of schizophrenia, whose postulated and interrelated causes include multigenetic factors; pre- and perinatal events such as maternal virus, winter birth, maternal toxemia or hypoxia; trauma exposure; substance use; and household and environmental stress (Tamminga & Medoff, 2000). Still other theories imply that a virus exposure leads to schizophrenia (Fox, 2010).

The root of Schizo, Possible cause

Treatment for schizophrenia is just as complex. Medication management for schizophrenia has long been debated, as some people with schizophrenia recover without medications and others require it throughout their lives (Torrey, 2014). Psychosocial services, such as individualized resiliency training, case management and supportive employment and education services, are also evidence based through studies that demonstrate their effectiveness. As with other illnesses, the range and intensity of services varies greatly and may include anything from casual office visits to long-term hospitalization. Perhaps the greatest difference is that there is no metric in schizophrenia symptoms to assist in making these decisions. In treating an illness like asthma, heart failure, or diabetes, there are clear lab values and objective data to guide treatment protocols. These do not exist as clearly in behavioral health. Thus, the range of presentation and outcome in the illness is varied, and the treatment relies more heavily on professional judgment and assessment, which is compounded by the *behavioral* symptoms of mental illness that make it a more socially bound disease phenomenon.

Treatments

Rosenhan (1973) has perhaps the best-known example of the social constructs that undergird our definitions of mental illness. In his landmark *On Being Sane in Insane Places,* Rosenhan demonstrated, quite adeptly, that "sane" and "insane" are labels that can alter humans' abilities to reason clearly about patients in a health care setting. In two experiments, he demonstrated that "sane" people could be admitted to long-term behavioral health care without detection by health care professionals, and that patients presenting to emergency rooms for behavioral health support were found to be "pseudopatients"—they were suspected of impersonating mental illness—simply by the power of suggestion. Readers should recall how they've felt when hearing the labels of "schizo," "sicko," "psycho," "serial killer," or "whacko" to understand the power these labels have on our ability to think clearly about mental illness. These labels shape both treatment seeking, as people may avoid treatment due to shame and stigma, and may shape treatment provision, due to biases, depersonalization, and stigma.

When we reflect that our knowledge on what causes mental illness and how to treat it remains imperfect, and we consider that the social stigma persists, it is reasonable to assume the social conversation on institutionalization will continue. Like any other evolving phenomenon, we are not done. This implies that even a radical policy shift, such as the move to institutionalization and the subsequent positive deinsitutionalization, should be revisited and reworked as needed. We can see these as opportunities for policy lessons and changes that better meet the needs of those in our society, particularly those most vulnerable.

A third compelling factor in debating deinstitutionalization is found in the poor outcomes of many people with serious mental illness who are living in our communities, even while so many succeed. It is challenging to balance the positive outcomes we have gained in mental health while still attending to the remaining problems, but we must think critically if we are to truly help the most people. Suicide rates in the United States continue to grow (Sullivan, Annest, Simon, Luo, & Dahlberg, 2013 & 2015). Likewise, people with serious mental illness, schizophrenia particularly, lead shorter and sicker lives. Olfson, Gerhard, Huang, Crystal, and Stroup (2015) followed data on more than one million people living with schizophrenia. Findings indicated that those with schizophrenia were more than 3.5 times as likely to die prematurely as compared to the general population. This was *not* primarily explained by suicide; natural diseases and accidents contributed significantly more. Overall, those with schizophrenia lived lives more than 25 years shorter than those in the general population.

SAMHSA indicates that approximately 26% of homeless people are living with mental illness (SAMHSA, 2011). The link between poverty and mental illness is long established. While poverty is known to increase risks for mental illness, being mentally ill is also a major risk factor for unemployment, disability, and living in impoverished conditions (World Health Organization, 2007).

Social isolation, disability, disease, and poverty impact the lives of many with serious mental illness. While a tremendous number of individuals recover successfully and are the champions of community-based living, we cannot ignore the segment of the population that is so negatively affected and clearly needs a more effective strategy to share in recovery. The debate about how to systematically assist this group of those most impacted raises questions about what intensity of support would be most helpful. In light of the housing, medical, social, and vocational needs, institutionalization continues to be a topic of debate as a potential solution for a small segment of people. What that institution might look like as the least restrictive option also remains debatable.

A final point to consider is the challenge of our current system and the variation in what people need. While this chapter has largely focused on the initial problems of both institutionalization and deinstitutionalization, it is important to note that it is likely that *neither are wholly satisfying, largely because one solution is unlikely to adequately address every variation in need.* The concept of recovery that leads to an ability to deinstitutionalize is important and should neither overshadow nor be underrepresented in our discussion. According to SAMHSA (2010), a working definition of recovery is "a process of change through which individuals improve their health and wellness, live a self-directed life, and strive to reach their full potential" (p. 3). In recovery, a person finds home, health, purposeful living, and community integration (p. 3). SAMHSA has provided ten guiding principles of recovery and has pushed behavioral health care providers to promote this hopeful and collaborative approach. *Most* people with mental illness significantly recover. A message of hope and reintegration is fundamental, given that a social welfare tenet of any solution should be the least restrictive environment and the most socially integrated system possible. Still, we find that a segment of people with serious mental illness need intense support and are at risk for negative outcomes without these supports. Productive conversation about solutions should be as nuanced as the people it purports to help. A range of possibilities to support acute and chronic needs at a variety of levels is needed.

Internationally, for instance, people with schizophrenia have different types of outcomes. Jablensky and Sartorius (2007), who participated in a large World Health Organization study, caution that developed nations do not have systematically better outcomes for their populations living with schizophrenia. They conclude there are cultural and social factors predictive of wellness that should not be ignored. In light of this, any possible solutions should not rely on a biased belief that modern medicine is the answer or that the social environment can be ignored.

The wheels of social policy can turn slowly, and health care is a large and critical social institution. The U.S. health care economy is about 18% of the U.S. gross domestic product. The size and growth of this economy was one of the main arguments for health care reform (White House, n.d.). At the same time, such a giant institution lacks agility for rapid change if it is to be safely implemented, and such critical infrastructure becomes a national security matter when we consider the number of jobs, organizations, and lives interwoven in this system. Thus, the system, as a whole, may lag behind the needs of people on the ground or be less flexible to adjusting to their variation in needs.

There are no easy answers to addressing the needs of those with serious mental illness. Yet the needs remain, and the current system is clearly inadequate. Solutions must be brought forward to address these complex needs, as the social policies of prior generations, namely deinstitutionalization efforts, lack the infrastructure and longevity to sustain their intended consequences.

Social work, with its unique focus on person in the social environment, can play a significant role in the myriad resolutions brought to bear, from the microlevel role of a case manager to the macrolevel work of a policy maker or administrator revising institutional care. Without this effort, the promise of recovery cannot be brought to reality for the thousands caught between institutions, stigmatized, and at extreme risk.

INSTITUTIONS COLLIDE

Brent and Regan didn't take long to decide what to do about Simon.

"I just wonder what his life was like before all this," Regan said, sadly.

"I know. I can't imagine what this does to families. I just look at the baby sometimes when I get home and . . ." Brent trailed off.

"You just have to set it aside if you're going to go on. You know you can just do what you can do." Regan advised, "I'll start the petition. We can cosign to make it stronger." Regan began filling out the form that she would use to petition, or ask, the court-appointed reviewer to approve to help get Simon to the hospital for an evaluation.

"Yeah, OK," Brent sighed. He could see Simon from where they were sitting, and his thoughts began to wander. How old was Simon when he first got sick? Was he like some clients Brent had worked with? Was he away in the army and suddenly started hearing voices, unable to complete tasks, and being told to leave? Had he been terrified by what was happening and losing his whole world at the same time? Were his parents grieving the loss of their baby? What was it like in the period of time when Simon got well and began to rebuild? What happened to Simon's son, who lost his father to an illness that might have led him to think of his father as a scary monster, or did he think that Simon somehow chose to leave? Brent thought about his own son, who had been born earlier in the year, and was grateful for what he had, yet bereft for families living with mental illness.

"All done." Regan handed him the stack of papers. Brent took the forms and began to add what he observed, concentrating on documenting why he believed Simon was in immediate need of emergency attention and could not safely remain on the streets. He finished and handed it back to Regan.

"So, I guess I'm calling it in?" she smiled. "Always dumping the work on me."

"Uh-huh. I think I still owe you for that mess last week," Brent retorted. He briefly acknowledged to himself how their banter was one of the ways he knew they both coped with how stressful the job got at times and helped to counterbalance the sadness that could break in.

"Point taken. OK, I'll call. I just realized, though, the call came from the township. Someone must have been calling them. But I think this park is the city, right? It's so close."

"Yep, it's the city. That's a relief." Brent listened as Regan spoke to the court-appointed on-call staff member, explaining the situation and reading their petition. It was an efficient process but one that still took time in a precarious situation. If the court-appointed staff member approved their petition, it would mean Simon could be picked up by the police and taken for an involuntary emergency examination at a local hospital. During that exam, a doctor would decide if Simon would be kept in the hospital or if he would be discharged home. Brent kept his eyes on Simon, who appeared agitated but who was wandering in a confined area of space in front of the park's fountain. Brent was grateful that the police response would be swift in this jurisdiction, as he knew the variation in response time could be significant depending on the size and location of the department, as well as how the department prioritized behavioral health calls. Brent worried about Simon taking off.

"K, we can take him in, calling the police now," Regan said.

Regan and Brent sat together quietly as they waited for the police. They agreed that they would not try to approach Simon again, each fearing he would become agitated, and that would increase the risk of someone getting hurt when the police arrived. Brent began his paperwork, keeping one eye on Simon.

"They're here." Regan elbowed him and jerked her head toward the street. Three police cruisers had arrived, one more than the usual two for behavioral health calls in the city. Regan fleetingly wondered which car Simon would end up in. Three familiar officers exited and approached Regan and Brent.

"Well, hey, we must really rate if you three showed up." Brent casually greeted Officers Tate, Ford, and Matthews.

"You're on our list all right," said Tate, "I'll leave it to you to guess which one."

"Let's get this over with. You two aren't going to like this," Matthews began, "but when we ran him, he had three bench warrants from Judge Lee's office. We called him and . . ."

"You are *kidding me!*" interrupted Regan. "He didn't say to take him in. Please tell me that didn't happen." Brent watched as the red blotches crept up Regan's neck and onto her face, her outrage and concern apparent.

"Yeah," Matthews said, "I don't like it either. I told him there was the commitment, I told him he needed the hospital. He told me we had to take him in. He said he's seen this guy too many times and that the hospital doesn't seem to keep him long enough to get him straight, so he'll keep him in jail."

He paused and looked first at Regan and then turned to Brent.

"I tried to explain that he missed his last hearing because he was sick and in the hospital. Listen, my hands are tied. It's the judge's order. You can give me the commitment orders. I'll take it when we take him in." He held out his hand for the paperwork.

Brent felt his blood boil. Immediately, he went to an image of Simon being searched and showered and maybe hurt by the other inmates. He wondered how it was fair that Simon would be punished for his illness.

Regan clenched and unclenched her jaw. Brent watched as she intentionally took a deep breath and made eye contact with Brent. He could tell she was debating arguing more, but they both knew they had to obey the judge's orders. Officers Tate and Ford looked to Brent expectantly. Brent knew that to keep Simon safe, his best bet was just helping him make it to the squad car uninjured, and he hoped that Simon would somehow comply with the handcuffs that were part of standard operating procedures.

"OK," Brent sighed. "It goes without saying that this is complete bullshit, but I know we can't change it. As you probably know, his name is Simon, and he is really sick. He couldn't talk to us, so I'm not sure how he's going to do when he sees three cops. Let's just try to figure out a plan so we can get him to you, get him handcuffed, and get him in the back of the car without him getting hurt." He slammed his folder shut.

"Once we do that, we can call the mental health advocate for the jail. They won't be in until Monday, so he'll just have to be OK on his own over the weekend."

Regan added, "I'm going to call the warden's office when we get to the car. We can at least let them know how sick he is."

Tate shrugged. "OK, let's go get him into the car."

QUESTIONS FOR DISCUSSION

1. After reading the chapter, what do you see as the benefits and dangers of institutionalization in state hospitals, jails, and nursing homes?

2. What supports do you think are necessary for people who have significantly struggled with their mental illness to live successfully in the community? How are these connected to the concept of *recovery as defined in the chapter*? For additional information on recovery, you can visit http://www.samhsa.gov/recovery.

3. How would you explain to someone who has stereotypical views about mental illness what a mental illness really is? What are some ways you think our culture can challenge stigma?

4. How are workers like Brent and Regan, or the police officers, impacted by what they see on the job? How can we prepare to cope with these situations?

5. What might it be like for Simon's family members to experience his illness? How can families be supported?

6. Costs must be considered in delivering health care services. How would you prioritize funding to help people with mental illness? What is your reasoning?

7. Evaluate Judge Lee's decision to send Simon to jail. Do you agree? Disagree? What are the potential consequences of sending Simon to jail or to the hospital?

8. As you read, mental illness is very common. How are people impacted differently by their illnesses? For instance, how might someone's life be changed by moderate depression verses depression that doesn't respond to medications? Consider different populations, such as people who are also homeless, veterans, children in foster care, people in rural areas, or older adults. Consider how people might be impacted if they have overlapping concerns, such as being a veteran who is living with mental illness, substance use disorder, and homelessness.

9. What are the emergency supports available for behavioral health in your area? If you are not sure where your resources are, you can visit the Treatment Advocacy Center at http://www.treatmentadvocacycenter.org/browse-by-state and find your state's commitment laws. You can also visit the National Suicide Prevention Lifeline for a list of crisis centers at http://www.suicidepreventionlifeline.org. Another strategy is to do an Internet search for "mental health crisis center" and your nearest city.

10. People with mental illness are statistically no more violent than the general population. However, people with mental illness have committed awful crimes, including mass shootings. How would you try to help someone deal with their *irrational* fears about everyone with mental illness? Where can we get help when we have reason to believe someone with mental illness does pose a danger to others, for instance, because of a direct threat or frightening beliefs?

11. What is your reaction to the number of people with mental illness in jails? What other options might we have to help people in jail, to divert people from jail, or to help people when they are released?

CASE ANALYSIS WRITING ASSIGNMENT

Option A

1. Read the assigned case study thoroughly prior to class in order to be fully prepared to join in the discussion.

2. Regan gets into the crisis vehicle knowing she needs to call the warden at the county jail. She is concerned about Simon's welfare and knows she needs to communicate her concerns to the staff at the jail. For this essay, put yourself in the role of Regan and identify the issues you would want to convey to the warden. Be sure to address the concerns for Simon, recommendations for how Simon might be treated while incarcerated, and suggestions for how to best help Simon from this point. Be sure to support your ideas with supporting evidence and logic.

3. The analysis should be an approximately two-and-a-half- to three-page, typed, double-spaced essay. Your essay should reflect the standards and expectations of college-level writing: spelling, grammar, and appropriate use of paragraphs all matter. If you quote directly from the case study, use quotation marks, and at the end of the quote, indicate the page number the quote appeared on. For example, "With the advent of newer medications, most notably thorazine, and programming to move people to their communities, these numbers decreased to 154,000 in 1980" (Koyanagi (2007).

4. Your case analysis is due _____ and worth a maximum of ____ points.

Option B

1. Read the assigned case study thoroughly prior to class in order to be fully prepared to join in the discussion.

2. As Regan and Brent are walking back to the crisis vehicle, a man walks out of a storefront along the park. "Thank you," he says kindly. "That guy was scaring away my customers, and I was getting worried I was going to find him sleeping in the back one of these days. It's about time someone got him out of here." Brent and Regan looked at each other quickly, knowing they could

not acknowledge their role. Regan decided she would take the lead. "Sounds like a tough situation," she said, knowing the man probably didn't understand mental illness and was just concerned about the welfare of his business. She couldn't blame him. The situation wasn't easy for anyone. She and Brent kept walking. "Have a good one," Brent said with a nod as they reached the car, each getting in before the dialogue could progress. For this essay, put yourself in the role of the shopkeeper. Compose an essay that addresses the concerns you may have about your business and about Simon's well-being. Describe how you think people with needs similar to Simon's should be addressed by our society. Regardless of your personal opinion, make a case for how to best protect the rights of all parties involved.

3. The analysis should be an approximately two-and-a-half- to three-page, typed, double-spaced essay. Your essay should reflect the standards and expectations of college-level writing: spelling, grammar, and appropriate use of paragraphs all matter. If you quote directly from the case study, use quotation marks, and at the end of the quote, indicate the page number the quote appeared on. For example: "With the advent of newer medications, most notably thorazine, and programming to move people to their communities, these numbers decreased to 154,000 in 1980" (Koyanagi, 2007).

4. Your case analysis is due _____ and worth a maximum of ____ points.

INTERNET SOURCES

Copeland Center (http://copelandcenter.com)

Enhanced Treatment Court Offers an Alternative to Traditional Sentencing of the Mentally Ill (https://www.youtube.com/watch?v=pkUgzVizLM8)

Mental Health America (http://www.mentalhealthamerica.net)

National Alliance on Mental Illness (www.nami.org)

National Institute of Mental Health (http://www.nimh.nih.gov/health/topics/schizophrenia/raise/coordinated-specialty-care-for-first-episode-psychosis-resources.shtml)

Recovery Innovations (http://www.recoveryinnovations.org)

Schizophrenia and Related Disorders Alliance of America (http://www.sardaa.org)

S.L. County Crisis Response System: A Law Enforcement Training Video (http://www.youtube.com/embed/qeW2YBzzSRA)

REFERENCES

ADA.Gov. (n.d.). *Olmstead: Community integration for everyone.* Retrieved from http://www.ada .gov/olmstead/olmstead_about.htm

American Psychiatric Publishing. (n.d.). *Schizophrenia fact sheet.* Retrieved from http://www.dsm5.0rg/ Documents/Schizophrenia%20Fact%20Sheet.pdf

Barry, D. (2014, November 27). Restoring lost names, recapturing lost dignity. *New York Times.* Retrieved from http://www.nytimes.com/2014/11/28/us/restoring-lost-names-recapturing-lost-dignity.html?_r=0

Cassels, C. (2011, November 17). *America's use of psychotropic medications on the rise.* Retrieved from http://www.medscape.com/viewarticle/753789

Centers for Disease Control and Prevention. (2013, October 4). *Burden of mental illness.* Retrieved from http://www.cdc.gov/mentalhealth/basics/burden.htm

Centers for Disease Control and Prevention. (2014, November 28). *Morbidity and mortality weekly report.* Retrieved from http://www.cdc.gov/mmwr/preview/mmwrhtml/mm6347a6.htm

Centers for Disease Control and Prevention. (2015, February 6). *FastStats.* Retrieved from http://www .cdc.gov/nchs/fastats/suicide.htm

Cohen, E., & Bonifield, J. (2012, March 15). California's dark legacy of forced sterilization. *CNN.* Retrieved from http://www.cnn.com/2012/03/15/health/california-forced-sterilizations

Community Consortium. (2015). *The Willard suitcases.* Retrieved from http://www.suitcaseexhibit .org/index.php?section=about&subsection=suitcases

Craig, D. (2015, October 24). ACLU: Some Pa. inmates wait a year for mental health treatment. *Philly News.* Retrieved from http://www.phillyvoice.com/aclu-pa-inmates-wait-year-mental-health-treatment

Dokoupil, T. (2013, May 23). Why suicide has become an epidemic—and what we can do to help. *Newsweek.* Retrieved from http://www.newsweek.com/2013/05/22/why-suicide-has-become-epidemic-and-what-we-can-do-help-237434.html

Ford, M. (2015, June 8). America's largest mental hospital is a jail. *The Atlantic.* Retrieved from http://www .theatlantic.com/politics/archive/2015/06/americas-largest-mental-hospital-is-a-jail/395012

Fox, D. (2010, June). The insanity virus. *Discover Magazine.* Retrieved from http://discovermagazine .com/2010/jun/03-the-insanity-virus

Hertel, N. (2013, November 10). Mentally ill ex-inmates lack treatment, meds. *Wisconsin Watch.* Retrieved from http://wisconsinwatch.org/2013/11/mentally-ill-ex-inmates-lack-treatment-meds

Jablensky, A., & Sartorius, N. (2007). What did the WHO studies really find? *Schizophrenia Bulletin, 34*(2), 253–255. *Oxford Journals.* Retrieved from http://schizophreniabulletin.oxfordjournals.org/ content/34/2/253.10ng

James, D. J., & Glaze, L. E. (2006). Mental health problems of prison and jail inmates. *Bureau of Labor Statistics.* Retrieved from http://bjs.gov/content/pub/pdf/mhppji.pdf

Johnson, C. (2009, March 22). Mentally ill threat in nursing homes. *Associated Press.* Retrieved from http://phys.org/news/2009-03-mentally-ill-threat-nursing-homes.html

Koyanagi, C. (2007). Learning from history: Deinstitutionalization of people with mental illness as precursor to long term care reform. *Kaiser Family Foundation.* Retrieved from https://kaiserfamily foundation.files.wordpress.com/2013/01/7684.pdf

Lovett, I. (2015, August 5). Los Angeles agrees to overhaul jails to care for mentally ill and curb abuse. *New York Times.* Retrieved from http://www.nytimes.com/2015/08/06/us/los-angeles-agrees-to-overhaul-its-jail-system.html

Metzl, J. M., & MacLeish, K. T. (2015). Mental illness, mass shootings and the politics of American firearms. *American Journal of Public Health, 105*(2), 240–249. doi: 10.2105/AJPH.2014.302242

National Council for Behavioral Health. (2015). *Community mental health act.* Retrieved from http://www.thenationalcouncil.org/about/national-mental-health-association/overview/community-mental-health-act

National Institute of Mental Health. (n.d.a). *Major depression in adults.* Retrieved from http://www.nimh.nih.gov/health/statistics/prevalence/major-depression-among-adults.shtml

National Institute of Mental Health. (n.d.b). *Bipolar disorder among adults.* Retrieved from http://www.nimh.nih.gov/health/statistics/prevalence/bipolar-disorder-among-adults.shtml

National Public Radio. (2005, November 16). *Frequently asked questions about lobotomies.* Retrieved from http://www.npr.org/templates/story/story.php?storyId=5014565

National Public Radio. (2014, November 5). *Payments start for NC eugenics victims but many won't qualify.* Retrieved from http://www.npr.org/sections/health-shots/2014/10/31/360355784/payments-start-for-n-c-eugenics-victims-but-many-wont-qualify

Olfson, M., Gerhard, T., Huang, C., Crystal, S., & Stroup, S. (2015). Premature mortality among adults with schizophrenia in the United States. *JAMA Psychiatry, 72*(12), 1172–1181. doi:10.1001/jamapsychiatry.2015.1737

Prins, S. J., & Draper, L. (2009). Improving outcomes for people with mental illness under community corrections supervision: A guide to research-informed policy and practice. *Council of State Governments Justice Center.* Retrieved from: https://csgjusticecenter.org/wp-content/uploads/2012/12/Community-Corrections-Research-Guide.pdf

Romney, L. (2013, October 9). State hospitals remain violent, despite gains in safety. *Los Angeles Times.* Retrieved from http://articles.latimes.com/2013/oct/09/local/la-me-mental-hospital-safety-20131010

Rosenhan, D. L. (1973). On being sane in insane places. *Science, 179*(70), 250–258.

Substance Abuse and Mental Health Services Administration. (2010). *SAMHSA's working definition of recovery: 10 guiding principles of recovery.* Retrieved from http://content.samhsa.gov/ext/item?uri=/samhsa/content/item/10007447/10007447.pdf

Substance Abuse and Mental Health Services Administration. (2011). *Current statistics on the prevalence and characteristics of people experiencing homelessness in the United States.* Retrieved from http://homeless.samhsa.gov/ResourceFiles/hrc_factsheet.pdf

Sullivan, E. M., Annest, J. L., Luo, F., Simon, T. R., & Dahlberg, L. L. (2013, May 3). *Suicide among adults aged 35–64 years—United States, 1999–2010.* Retrieved from http://www.cdc.gov/mmwr/preview/mmwrhtml/mm6217a1.htm

Sullivan, E. M., Annest, J. L., Simon, T. R., Luo, F., & Dahlberg, L. L. (2015, March 6). *Suicide trends among persons aged 10–24 years—United States, 1994–2012.* Atlanta, GA: Centers for Disease Control. Retrieved from http://www.cdc.gov/mmwr/pdf/wk/mm6408.pdf

Tamminga, C. A., & Medoff, D. R. (2000). The biology of schizophrenia. *Dialogues in Clinical Neuroscience, 2*(4), 339–248.

Torrey, E. F. (2014, June 18). Better off without psychotropic drugs? *Psychiatric Times.* Retrieved from http://www.psychiatrictimes.com/psychopharmacology/better-without-antipsychotic-drugs

Torrey, E. F., Kennard, A. D., Eslinger, D., Lamb, R., & Pavle, J. (2010). More mentally ill people are in jails and prisons than hospitals: A survey of states. *Treatment Advocacy Center.* Retrieved from http://www.treatmentadvocacycenter.org/storage/documents/final_jails_v_hospitals_study.pdf

White House. (n.d.). *The economic case for health care reform.* Retrieved from https://www.whitehouse.gov/administration/eop/cea/TheEconomicCaseforHealthCareReform

World Health Organization. (2007). *Breaking the vicious cycle between mental-ill health and poverty.* Retrieved from http://www.who.int/mental_health/policy/development/1_Breakingviciouscycle_Infosheet.pdf

Chapter 6

Perplexing Challenges in Child Protective Services

Life on the Front Line

DR. KATIE CLEMONS

Sean looked at his schedule and sighed. His plan for the day had been to go through the usual e-mails and voice messages and then catch up on case notes, filing, and the three court reports due later this week. Yet, as too often happens, he had to abandon his plan to deal with a disrupted placement. Ely, 7, and Ethan, 5, had been living with their uncle until he called this morning saying he could no longer have the boys stay with him and requested that they be picked up and moved immediately.

Ely and Ethan had come into care when their mother, Dina, had been arrested for selling methamphetamines. There had been previous referrals of neglect and possible physical abuse, but previous investigations had not found enough evidence to warrant removal. However, when the police arrested Dina, they found the boys in a dirty home, with no food, and no viable caregiver around. Due to the circumstances, the police then signed an authorization for emergency placement, which started the legal process to have the boys in out-of-home placement and under custody of the state. Now they've been in out-of-home care for 6 months living with their uncle. Apparently they've been getting into physical altercations with his kids (their cousins), which prompted their uncle to request they be moved right away.

Their mother has been released from jail and, having completed intensive chemical dependency treatment in jail, is now working her case plan services of level one outpatient chemical dependency treatment, as well as twice weekly urinalysis tests (UAs), domestic violence classes, and supervised visits with a family therapist.[1]

Sean thought there was a good chance that Dina would go through the steps long enough to get her children back, but based on his recent interactions with Dina, he now had the sneaking suspicion that it would be short-lived. Dina didn't seem to truly accept the concerns for her children's safety or see a need for the services she was participating in. Sean had to think of where he could move the boys that could potentially be a long-term placement in case Dina fell off the wagon or simply disappeared. Parents, particularly with substance abuse issues, sometimes do. This is largely due, he knows, to so many parents he works with having been abused themselves, having mental health problems they are self-medicating, or simply having too much pain and trauma to be able to adequately care for their children and put their children's needs first.

So Sean mentally went through a list of Ely and Ethan's kin, since first prefer-ence for placement goes to relatives. The maternal grandmother had been ruled out due to her own previous child protective services[2] (CPS) involvement. This was a relief to Sean since she had been openly hostile and threatening when he met her. The paternal grandmother is also not an option since she is maxed out taking care of three other grandkids, who are half siblings to Ely and Ethan. There were no other kin in the picture. Feeling a bit discouraged, he kept considering options.

That's it! thought Sean. There are two more half-siblings, from a third mother with the same father. If Sean could place the boys with the foster family taking care of the half-siblings, Ely and Ethan would be with siblings. And they are a foster-adopt family,[3] so if things go south with Dina and the boys end up staying in or returning to care, it could be a long-term option. Sean was relieved he had come up with what appeared to be a good plan. He would need to run it by his supervisor, but he was sure she would be on board.

"Hey, you have a minute?" Sean asked as he popped his head into his supervisor Molly's office.

"Sure, what's up?" Molly asked.

---

[1] These are all common services for parents involved with child protective services. Visits are often supervised by a licensed social worker or counselor to work on attachment and parenting issues.

[2] This case study example is using child protective services to refer to child welfare work within the Department of Health and Human Services. Different states have various names for the division of child welfare, including child protective services, office of children and youth, and office of children and family. Additionally, within the same state, many terms are used interchangeably, including child welfare, children's administration, and division of children and family services.

[3] Foster-adopt refers to foster parents who are open to adoption and often hope to adopt rather than be only a short-term placement option for children in care.

"Well, Ely and Ethan's uncle asked that they be moved. They've been fighting with their cousins, so I have to go pick them up. He kept them home from school today so they could leave as soon as possible," Sean explained.

"Oh, geez, well, we weren't completely comfortable with this placement anyway, but you still hate to see them have to move. Do you have a plan for where to place them? Any other relatives?"

"There aren't any other relatives who are a placement option, but I have a call in to Homefinders to confirm that the foster-adopt parents who have placement of some of the paternal half-siblings have room and are open to the idea of two more children in their home."

"Good thinking. Have you scheduled a child protection team (CPT)[4] meeting?"

"Not yet, but I'll send a request in before I leave."

"Okay, I'll watch for the Outlook meeting notification to get it on my calendar. Good work, Sean. Be sure to sign out on the board when you leave."

"Will do. Thanks," Sean said as he left her office and went back to his cubicle to finalize plans before leaving. It bugged him that Molly mentioned the sign-out board, but in fairness to her, he knew he didn't always remember. Sean found a voice mail waiting for him from the Homefinders unit that confirmed that the foster parents with the other half-siblings had room and would be happy to have the boys placed with them as well. Breathing a sigh of relief, Sean felt grateful that something today was working out as he hoped. He then sent a quick e-mail to his contact at Treehouse, an education advocacy service that would help set up transportation for Ethan and Ely so they wouldn't have to change schools in the middle of the school year.[5] He then went to check out a state car and a couple of booster seats for the boys, signing out on the board as he did so.

While driving to pick up Ely and Ethan, Sean turned his attention to what he planned to write on one of his three court reports he still had to get back to. The Wilson case was the type of case he found most disconcerting. The bulk of his cases had to do with neglect, usually due to drug abuse. He also had the occasional physical or sexual abuse case, and as upsetting and scary as those cases were, the ones that got to him the most were the cases where parents had serious mental

---

[4] CPT meetings are mandatory in most states any time there is a placement change or before returning a child in out-of-home care back to the parents. This way a board of people who have varying expertise help the worker and supervisor come up with a plan and make sure everything has been thought of to ensure the child's safety and welfare. While it is ideal for it to happen prior to a placement change, as in this case, it is not always possible, and the CPT may happen after a placement disruption.

[5] The federal legislation of the McKinney-Vento Act ensures that homeless children and children in foster care are provided free transportation to and from school to allow them to continue to go to the same school regardless of what district the family resides in. This is extremely important as transferring schools is known to be detrimental to a child's education and can negatively impact mental health as well.

illnesses or intellectual or developmental disabilities (IDD), which was the situation with the Wilson case.

Rain Wilson had attended every service recommended by the court. She had completed a psychological evaluation and a parent-child assessment, and she was participating in individual counseling and supervised visits with a parent educator. Yet all the provider reports had come back with concerns that Rain was not capable of caring for her two young children. The test results indicated that she had severe impairments and was functioning at about a second-grade level. Her parent educator reported that during visits, Sara, the 4-year-old, took on the role of caring for 9-month-old Neal, telling Rain when he needed to be fed and changed. Rain would get upset easily, forget about the kids, and either rant about something or simply start rocking herself and staring into space. Rain clearly loved her children and had done all that was asked of her, but she still wasn't able to provide a safe home for them. Rain had no family support system, and there were no institutions that provided support for people with mental illnesses or IDD and their children. The father, who had not participated in any of his court-ordered services, indicated that he had no desire to be involved and wanted to relinquish his parental rights as soon as possible, and Sean had little hope of that changing.

If only there were a viable relative who could provide a safe home for Rain and her children to be together and ensure the kids were safe, Sean thought. *Why are there no services or living options for those with intellectual or developmental disabilities with kids?* "Because we expect them to be asexual beings and not procreate," Sean answered himself aloud.

Sean shook his head and thought, *I'm exhausted and talking to myself, and it's not even lunchtime yet. I better be sure to get to the gym this evening.* After 2 years of working as a child welfare worker, Sean knew that self-care was an absolute must, but no matter how much he worked out or kicked back on a Sunday, he feared he was fighting a losing battle against burnout. He laughed thinking of when one of his master's in social work (MSW) professors said CPS stood for a bureaucracy marked by complexity, problems, and stress. *He got that right,* he thought.

Some of his colleagues were great role models, and he made a mental note to talk to them more about how they dealt with work stressors. Other colleagues seemed to be dangerously burned out, which just added to his stress. He resented the fact that some cases transferred to him had incomplete casework and case notes. Those cases came from the same colleagues who he would hear chatting with each other way too often about nonwork issues, gossiping about other people, complaining, and sometimes talking inappropriately about clients. Sean knew he needed to get a better handle on dealing with his emotions and on figuring out how to avoid getting irritated by colleagues who didn't appear as invested as he was. He had promised himself he would never become a burned-out social worker giving less than a 100%. The job was too important. Children's well-being and lives were at stake. It wasn't easy, and he'd quit before he'd forget that he was making a real difference in lives and for society.

BACKGROUND INFORMATION

History of Child Protection

State-employed workers, such as Sean, whose job is to ensure child safety and well-being have not always existed. Prior to the mid-1800s, child protection from abuse and neglect was sporadic and not formerly organized. Parents could be prosecuted for extreme cases of physical abuse, and police could remove children they knew to be abused, but there was no formal process or organization to prevent child abuse. Formal programs to address these issues can be traced back to Charles Loring Brace, who initiated the orphan train movement that sent more than 150,000 children who were abused, abandoned, or orphaned from New York City to families living in the country, primarily in the Midwest. Brace founded the Children's Aid Society in 1853, which was incredibly influential in the movement away from institutionalized care and the emphasis toward placement with families (Children's Aid Society, n.d.).

Further progress was made in 1875 when, appalled that there were no resources for a severely beaten and neglected child, and knowing a system was in place to address animal cruelty, Etta Wheeler sought out Henry Bergh, who had helped found the American Society for the Prevention of Cruelty to Animals. With Bergh's assistance, Wheeler launched the New York Society for the Prevention of Cruelty to Children. Soon many other private nonprofit organizations started all over the country. Through a combination of factors, including the beginning of the juvenile court system and the Great Depression that made it hard for private nonprofit organizations to stay in business, the oversight of child welfare began to be taken over by the government. The process was slow, but states began implementing laws regarding the reporting of child abuse, and the U.S. Congress included amendments focusing on child protection to the Social Security Act of 1962 (Myers, 2008).

In 1974, the passage of the Child Abuse Prevention and Treatment Act (CAPTA) truly marked the beginning of the child welfare system as we know it today. CAPTA authorized federal funding to help the states address abuse and neglect. Most private nongovernmental child protection organizations were closed or reorganized to provide contract services to the state-run child welfare organizations. While CAPTA has been amended many times over the years, it continues to be a key piece of legislation that informs child welfare practices (Myers, 2008; Child Welfare Information Gateway, 2011).

Additional Key Federal Child Welfare Legislation

In addition to CAPTA, there are two other major federal pieces of legislation that inform practices: the Indian Child Welfare Act (ICWA) and the Adoption and Safe Families Act of 1997 (ASFA).

The Indian Child Welfare Act of 1978 was a response to the fact that up to 35% of children removed from Native American/American Indian families by child welfare services were placed in nonnative homes. This was viewed by many as a renewal of the cultural genocide that had occurred previously when for decades children of Native American families were removed and placed in boarding schools. In order to avoid this continued discrimination, and to respect the sovereignty of Native American tribes, they were given the right to have separate jurisdiction in child welfare cases. ICWA recognizes Tribal jurisdiction to make custody decisions involving the removal of Native children from their homes and provides minimum federal standards for states to follow when Native children are removed from their homes in all Native cases, whether the tribe chooses to take jurisdiction or not (National Indian Child Welfare Association, 2015).

The Adoption and Safe Families Act of 1997 (ASFA) was a significant change to federal child protection policies. ASFA moved child welfare services from a child rescue approach to a focus on both child safety and family preservation. It implemented timelines in an attempt to get children to permanent placements sooner rather than have so many in foster care for years. In short, states must file termination of parental rights if a child has been out of home for 15 of the last 22 months. This change required welfare workers to do concurrent planning, which means that while working on reunification whenever possible and reasonable, there is also the goal of the child being able to have permanency as soon as possible for their well-being. This legislation does allow states to forgo "reasonable efforts" of reunification for extreme cases, such as when a parent has committed murder or felony assault or previously had their parental rights terminated (Adoptions and Safe Families Act of 1997, 1997).

Definition

While all 50 states, the District of Columbia, and U.S. territories have child abuse and neglect laws and require certain professionals to report suspected child maltreatment to a child protection services (CPS) agency, the definition of child abuse and neglect varies by state. These laws are, however, guided by a federal standard identifying certain acts or behaviors that qualify as child abuse and neglect. The Child Abuse Prevention and Treatment Act (CAPTA), discussed above, legislates that the existing definition of child abuse and neglect is, at a minimum:

Any recent act or failure to act on the part of a parent or caretaker which results in death, serious physical or emotional harm, sexual abuse or exploitation; or an act or failure to act, which presents an imminent risk of serious harm. (Child Welfare Information Gateway, n.d.a)

Most states recognize four major types of maltreatment: neglect, physical abuse, psychological maltreatment, and sexual abuse. Although any of the forms of child maltreatment may be found separately, they can occur in combination.

Prevalence and Statistics

There is some good news in the area of prevalence and statistics in that there is some evidence that physical and sexual abuse are declining. An article released by the Crimes Against Children Research Center, University of New Hampshire, examined whether declines in child physical and sexual abuse since the 1990s as reported to National Child Abuse and Neglect Data System (NCANDS) reflect a true decline in the prevalence of child maltreatment. The study compared data from a number of sources against NCANDS, which showed a 56% decline in physical abuse and 62% decline in sexual abuse from 1992 to 2010 (Jones, Finkelhor, & Halter, 2006).

The decline in sexual abuse was consistent across data sources, including the National Incidence Study, FBI data from the Uniform Crime Report, the National Crime Victimization Survey, the Minnesota Student Survey, the National Survey of Family Growth, and the National Survey of Children Exposed to Violence. They all showed declines in child sexual abuse during one or more parts of the period from 1992 to 2010. However, the declines seen in NCANDS from 1995 to 2010 for physical abuse were not fully supported. While the National Incidence Study and one state victimization survey showed a similar decline, data from two national victimization surveys and hospitals did not (Jones et al., 2006).

Despite these decreases, in 2012, U.S. state and local CPS still received an estimated 3.4 million referrals of children being abused or neglected. Of these referrals, CPS estimated that 686,000 children (9.2 per 1,000) were victims of maltreatment. The majority of these children (78%) were victims of neglect; 18% experienced physical abuse; 9% experienced sexual abuse; and 11% were victims of other types of maltreatment, including emotional and threatened abuse, parent's drug/alcohol abuse, or lack of supervision. The total adds up to over 100% as many of the children experienced multiple forms of maltreatment (U.S. HHS, 2012). As these are only the cases reported to CPS and/or the police, studies show this to be a vast underrepresentation of children who experience abuse and neglect (Finkelhor, Turner, Shattuck, & Hamby, 2013). In fact, it is estimated that as many as one in four children may experience child maltreatment at some point in their life (Centers for Disease Control and Prevention, 2016).

Based on the 2012 report from the U.S. Department of Health and Human Services (HHS), 27% of victims were younger than 3 years, and 20% of victims were aged 3 to 5 years, with children younger than 1 year having the highest rate of victimization (21.9 per 1,000 children). The majority of perpetrators (80.3%) were parents, 6.1 percent were relatives other than parents, and 4.2 percent were unmarried partners of parents. Child abuse is different from most violent offenses in that it is one area where there are more female perpetrators than males; 54% of perpetrators were women and 45% of perpetrators were men.

Many neglected and abused children end up in foster care. At the end of 2012, there were approximately 397,000 children in foster care on the last day of the fiscal year. During that year, an estimated 252,000 children entered foster care, and 241,000 children exited foster care. Between 2002 and 2012, the number of children in care on the last day of the year decreased by 24.2%, from 524,000 to 397,000 (U.S. HHS, 2012). This may be a result of the decline in abuse noted above or due to the guidelines set out in ASFA that required states to implement concurrent planning and more quickly get children into permanent homes.

Rates of child abuse are also influenced by macroforces such as socioeconomic factors. The vast majority of people who are low income do not neglect or abuse their children. However, research indicated that child abuse and neglect is more prevalent in low-income neighborhoods. Poverty increases risk for maltreatment for a variety of reasons, including the increased stress and inadequate access to resources, including safe child care.

Bivariate analysis has shown strong relationships between child maltreatment and poverty as well as income inequality. These relationships held true in regression models controlling for possible confounding variables such as ethnicity, education, public assistance, and infant mortality rate. The models showed an interaction effect where income inequality increased the risk of child maltreatment, but the highest impact was at high levels of poverty (Eckenrode, Smith, McCarthy, & Dineen, 2014). The increased risk of maltreatment for children living in poverty is exponential. Children living in families with annual incomes below $15,000 are 22 times more likely to be abused and 44 times more likely to be neglected than children living in families with annual incomes greater than $30,000 (Sedalk & Broadhurst, 1996). If poverty were to be decreased, there would very likely be a corresponding decrease in child neglect and abuse.

Impact

The impact of child abuse is wide and varied. It includes physical, psychological, emotional, and financial consequences both for the victim and society at large. The most severe physical impact is obviously death. In 2012, an estimated 1,640 children died from child maltreatment (rate of 2.2 per 100,000 children).

This figure is estimated based on 49 states that reported 1,593 child fatalities. Of the child death victims, 70% experienced neglect, and 44% experienced physical abuse either exclusively or in combination with another form of maltreatment. Most of the victims (70%) were children under the age of 3. The fatality rate for boys was higher at 2.5 per 100,000 than the rate for girls, which was 1.9 per 100,000 (U.S. HHS, 2012).

Child death cases are horrific but not the norm. The severest cases of physical abuse and neglect are more likely to result in long-term brain damage of various degrees, which can include cognitive, motor, and visual impairments, in addition to psychological and behavioral problems. These problems then also have an economic impact on top of the money spent providing services to parents, children, and support for caregivers. According to the Centers for Disease Control and Prevention (CDC), total lifetime costs of abuse are $124 billion a year (Centers for Disease Control, 2016). These costs are a result of improper brain development; impaired cognitive (learning ability) and socio-emotional skills; decreased language development; blindness; higher risk for heart, lung, and liver disease; higher risk for obesity, cancer, high blood pressure and cholesterol; anxiety, smoking, alcoholism, and drug abuse (Fang, Brown, Florence, & Mercy, 2012).

Research on Child Maltreatment Consequences

The most prominent study completed on the impact of childhood trauma is known as the Adverse Childhood Experiences Study (ACES). The study, conducted in the late 1990s, included more than 17,000 members of a health maintenance organization undergoing a physical examination who provided details of their childhood experiences, including abuse and neglect. While the connection between childhood abuse and long-term consequences had previously been written about and studied by social scientists, this was the first large-scale study examining the breadth of exposure to childhood emotional, physical, or sexual abuse and their relationship to health risk behavior and disease in adulthood. The study examined seven adverse childhood experiences: psychological, physical, or sexual abuse; domestic violence (against the mother); living with household members who were substance abusers, mentally ill or suicidal, or imprisoned.

The prevalence of adverse childhood experiences was pervasive and occurred across racial and socioeconomic backgrounds. More than half the respondents reported at least one ACE, and a quarter of the respondents reported more than two. Results indicated that the more adverse childhood experiences, the higher the likelihood of such issues as alcoholism, drug abuse, criminal activity, depression, obesity, heart disease, cancer, liver disease, and premature death (Centers for Disease Control and Prevention, 2016; Felitti et al., 1998). In addition, research consistently indicates links to cognitive, behavioral, and social difficulties for children and adults who experienced childhood abuse or neglect (Child Welfare Information Gateway, 2013).

Child Maltreatment Referral Process and Case Outcomes

As stated above, in 2012 there were about 3.4 million referrals of abuse or neglect, and 686,000 children were found to be victims of child abuse or neglect. There is a long process that occurs after a referral is made to the child welfare agency. There are a variety of workers who specialize in one part of the process or another, but in smaller communities sometimes one worker will take on multiple roles or even follow the same cases from referral to outcome. While it varies from state to state, in general the process is as follows.

1. The process begins with a concerned citizen, relative, or mandated reporter[6] calling in a referral. An intake worker completes a risk assessment for each referral. Based on the information received and varying state definitions of child abuse, it is determined whether further investigation is called for.

2. If it is determined that further investigation is needed, a child protection worker completes an initial investigation. The worker will do one of three things: pursue out-of-home placement if the child is in imminent danger, put together a plan for support services to try to maintain family unification, or dismiss the case based on a low-risk assessment.

3. If the worker either sets up a plan for support services or out-of-home place-ment, the case usually moves on to a worker who will provide services to parents to maintain unification or move toward reunification if the child has been removed. At all times, ensuring that the child is safe is paramount, and if removed, the child is ideally placed in a potential long-term home.

4. If parents make progress in services, the child is returned home (or stays in the home as the case may be), and progress is monitored for a period of time determined by the state to ensure the continued safety of the child. Social workers perform in-home visits as part of this process to ensure child safety and ongoing progress.

   A. However, if parents do not complete services or do not show progress in services that indicates they can provide a safe home for their child, then

---

[6] Mandatory reporting laws vary from state to state. Some states require that anyone who suspects child abuse or neglect report it, and some states include a wide array of school employees as mandated reporters, such as staff, administrators, or volunteers. There are many similarities though, as nearly every state has statutes regulating that teachers, law enforcement officers, child care providers, health care providers, counselors, social workers, and other mental health professionals are all mandated reporters.

their child will remain in out-of-home care. A permanent plan, such as termination of parental rights and a subsequent adoption, will be pursued. In the case of service plans for children remaining in the home, out-of-home placement would be sought.

Current practices have been influenced by the push in social work to move toward evidence-based practices. The field is working to build more empirical evidence about specific child welfare practices, as this has been somewhat lacking for child welfare until recently. Due to the nature of quick intervention and mandated responses, controlled clinical studies are difficult in child welfare. Still, the new model of evidence-based practice is influencing services and interventions for children and families in addition to social workers' practice-based knowledge (Child Welfare Information Gateway, n.d.b).

RUNNING IN PLACE?

Sean was relieved that running on the treadmill had alleviated some of the tension he was feeling. His mission to destress was working until, while stretching in the sauna, he heard a group of guys discussing how parents have no rights these days, and if kids would only be spanked, things would be better. We have so many problems with kids these days because the parents can't do anything to control them was the perspective being promoted. Sean had heard it all before, and he was tempted to explain that the kids he worked with were good kids who experienced countless traumatic experiences. And parents having no rights? Ha! Parents can still legally spank their children despite the great amount of research showing it is no more effective than other disciplinary action such as time-outs and may have negative consequences (Straus, 2005). He contemplated sharing this information and the fact that it was only illegal to hit your child with a closed fist, an object, or to leave more than a "transient" mark. He wondered if it would change the tune of these men at all if he explained that their tax dollars went to providing parents with services to ensure they have every opportunity to preserve their families, and in the cases where kids have been removed, to be reunited. Of course, Sean was worried this information may just move the negativity toward the parents and make it sound as if parents were the enemy, which they are not. The services are necessary; many of these parents were previously children under stress that the system had failed, and these services are a chance to help them address their own trauma. Anyway, he was too tired to get into it and figured his words would fall on deaf ears, so he let it go. He told himself, I can only deal with so much right now. It doesn't make any difference to the kids I'm supposed to be helping. So much for relaxing, he mused to himself.

Sean left the sauna, showered, dressed, and headed home. When he got there, he got online to check his work e-mail. He knew he should leave work at work, but since his entire day had gone into moving Ely and Ethan and writing the court report for Sara and Neal, he had spent no time working the cases or catching up on paperwork on the other 28 kids currently on his caseload. While Sean knew 32 wasn't terribly high for a caseload, he still found it to be too much to do quality social work on each case in a supposed 40-hour workweek. He had actually had over 40 children assigned to him during a previous hiring freeze when there were even fewer social workers, and the guardian ad litems[7] he knew had over 100 cases each. Remembering this, Sean tried to be grateful that his caseload wasn't higher and he had some cases that were going smoothly for the moment. *Knock on wood!* he thought.

When Sean was hired, he thought he was going to get to spend a lot of time working directly with kids. Now he estimates he spends less than 10% of his work time with kids and perhaps another 10% with parents. The rest of it is spent completing mandatory paperwork and attending meetings and court dates. He often asked himself how he could do real influential social work when his time wasn't being spent where it should be.

In a policy class that Sean had taken as part of his MSW program, taught by a previous regional administrator (RA) for the Children's Administration, the instructor and former RA explained that "we don't have a child welfare system. We have a child abuse system." *Isn't that the truth?* Sean thought to himself, and he continued ruminating: *We only get the cases that come to the state's attention, and then intervention is only made in the worst of the worst. How can we help all the kids who never even get reported, or the kid whose referral doesn't meet a high enough level of safety concern for an intervention? How can we provide better services to our parents, especially those who are trying but just need more support in order to raise their kids safely and successfully? And how the hell am I supposed to do any of this when I'm already putting in extra hours and feel physically and emotionally exhausted?*

Shaking his head, Sean tried to clear his mind. He wasn't going to come up with any brilliant solutions at 10:30 p.m., and he needed a good night's sleep as he knew he would have a busy day again tomorrow. Fortunately, he was asleep the second his head hit the pillow.

---

[7] A guardian ad litem (GAL), or court-appointed special advocate (CASA), is appointed by the court as an independent observer and voice for the child. CASAs are usually volunteers and GALs are usually trained employees of juvenile court or lawyers. Their sole purpose is to advocate for the child's best interests.

After 7 solid hours of sleep, Sean woke more refreshed than anticipated and was at his desk by 7:00 a.m. hoping to catch up a bit and get a couple of his court reports submitted. As he went through his voice mail, he had a few extra tasks added to his to-do list. One foster parent had called stating the child was too sick to come for a visit today with her biological mother and would need to reschedule it. Fortunately, it was on a case with an agreeable parent who would be more concerned about the child being ill than upset about a changed visit. He also had a parent who had lost her bus pass and needed a new one and a counselor who thought a family team meeting[8] should be scheduled. Most of the rest of the voice mails simply needed to be documented and didn't require anything else from Sean. The foster mother who had taken placement of Ely and Ethan reported that the first night had gone smoothly, and the kids seemed to be excited about being with their half-siblings full time.

His attention then turned to an e-mail that he knew he had to respond to before finalizing his court report on the Wilson family. Janet, the children's CASA, said she wanted to discuss a possible idea for a permanent placement for Sara and Neal. Sean perked up. Not all CASAs were as involved as Janet was, and Sean had a good working relationship with her. A possible long-term placement option would definitely make the case review in court go more smoothly. As much as it bothered him, he knew he had to recommend termination of parental rights based on the providers' reports, and Sara and Neal were not currently in a foster-adopt home. Sean e-mailed back and forth with Janet and set up a meeting with her at the office later.

Feeling relieved he was actually getting some paperwork done, Sean was startled when he heard, "Hey there, ready for me?" as Janet poked her head in his cubicle. "What are you doing here already?" responded Sean with a smile, as he simultaneously looked at his clock to see that Janet wasn't early. "Oh man, I don't know where the last couple of hours went. Let's go in the meeting room just across the hall."

Grabbing his lunch that he had forgotten to eat, he followed her into the room. He pulled out a sandwich and offered half to Janet. Motioning "No thanks," she cleared her throat. "I have an idea for a long-term placement for Sara and Neal." Sean waited, as this much he already knew. Silence, as with most people, prompted Janet to keep talking. "I want to take placement of Sara and Neal." Now Sean was

---

[8] Family team meetings also go by various names. The concept is a group staffing where a facilitator or the assigned social worker meets with all the involved parties to try to come up with an agreed-upon safety plan or intervention to meet the family's and children's needs. These sorts of meetings would usually include a social worker; a supervisor; parents; attorneys; service providers for the parents and children, such as counselors, attachment specialists, and school social workers; and whoever had placement of the child, such as foster parents, kin providers, or a group home representative.

silent because he wasn't sure what to say. He had never heard of such a thing. A CASA taking custody? What would the public defenders or the judge have to say? This is a serious conflict of interest.

"Wow," Sean finally responded, trying not to sound too surprised, "that's a generous thought, but I'm just not sure it's feasible." "I know," said Janet. "But I really have thought this through. I would obviously resign as a CASA. I started the process to become a foster parent a couple of years ago but didn't complete the home study, as I decided to help by being a CASA instead. I've grown attached to Sara and Neal, and Rain, too, actually. There is no viable family member who would help Rain maintain a relationship with the kids, and I would want to do that. I know that I could provide the next best option. I know it's unprecedented, and from the look on your face, I'd say you think it's a crazy idea."

Sean's mind began to race. He let Janet sit there while he took a few minutes to wrap his head around the idea. Yes, it was a conflict of interest, but on the other hand, Janet had a preexisting relationship with the children now and was even suggesting she wanted an open adoption, which another foster-adopt parent who the kids didn't know might not. "You know what? It might not be that crazy. Let me run it by my supervisor and the assistant attorney general (AAG). If it's okay by them, then I'm happy to support it. Hopefully, the public defenders will be on board. Dad definitely wants to relinquish his rights to stop having child support payments, and Rain's attorney just may be okay with it based on your offering a lot of communication and visits. It might be complicated, but if it is in the best interest of the children, which I think it is, I'm willing to advocate it."

"Great. I'll let my supervisor know that I'm resigning as a volunteer CASA and get going on completing the home-study for my foster-adopt license," Janet said.

"Janet, I support the idea, but please don't get your hopes up. Your idea caught me off guard, and it didn't take me long to see the benefit of your taking the children, but that doesn't mean others will come to the same conclusion. Even if you get placement, and that's still a big *if* right now, the case is far from over, and you just never know what can happen." Sean didn't want to discourage Janet, but he also was well aware that setting realistic expectations for all foster parents or potential foster parents was an important part of his job.

"Yes, I realize that. I just really feel this is the right thing to do and best for Sara and Neal and Rain, too."

"All right, Janet, let's get started and see if this is an option." Sean said goodbye to Janet and headed back to his cubicle. *Who knows,* Sean thought to himself, *maybe this will be one of the success cases.*

As he drove to the first of the two health and safety visits[9] he had scheduled for the afternoon, Sean thought about how best to approach his supervisor with Janet's idea. He wasn't sure she would like the plan, and he wanted to make sure he thought through all the possible concerns.

QUESTIONS FOR DISCUSSION

1. What do you see as the top three challenges faced by Sean as a child welfare worker?

2. In addition to what you might have included in your answer above, what are the system issues that need to be addressed? Include services or programs you see a need to better serve the clients of the children's administration.

3. How can one avoid getting too discouraged when he or she sees others not acting professionally?

4. If a mother loves her children but is intellectually or developmentally disabled, under what circumstances is it appropriate to remove children from her care? What other options would the worker want to consider?

5. What are the ethical dilemmas that you noticed in the case? What other ethical dilemmas do you think a child welfare worker may face?

6. Would you recommend services for Ethan and Ely based on what you learned about them in this chapter?

7. Based on the information in this case, can you think of any legislative policy changes that might improve the child welfare system?

8. What do you think about the possibility of privatization of child welfare? What would be the strengths and weaknesses?

9. Rather than focus on addressing child abuse after it has been reported, how might social workers work to move toward a focus on child abuse and neglect prevention?

10. What forms of inequality do you think might influence the occurrence of child abuse and neglect? How do you think inequality impacts intervention in cases of child abuse and neglect? For example, do you think parental wealth and status impact how a case might be addressed?

---

[9] Health and safety visits are when the caseworker checks in on the children in placement and spends time observing them and talking to them to ensure they feel safe and secure. This is an essential part of the job but unfortunately not one that always gets the time and attention it should.

CASE ANALYSIS WRITING ASSIGNMENT

1. Read the assigned case study thoroughly prior to class in order to be fully prepared to join in the discussion.

2. Imagine you have been asked to speak to a group of foster parents at their monthly support group meeting. The title of your speech is "A Day in the Life of a Child Welfare Service Worker." Write an essay that explains to foster parents what the job entails, key policy that influences the work, and what challenges and ethical dilemmas you may face on any given day.

3. The essay should be approximately two pages, typed, and double-spaced. Your essay should reflect the standards and expectations of college-level writing: spelling, grammar, appropriate use of paragraphs, and so on all matter. If you quote directly from the case study, use quotation marks, and at the end of the quote, indicate the page number the quote appeared on. For example, "The process was slow but states began implementing laws regarding the reporting of child abuse, and the U.S. Congress included amendments focusing on child protection to the Social Security Act of 1962" (Myers, 2008, as cited in Clemons, 2016, p. 6).

4. Your case analysis is due _____ and worth a maximum of _____ points.

INTERNET SOURCES

Administration for Children and Families (http://www.acf.hhs.gov/program-topics/children-youth-0)

Adverse Childhood Experiences (https://www.youtube.com/watch?v=GQwJCWPG478)

Annie E. Casey Foundation (www.aecf.org)

CASA: Court Appointed Special Advocates for Children (http://www.casafor children.org/site/c.mtJSJ7MPIsE/b.6367905/k.7D91/Child_Welfare.htm)

Children's Aid Society (http://www.childrensaidsociety.org)

Child Maltreatment and Brain Consequences: Academy of Violence and Abuse (https://www.youtube.com/watch?v=r6_nindqsTs)

Child Welfare Information Gateway (https://www.childwelfare.gov)

Child Welfare League of America (www.cwla.org)

Family Violence, Child Abuse and the Brain (https://www.youtube.com/watch?v=r9jWyVKPJ70)

Nadine Burke Harris: How Childhood Trauma Affects Health Across a Lifetime (https://www.youtube.com/watch?v=950vIJ3dsNk)

Prevent Child Abuse America (http://preventchildabuse.org)

REFERENCES

Adoptions and Safe Families Act of 1997 (H.R. 867). (1997). Retrieved from https://www.socialworkers.org/archives/advocacy/updates/1997/safeadop.htm

Centers for Disease Control and Prevention. (2016). *Child abuse and neglect prevention.* Retrieved from http://www.cdc.gov/violenceprevention/childmaltreatment/index.html

Children's Aid Society (n.d.). *History.* Retrieved from http://www.childrensaidsociety.org/about/history

Child Welfare Information Gateway. (2011). *About CAPTA: A legislative history.* Washington, DC: U.S. Department of Health and Human Services, Children's Bureau. Retrieved from https://www.childwelfare.gov/pubs/factsheets/about

Child Welfare Information Gateway. (2013). *Long-term consequences of child abuse and neglect.* Washington, DC: U.S. Department of Health and Human Services, Children's Bureau. Retrieved from https://www.childwelfare.gov/pubpdfs/long_term_consequences.pdf

Child Welfare Information Gateway. (n.d.a). *Definitions of child abuse and neglect in federal law.* Retrieved from https://www.childwelfare.gov/topics/can/defining/federal

Child Welfare Information Gateway. (n.d.b). *Evidence-based practice.* Retrieved April 18, 2016, from https://www.childwelfare.gov/topics/management/practice-improvement/evidence

Eckenrode, J., Smith, E., McCarthy, M., & Dineen, M. (2014). Income inequality and child maltreatment in the United States. *Pediatrics, 133*(3), 454–461.

Fang, X., Brown, D. S., Florence, C. S., & Mercy, J. A. (2012). The economic burden of child maltreatment in the United States and implications for prevention. *Child Abuse & Neglect, 36*(2), 156–165.

Felitti, V., Anda, R. F., Nordenberg, D., Williamson, D., Spitz, A., Edwards, V., Koss, M., & Marks, J. (1998). Relationship of childhood abuse and household dysfunction to many of the leading causes of death in adults: The adverse childhood experiences (ACE) study. *American Journal of Preventive Medicine, 14*(4), 245–258.

Finkelhor, D., Turner, H., Shattuck, A., & Hamby, S. (2013). Violence, crime, and abuse exposure in a national sample of children and youth. *JAMA Pediatrics, 167*(7), 614–621.

Jones, L., Finkelhor, D., & Halter, S. (2006). Child maltreatment trends in the 1990s: Why does neglect differ from sexual and physical abuse? *Child Maltreatment, 11*(2), 107–120.

Myers, J. (2008). A short history of child protection in America. *Family Law Quarterly, 42*(3), 449–463. Retrieved from https://www.americanbar.org/content/dam/aba/publishing/insights_law_society/ChildProtectionHistory.authcheckdam.pdf

National Indian Child Welfare Association. (2015, September). *Setting the record straight: The Indian Child Welfare Act fact sheet.* Retrieved from http://www.nicwa.org/government/documents/Setting-Record-Straight-About-ICWA_Sep2015.pdf

Sedalk, A., & Broadhurst, D. (1996). *Third national incidence study of child abuse and neglect, final report.* U.S. Department of Health and Human Services. Retrieved from https://www.childwelfare.gov/topics/systemwide/statistics/nis

Straus, M. A. (2005). Children should never, ever, be spanked no matter what the circumstances. In D. R. Loseke, R. J. Gelles, & M. M. Cavanaugh (Eds.), *Current controversies about family violence* (2nd ed., pp. 137–157). Thousand Oaks, CA: SAGE.

U.S. Department of Health and Human Services, Administration for Children and Families, Administration on Children, Youth and Families, Children's Bureau. (2012). *Child maltreatment 2012.* Washington, DC: Government Printing Office. Retrieved from http://www.acf.hhs.gov/sites/default/files/cb/cm2012.pdf

Chapter 7

Society's Evolving Understanding of Chemical Addiction and the Subsequent Changes in Policy and Treatment Approaches

The Struggle to Stay Clean

***O**h no, this can't be good,* thought Olivia, as she impatiently waited for Carolyn to show up at the Narcotics Anonymous (NA) meeting. Olivia had a bad feeling as she hadn't heard from Carolyn for about week, and now, 15 minutes into the meeting, she was downright worried. Carolyn had missed the NA meeting last Friday that they typically attended together but had told Olivia she'd gone to meetings on Tuesday and Thursday nights last week so was giving Friday a miss as she had a head cold. She had promised Olivia she'd be back tonight. Lie #2

A half hour into the meeting, Olivia couldn't sit still another second, so she left as quietly as possible and headed to Carolyn's house. She knew she wasn't responsible for keeping her young friend clean, but she also knew all too well what the pull to the dark side was like. If not for the support of a relative and a caring social worker, she would likely be in jail or dead. Paying forward the support she'd received had helped Olivia in her recovery, but she knew there were limits.

"Damn it," Olivia shouted, when her repeated knocks on the door went unanswered. She headed around back and found the back door slightly ajar. Pushing it

Lie #1 →

open, she crossed the kitchen, sidestepping the garbage strewn across the floor. Once in the living room, she saw Carolyn lying on the couch, looking pretty out of it, her bare arms and legs scratched raw. A syringe was on the floor, and a dirty spoon was on the coffee table. Olivia knew there was no point in talking to Carolyn at that moment, but she was angry, disappointed, and scared for Carolyn, so she let loose.

"Back at it, I see. I thought you were tired of being sick and tired. I thought you didn't want to go back to prison. I thought you wanted to get your kids back. I figured that this time you'd stay away from this poison. C'mon Carolyn, think about somebody besides yourself."

"F-you, just leave me alone," Carolyn spewed back before nodding off. Rather than irritating Olivia, the response made her reflect on how unhelpful she was being. "I won't leave you alone, Carolyn, because I'm your friend and I care, but I will shut up and let you sleep. We can talk later." Olivia didn't expect or get a response and decided that she might as well see if she could clean up enough to get rid of the horrid smell.

Olivia figured that Carolyn would be remorseful and angry at herself for using again. But feeling remorse was no guarantee that she'd get back on track with her recovery program. *Maybe being sent back to prison would be the best thing for her,* Olivia thought, *but I don't know, and it's not my call anyway. My job is to be her friend, not her social worker.* As she cleaned, Olivia reflected on a couple of her many conversations with Carolyn in the past six months.

After the third Friday night NA meeting that Carolyn attended, Olivia had asked her if she wanted to meet for coffee and had been surprised when Carolyn readily accepted the offer. Although quiet at the meetings, when it was just the two of them, Carolyn had opened up immediately, confiding that "all I used to want was to stay high. It was the only time I didn't feel self-hatred, self-pity, and anger toward everyone, even my children. It was like I was stuck living in a world without sunshine or hope; a world of sadness, of gray, of losing, and especially pain. I was desperate to escape the pain I felt and actually still do feel. It didn't seem to matter if I lived or died, so I didn't worry about dirty needles or a contaminated batch. Thinking about that and how I didn't care that it would hurt my kids makes me cry a lot. Part of me still wants to get high; I crave it bad, but NA is helping me stay clean."

It was during this first coffee together that Carolyn had shared some of the childhood memories that she used drugs to avoid thinking about. "I watched my mother be physically abused by my father, who punched her regularly, and hard. He was a brute and hit me as well and would drag me by my hair. Then, after my parents divorced when I was 10, my mom got involved with another abusive scumbag. My parents were heavy drinkers and not what one would call responsible, but at least when they were together my uncle wasn't around all the time and wasn't sexually abusing me. That started after the divorce. I don't know—maybe that creepy asshole was waiting until I was at least 11. When my father left, my uncle came by a lot under the pretense

He groomed her.

of helping my mom. He gave me presents, asked me about school, and even took me on trips. He was the only adult family member who paid attention to me." Carolyn had grown more upset telling the story and was almost in hysterics, sobbing loudly, her chest heaving. Olivia had a hard time making out the exact stream of words, but the gist of it was that "I hated myself for 'allowing' it to go on and not telling my mom. I hated my mom for being oblivious to it and too caught up in her worthless boyfriend to notice me. I was all alone. I had no one to turn to. When my so-called friend offered me drugs, I figured, why not? The drugs helped numb the pain and self-loathing. At first I mainly used alcohol, pot, and cocaine. I even backed off coke when I was pregnant. After my children were born is when I got into heroin."

neglect, Isolated, trapped.

Drugs helped – numb pain & self-loathing

Carolyn went on, "It was in prison, after getting caught stealing to feed my drug habit, that I decided I didn't want to go on living just to get high. My children, who were living with my mom, came to the prison to visit. I hated my mom for bringing them, but on the other hand, it was a wake-up call that I didn't want to lose my kids, and I didn't want their memories of their mom to be prison visits. I only had to spend a couple of months in prison, and despite all those good intentions, the day I got out I got high. Stupid, I know, but it was like I needed it, and I thought I deserved to not feel like crap. So much for the wake-up call.

"A week after my release, my parole officer called and told me I needed to stop at NewWay for a random drug screen. I told her I wouldn't pass it. To my surprise, instead of sending me back to prison she offered me the opportunity to enter drug court. Like I said, part of me really wanted to get clean for my kids, but a big part of me just wanted my fix, my escape. I really didn't think I could live without it. I didn't know how to handle the hurt and pain. I also didn't, and don't, want my kids with my mom. She is well meaning, but she's a mess. And now she's got a new boyfriend, and that freaks me out given my experience with her choice in men. I'm surprised that child welfare even considered her appropriate for kinship care."

Those early talks, and then her convincing Carolyn to try out Sophia, the social worker Olivia herself had gone to for years, seemed like a long time ago. Sophia was employed at a facility the drug court worked with, so there was no waiting to get in to see her. Olivia believed Sophia was a godsend. She had helped Olivia reframe how she thought about herself and work on forgiving herself little by little for the death of her daughter, Lizzie. Olivia was Carolyn's friend and would continue to support her, but she knew that she didn't have the skill set to be her social worker, nor did she have the emotional distance.

Olivia was thinking about how much Sophia had helped her when she discovered at least a partial source of the disgusting smell: a pile of runny dog poop. She simultaneously heard Jake, a dachshund, whimpering quietly on the bed of Carolyn's 3-year-old son, Travis. Travis was still in kinship care with Carolyn's mom, along with his 4-year-old sister. "Come on Jake, poor little guy, let's get you some water and food.

Who knows when you last ate, and from the smell of this place, you have definitely been doing your business inside." Olivia continued talking to Jake as she fed him and then grabbed a bucket of soapy water and a hose to wash off some of the muck caked on him. Jake replaced his whimpering with yelping, but Olivia continued unabated.

"Jake, if only getting clean was this quick and painless, despite your protests, for Carolyn. I just hope she'll call her parole officer and Sophia. Better that she reports she messed up again than let it show up on a random drug test. Maybe the consequence for using again won't be prison time, since she's had no dirty urines for over 4 months, and the drug court staff all believe she's been working her program. They also know that relapse is not unusual. Judge Meisner warned her early on to stay away from her old crowd. I knew last week she had been in contact with some old friends who are still using, and that was a red flag for me, but I can't control her, can I?" *Good grief,* Olivia thought, *I'm resorting to talking to a dog.*

After changing bedding, throwing a urine-soaked rug outside on the fence, and making sure Jake had left no other surprises, Olivia was exhausted, and despite the grossness of these tasks, she was hungry. She had checked on Carolyn periodically, and each time found her still sleeping fitfully on the couch. Her breathing had seemed more normal the last time Olivia looked in on her. After grabbing a spoonful of peanut butter and a bowl of stale, dry Captain Crunch, Olivia crashed in Carolyn's room. It was the only room where she could mostly escape the lingering bad smell.

A noise awakened Olivia, and once her eyes adjusted to the dark, she saw Carolyn rummaging through her purse. As calmly she could, Olivia said, "Put it down, Carolyn. There are maybe two dollars max in there."

"Get out of my house," Carolyn yelled. Then she started shaking and sobbing. "You don't know what it's like for me. I can't do it. I tried. Just leave me alone. You can't save me, so stop trying. I'm sick of you."

Olivia was well aware that part of her need to try to "save" Carolyn stemmed from watching her own daughter, Lizzie, die from a cocaine overdose that she was too high herself to prevent, or so she still told herself. That was 12 years ago and the reason that Olivia got clean. The guilt was something she was still working at letting go of. Olivia tried to push thoughts of her daughter away and be there for Carolyn, who had sat down on the bed beside her, appearing agitated and anxious. Olivia knew the agitation and anxiety were mostly the body's reaction to coming down from the drug and craving more. She figured Carolyn had most likely been getting high a lot over the last week and maybe longer, so the need was strong.

Olivia calmly turned to Carolyn and said, "Carolyn, you're the only one who can save yourself and get your kids back, which I know you want. I figure you're out of drugs and money or you wouldn't have been trying to steal from me. Given how badly beaten you were the last time you sold your body for drug money, that doesn't seem like an option you'd want to choose."

Another "F-you" was the only response from Carolyn before she crawled onto the bed and slept. Two hours later when she woke up, although still sounding agitated, Carolyn's first question to Olivia was, "Do you think Judge Meisner will send me back to prison?" Then she started sobbing again, repeating over and over, "I just know I'm never going to get my kids back, but they're better off without me anyway. I don't know why I even bother."

"I tried self-pity, too, but it didn't get me anywhere, Carolyn. You were clean for over 4 months, then had a relapse, so get up, deal with the consequences, make the amends needed, and move forward."

Carolyn didn't respond, so Olivia continued. "If you call Sophia, she can probably pull some strings and get you into detox right away."

"I don't need detox. I can handle it."

"Give it a break, Carolyn. If you get up and say that to Judge Meisner, you'll be spending time in a cell, and your children will be visiting you behind bars, which you know is traumatic for them. You've been lying to me and just tried to steal money from me. Having a relapse is one thing; not admitting you need help is quite another."

"I know, I know. I'll call Sophia and tell her what happened. That's our contract. I'm to let her know immediately if I'm not following my program. Oh *#*#, I'm just tired, and I feel so horrible. I need some H bad."

She's not making a lot of sense, thought Olivia, regarding the conflicting messages, but she attributed it to Carolyn desperately wanting to be a better mother than hers was, while at the same time physically craving opioids on top of the psychological addiction. "I'll stay until you connect with Sophia and have a plan. I can take you to wherever you need to go."

Olivia made a mental note that she would talk to Sophia next week, yet again, about her overwhelming need to save Carolyn and her fear that she sometimes went overboard in trying to make sure Carolyn stopped messing up. Until yesterday, she'd thought she was further along in letting go of the guilt about her daughter. This incident made her realize that she still had a way to go—she was still trying to make up for the role she believed her negligence as a mother had played in Lizzie's death.

BACKGROUND INFORMATION

The consequences of the ravage of substance abuse on individuals, family members, friends, communities, and society as a whole are profound and utterly tragic. Losing custody of children, broken relationships with family and friends, dropping out of school, being fired from a job, prison time, significant health problems, destitution, and death are examples of the wide-ranging and dire consequences of substance abuse. The economic costs alone of illicit drug abuse and alcohol abuse carry a price tag of over $400 billion per year in health care, crime-related expenses, and lost productivity (National Institute on Drug Abuse, 2015a).[1]

This section provides the foundational information necessary for you to gain a better understanding of the scope of the issue of substance use and abuse; the key philosophy and approach taken during the 40-plus year "war on drugs" and the outcomes of this war; the swinging pendulum on our approach to addressing illicit drug use; and the factors informing this approach. While the primary focus is on illicit drugs (and opiods, in particular), given the human, social, and economic costs of alcohol abuse, it too will be touched upon. With the information in this section in hand, you will be better prepared to discuss and evaluate policy choices relative to efforts to address substance abuse effectively.

Scope of the Problem

The Substance Abuse and Mental Health Services Administration (SAMHSA), reporting on a 2014 trend study, states that approximately 10.2% of the U.S. population ages 12 and older had used an illicit drug within the past 30 days. This equates to 27.0 million people, which is higher than in any year from 2002 to 2013. Marijuana use, and the use of prescription painkillers for nonmedical reasons, accounts for 26.5 million of the total. While the use of some illicit drugs was down, the use of heroin was higher in 2014 than in most years from 2002 to 2013 (Hedden, Kennet, Lipari, Medley, & Tic, 2014, p. 1).

Alcohol, although not an illicit drug for the adult population, is a drug nonetheless that, when abused, can lead to harmful consequences. And it is often abused by minors. Of the 139.7 million people who indicated in the 2014 SAMHSA study that they drank alcohol in the past month, 60.9 million were binge drinkers and 16.3 million were heavy alcohol users.[2] Underage binge and heavy drinking showed a decline in 2014, compared to 2002 to 2013. Still, 23% of 12- to 20-year-olds reported drinking, and of those, 17.2% were either "binge" or "heavy users." In the 18- to 25-year-old age group, the study found that 37.7% were binge drinkers and 10.8% were heavy alcohol users (Hedden et al., 2014, p.1). It is estimated that there are 88,000 deaths per year from alcohol abuse (Centers for Disease Control and Prevention, 2016a). These deaths are largely due to traffic accidents.

---

[1] Some government sources put the economic costs at over $416 billion for alcohol and illicit drugs.

[2] "Binge alcohol use is defined as drinking five or more drinks on the same occasion on at least 1 day in the past 30 days, and heavy alcohol use is defined as having this number of drinks on the same occasion on 5 or more days in the past 30 days" (Hedden et al., 2014, p. 1).

There is a difference between using an illicit substance, or engaging in binge or heavy drinking, and being considered to have a substance use disorder (SUD). SUD, a clinical diagnosis found in the *Diagnostic and Statistical Manual 5,* is given to those who meet certain criteria such as significant impairment, major substance-related health issues, and not being able to carry out responsibilities (such as going to class or work). In 2014, the National Survey on Drug Use and Health found that approximately 21.5 million people age 12 or older suffered from an SUD in the past year. The breakdown of the 21.5 million is 17 million with an alcohol use disorder and 7.1 million with an illicit drug disorder, as 2.6 million had both alcohol and illicit drug disorders (Hedden et al., 2014, p. 22).

Another key grouping that provides us with evidence of the scope of the issue at hand and its complexity are those who experience both a serious mental illness (SMI)[3] and an SUD. In 2014, this included approximately 1% of the adult population in the United States and 1.4% of youth ages 12 to 17. If we add in adults with both SUD and any mental illness, this percentage increases to 3.3% of the total adult population (Hedden et al., 2014, p. 2). Oftentimes, individuals with mental illness use illicit drugs as a means of coping, however ineffective, with symptoms of their illness.

Increase in Opioid Abuse

There are those who say we are experiencing an opioid epidemic, while others are not so quick to use the term *epidemic* and question if the increased attention on opiate overdoses is because of the increase in White suburban and rural women using the substance (Wood, 2014). History informs us that which subgroup in our population is using a drug greatly impacts how it is portrayed and subsequently responded to. We will return to the topic of perception and response, but for now we will cover the rising number of overdoses and deaths from drugs, especially opiods.

There were approximately half a million deaths from 2000 to 2014 attributed to drug overdoses. In 2014, the number of deaths at 43,255 was the highest ever recorded, exceeding by one and a half times the number of motor vehicle fatalities. The biggest culprit in the deaths were prescription pain relievers and heroin (accounting for 29,467 deaths), with the rate of opioid overdoses tripling in the past 4 years (National Institute on Drug Abuse, 2015b). "Every day in the United

---

[3] "Serious mental illness includes diagnoses which typically involve psychosis (losing touch with reality or experiencing delusions) or high levels of care, and which may require hospital treatment. Here we look at two of the most common severe mental illnesses: schizophrenia and bipolar disorder (or manic depression)" (Mental Health Wales, n.d.).

States, 44 people die as a result of prescription opioid overdose" (Centers for Disease Control and Prevention, 2016b, p. 1). In regard to the upward trend in heroin use and overdose, the key factors for this are its increased availability coupled with relatively low prices and high purity (Rudd, Aleshire, Zibbell, & Gladden, 2016, p. 1). Moreover, it is generally believed that efforts to make it harder to obtain prescription opioid drugs increased their price and drove many addicts to heroin.

The newest player in the opioid abuse arena is fentanyl, a powerful synthetic painkiller that looks like heroin but is up to 50 times more potent. It is cheap, extremely strong, and fast-acting, leaving little time for naloxone[4] to be administered in the case of an overdose. Fentanyl is most present in the Northeast, Mid-Atlantic, and Appalachia though it has started to infiltrate the Midwest. While there are no nationwide statistics, as state laboratories do not track fentanyl-related deaths, the drug killed 336 people in Massachusetts from 2014 to 2015, an increase of 53% from the year before (Seelye, 2016, para. 17). As users seek out a cheaper, more intense high, it is possible that fentanyl will be the next epidemic.

The numbers regarding the prevalence and economic costs of substance abuse, even without the full picture of the tremendous pain and suffering experienced by millions, beg for an effective societal response to address the negative consequences of drug abuse. A historical look at our nation's drug policies provides valuable lessons that have impacted thinking and policy action by the Obama administration.

Drug Policy and Race

Historian Richard Miller claims that U.S. drug policies have always been associated with race. In 1907, the smoking of opium was criminalized in California. Chinese were known for their opium dens, and they were also viewed with animosity by many. Miller believes that outlawing opium was used as a way to lock up the Chinese since they weren't breaking any other laws. States, Miller says, started criminalizing cocaine when it began to be associated with Blacks using it at the turn of the 20th century. And marijuana was outlawed in the 1930s after Mexican Americans started using it for recreational purposes (Fuchs, 2013). While one might argue about the racial underpinnings of early drug laws, if we look at the drug policy during the war on drugs there is clear evidence of racial disparity.

---

[4] Naloxone (Narcan) is administered to reverse the effects of a heroin overdose and prevent death. It is sometimes administered in hospitals to patients after surgery to counter the effects of the narcotics administered during surgery (National Institute of Health, 2016).

Studies show that Blacks and Whites use drugs at the same rate, and Whites are more likely to sell drugs than Blacks. Yet Blacks are far more likely to be arrested for selling or possessing drugs than Whites (Ingraham, 2014). Moreover, when convicted, the sentences received by Blacks are longer than those of Whites. According to the U.S. Sentencing Commission, the sentences for Blacks in the federal system are 10% longer for the same offense than if the offender is White. Findings from the Sentencing Project indicate that Blacks are 21% more likely than Whites to receive mandatory-minimums and 20% more likely to get prison time (Kerby, 2012). It is no wonder that many question whether it is just coincidence that the shift away from harsh and punitive policy for drug users comes at the same time that those affected by heroin addiction are largely White, not people of color (Haberman, 2015).

War on Drugs

In 1971, the Nixon administration launched the war on drugs and set the wheels in motion for a long fight. Referring to it as "a serious national threat," Nixon successfully crafted a narrative that shifted public perception of drug users to "dangerous criminals" who were "attacking the moral fiber of the nation, people who deserved only incarceration and punishment" (Dufton, 2012, para. 3). The irony is that during the Nixon administration, before the war was in full swing, more money was spent on prevention and rehabilitation than on enforcement in any administration since.

In the 1980s, under President Reagan, the war on drugs escalated. By the mid-80s, mandatory-minimum sentences for drug offenders, supported on both sides of the aisle, resulted in thousands of nonviolent offenders being sent to prison. First Lady Nancy Reagan had started her "Just Say No" campaign, and President Reagan was effectively convincing Americans that drug use was "public enemy number one." (There was indeed a rise in crack cocaine use.) In 1985, a poll indicated that between 2% and 6% of those in the United States saw drug use as our number one problem, but by September 1989, 64% believed it was the number one problem we faced. It is important to note that not even a year later, fewer than 10% polled indicated drugs were our number one problem. The power of this narrative told and repeated over and over again by the media cannot be overlooked in understanding how people are influenced and public policy is made (Drug Policy Alliance, 2016).

The "tough on crime" rhetoric pervaded policy discussions, and although evidence of its ineffectiveness was well known, the war on drugs continued unabated under President George H. W. Bush, President Clinton, and President George W. Bush. Finally, a shift in the rhetoric of how best to deal with drug abuse began during President Obama's first term.

The Changing Tide

President Obama called for adopting a public health/harm reduction approach[5] to drug abuse and argued that criminal justice reforms to reduce incarceration rates were needed. He also called for "boosting community-based prevention, expanding treatment, strengthening law enforcement and working collaboratively with our global partners" (Obama Drug Control, 2010, p. 1). There are many advocates for reform who support the approach President Obama proposed, but they want to see more evidence that the budget matches the improved rhetoric. They point out that, still today, less than half of drug control funds are being used for prevention. In its early assessment of the Obama administration's approach, the General Accounting Office (GAO) was not overly positive about the progress made, noting that prevention services were fragmented across 13 agencies (Sledge, 2013).

Although slower than many would like, there have been changes in how the government is addressing drug abuse that go beyond rhetoric, even if they don't go far enough. In 2010, the Fair Sentencing Act was signed into law by President Obama. This act reduced the disparity in the penalties between crack cocaine and powder cocaine from a 100:1 weight ratio to an 18:1 ratio. It also struck down the mandatory-minimum of 5 years of imprisonment for possession of crack cocaine. In 2014, the U.S. Sentencing Commission reduced penalties for many nonviolent drug crimes, and in 2015, approximately 6,000 inmates who had been charged with nonviolent low-level drug deals in the 1980s and 1990s were given early release from federal prisons (Schmidt, 2015). In 2015, a bipartisan group of senators joined forces and proposed the Sentencing Reform and Corrections Act that would, if it becomes law, be a step forward in bringing about an array of changes such as reducing the number of low-level drug offenders sentenced to prison, replacing life in prison sentences for third-time offenders under "three strikes" laws, giving judges discretion in sentencing and increasing funding for re-entry programs (Smith, 2015).

Michael Botticelli, who became director of the Office of National Drug Control Policy in 2015, stated that "the drug epidemic in America is at its worst ever, because the war on drugs was all wrong" (Top Drug Official, 2015, para. 1). After more than 40 years of ineffective policies that (1) cost over a trillion dollars, (2) resulted in hundreds of thousands of people (disproportionately African

---

[5] Harm reduction is aligned with a public health approach. It entails strategies that seek to reduce the negative outcomes associated with drug use and ineffective drug policies. It recognizes that drug use and abuse should be treated as a health issue, not a criminal issue (this approach is not aimed at those who traffic drugs, which is still seen as a criminal act). This approach does not minimize the tragic consequences and great harm that results in drug abuse but focuses on reducing the harm through education, services, and various forms of treatment.

Americans) being locked up, (3) destroyed lives, (4) negatively impacted entire communities, and (5) harmed police-community relations, the pendulum is swinging toward an approach that changes how drug abuse is defined. Botticelli, by defining drug addiction as a public health issue rather than a criminal issue, reinforced the change in language President Obama began in 2008 that put in motion legislative changes. Changing the definition of the problem will result in changing the policy prescriptions.

What Botticelli is calling for is consistent with the public health approach to drug addiction. He states that "we can't arrest and incarcerate addiction out of people. Not only do I think it's really inhumane, but it's ineffective and it cost us billions upon billions of dollars to keep doing this" (Top Drug Official, 2015, para. 3). Mr. Botticelli summarizes the White House policy changes as follows:

Using a public health framework as its foundation, our strategy also acknowledges the vital role that federal, state and local law enforcement play in reducing the availability of drugs—another risk factor for drug use. It underscores the vital importance of primary prevention in stopping drug use before it ever begins by funding prevention efforts across the country. It sets forth an agenda aimed at stripping away the systemic challenges that have accumulated like plaque over the decades: over-criminalization, lack of integration with mainstream medical care, insurance coverage and the legal barriers that make it difficult for people once involved with the criminal justice system to rebuild their lives. (Botticelli, 2015, para. 9)

Past leaders, with the help of the media, shaped public perception of drug abusers as criminals destroying our country. Botticelli aims to reshape public perception, believing it is vital that "we fundamentally change the way we think about people with addiction" (Botticelli, 2015, para. 10). He states:

Addiction is a brain disease. This is not a moral failing. This is not about bad people who are choosing to continue to use drugs because they lack willpower. You know, we don't expect people with cancer just to stop having cancer. (Top Drug Official, 2015, p.1)

Maia Szalavitz, author of *Unbroken Brain: A Revolutionary New Way of Understanding Addiction,* calls for a further paradigm shift in how we view addiction. She relies on neuroscience findings to support her position that addiction is a learning disorder. Yes, she says, it is a brain problem, but it is not necessarily a progressive one. What is needed is for the addicted person to redirect their compulsive drive to use a substance into healthier channels. Referring to her personal experience with drug addiction, she states that "heroin provided a sense of comfort, safety and love that I couldn't get from other people. . . . Once I'd experienced the relief heroin gave me, I felt as though I couldn't survive without it" (Szalavitz, 2016, para. 10). She likens addiction to healing a broken heart and believes those who rely on drugs for emotional needs can find other ways of getting those needs met.[6]

What Science Tells Us About Addiction

Neuroscience, the study of brain mechanisms, has greatly expanded our understanding of addiction. Recent research findings based on advances in brain imaging, genetic studies, and molecular biology provide evidence to make better informed policy decisions (Nutt & McLellan, 2014, p. 6). Simply put, research, using the tools of neuroscience, informs us that while the decision to take a drug is initially voluntary, over time brain changes occur that impair an addicted person's self-control and hamper his or her ability to resist intense impulses to take drugs. Therefore, addiction is defined as "a chronic, often relapsing brain disease that causes compulsive drug seeking and use, despite harmful consequences to the addicted individual and to those around him or her" (SAMHSA, 2011, para. 1). This evidence-based definition of addiction is information that should be used in the message to foster a change in the public perception, which is exactly what Mr. Botticelli is adamant needs to happen. More important, recent findings from research must inform public policy. Writing about the advances in neuroscience, Nutt & McLellan conclude:

> [The advances] mean that the addiction potential of existing and new "designer" drugs can now be assessed—offering the potential for the design of more effective prevention and early interventions; and more sensible and sensitive public policies to reduce the risks and harms of drug abuse. (2014, p.10)

We still need more research to better understand the interactive effects of, for example, drug use and one's emotional experiences or drug use and the interactive effect on the developing brain (Weiss, 2015).

If everyone who used drugs became addicted, it might be easier to change public perception and influence policy, but that is not the case, and leads too many to think addiction is simply about will power. (That is not to say that there is no ability to change the choices one is making.) One's risk of addiction is influenced by various factors, including genetics, environment, and development. Evidence suggests that genetics account for about half of a person's vulnerability to addiction. Genetic

---

[6] A *New York Times* article (http://www.nytimes.com/2016/06/26/opinion/sunday/can-you-get-over-an addiction.html) provides an overview of Szalavitz's perspective on addiction and recovery.

factors combine with environmental factors (e.g., stress, peer pressure, family, parenting, abuse) and developmental factors that increase the likelihood of addiction for some (SAMHSA, 2015).

There is ample evidence to argue for more effective prevention and intervention programs involving not just individuals but families, schools, and communities. Since the media conveys the message, media sources discussing drug use and abuse need to be informed. In regard to intervention, there are evidence-based practices that fall under two broad categories: pharmacotherapies and behavioral therapies. Pharmacotherapies include medication and are more effective when combined with behavioral therapy or some form of counseling. (As with any treatment, it is more effective when it is holistic. All the needs of the person, for example, medical, psychological, employment, and housing, must be addressed, not just the drug abuse.) Some of the primary behavioral approaches include motivational interviews, motivational enhancement therapy, cognitive behavioral therapy, safety seeking and prize-based contingency management, and 12-step facilitation therapy (Centers for Disease Control and Prevention, 2012; Society of Clinical Psychology, 2016).

The good news is that there are many effective prevention and intervention programs (noted in previous paragraph) being implemented, and, as noted, the Obama administration took steps to treat addiction as a public health issue rather than a criminal issue. Still, we have a long way to go in terms of having a public that understands the dynamics of addiction, how important prevention is, and ensuring that those in need of treatment receive the services needed.[7]

CAROLYN'S JOURNEY

Carolyn waited nervously for her turn to stand in front of Judge Meisner. The drug court participants had gone before her all had good reports and were applauded. Carolyn knew that would not be the case for her. When her name was called, she approached the bench thinking over what she and Sophia had discussed. Carolyn had actually missed her last drug court appointment as she was in detox. She knew Sophia, and really the whole drug court team, were on her side. But she also knew they would all hold her accountable.

"Hello, Carolyn, how's it going?" asked the judge. She was aware that the judge knew all about her relapse and what had transpired since. She had watched a few times as drug court participants had been handcuffed and hauled off to jail for lying about their drug use, for not following their program, or for exhibiting an indignant attitude.

---

[7] There is no one-size-fits-all approach to intervention, and there are many people who at one time met the *Diagnostic and Statistical Manual* criteria for substance abuse but are no longer using and never received treatment.

A what-the-hell-do-you-know attitude was one Carolyn herself exhibited before her first prison stay. Through her sessions with Sophia she knew it was, for her at least, just a defense mechanism, a cover for not wanting to deal with her own issues.

"I think I'm back on track, Judge Meisner. I messed up pretty bad. I was doing so good for over 4 months, then instead of using the coping strategies Sophia and I have talked about, I let myself give in to old and familiar habits. I told myself this time it would be different, that I would just use drugs once in a while. I wasn't being honest with myself. The only reason I wanted to hang out with my old crowd was so that they could supply me with drugs, and I gave in to the craving for a good high. I admit I'm scared; I really don't want to mess up again. The difference now is I know even if I stay away for a while, it's easy to relapse. I'm an addict and can't just use stuff a little. That desire to use is there, and I know I need to stay away from the people I used to get high with. I started working my program again, which now includes going to Begin ANEW every morning for Suboxone.[8] I have to meet with a counselor there as well as attend my other meetings.

"Carolyn," responded Judge Meisner, after each of the members of the treatment team weighed in mentioning the revised treatment plans and some of the positive steps Carolyn was taking. "You have a lot of support here, but the hard work it up to you. Is there anything else you need?"

"No, judge," Carolyn quickly said.

"Okay, well, we'll see you in 2 weeks, and I expect a good report."

That was it. No jail. Carolyn breathed a sigh of relief as she left the courtroom. She was extremely relieved but, at the same time, disappointed that the usual clapping that always lifted her spirits didn't happen. The judge had not asked for a round of applause for her. She knew she had let not only herself down but the whole drug court team who had invested in her. Four months ago she didn't care what others on the treatment team thought, but today, although she was not quite sure why, it mattered a lot to her.

Five Weeks Later

"Carolyn, I'll be right with you," shouted Sophia from her office when she heard the outer door to the waiting area slam shut. Carolyn had not missed a session since she had gone through detox again and started on Suboxone. During the past session, Sophia's intuition told her that Carolyn was struggling, although verbally Carolyn indicated that all was good, and she had not missed any of her

---

[8] Suboxone is one of the prescription medications, as are methadone and naltrexone, currently used as part of medically-assisted treatment approaches for opioid addiction. Suboxone contains buprenorphine and naloxone. Medically-assisted treatment includes counseling and other supports along with the medication to suppress withdrawal symptoms and reduce the cravings (National Institute of Drug Abuse, 2016).

appointments or work. Before calling her in, Sophia wanted to take a couple minutes to make extra sure she was centered for the session with Carolyn and able to be keenly alert to nonverbal as well as verbal messages.

Sophia knows that she overidentifies with Carolyn, probably because Carolyn strongly reminds her so much of an earlier "messed-up" version of herself. That seems like a lifetime ago, and Sophia is thankful she has grown so much and can truly be there for others. She is also keenly aware of how important it is for her to continue working on taking care of herself and not "overinvesting" in her clients as she did early in her career. Though it was long ago, she clearly remembers a time when she allowed a few clients, who claimed to have "no other supports," to call her at home at night. It was on her work phone, but still it quickly got out of hand with a couple of them. She recalls many talks with her supervisor regarding her role and responsibilities versus those of the people she was working with. Her supervisor was fond of saying, "As much as we may want to, we can't make the change for them."

In theory, Sophia fully believes in the concept of self-determination, but, in practice, she sometimes still finds herself wanting to "fix" clients and believing she knows what is best for them. The bottom line is that she really just wants them to make the choices she thinks will bring them contentment, and at times sees it as her fault when clients don't make progress toward their goals. It is a constant struggle. On the one hand, she knows that only Carolyn can make the changes necessary to get her children back, but on the other hand, she wants so badly for that to happen that she fears it interferes with her ability to effectively carry out her role. A year ago, Sophia considered quitting her job because she started again to allow poor choices made by clients to gnaw at her. She went back to meet with her former social worker about this struggle and has made great progress.

Sophia steps out into the waiting area to greet Carolyn and immediately sees that something is not right. Carolyn looks upset, unkempt, and she has a bruise on her cheek. Just yesterday, Sophia spoke to Carolyn's counselor at the Suboxone clinic and was told Carolyn was compliant with the medication part of the treatment and appeared to be doing well. Clearly, she's not doing well today. *Crap*, Sophia thinks, *not again*.

"Carolyn, please come in," Sophia said calmly but with concern in her voice. Before Carolyn is all the way into Sophia's office, the tears are flowing as she meekly says, "I started seeing Jeremy again a couple weeks ago. He told me he wanted to stop using and even attended a couple NA meetings with me, but it was only a ploy to get me back. Last night we got into a fight when he accused me of just substituting one drug for another. I told him he didn't know what he was talking about and called him a loser and all sorts of vile names. As the fight escalated, I pushed him, and he shoved me back. I lost my balance, fell, and hit my face on the table. I don't know what to do. I know Jeremy may be bad for me in some ways, and that I'm supposed to stay away from him since he's using, but, despite the fight, I still want to be with him, and he is the father of my daughter.

While I'm making confessions, I better tell you that it didn't help that before the fight we each had a few beers. Well, I had a few, Jeremy had quite a few. That's part of what made me mad about his comment. I know that drinking is against my treatment plan. I don't even know why I had those beers as they didn't really give me a buzz. I just fell back into old habits, but I didn't use anything else, I swear."

Carolyn looks at Sophia for a response. Sophia doesn't want to put Carolyn on the defensive so knows she needs to be careful. "Carolyn, I'm glad you kept your appointment and want to talk about what's going on. You bring up some important issues we definitely need to discuss, but how about if we do our standard 'things I did well this past week' first and then get back to the issues at hand?" Sophia is a little hesitant to switch gears, but it accomplishes what she hoped it would. Carolyn isn't too upset to rattle off a number of positive things she has done during the week, including working an extra shift and using the money to buy her kids gifts. She sits up taller as she speaks, and her voice grows stronger and more confident.

Sophia returns to the serious issues of Carolyn's appearance and confession. "Carolyn, despite continued struggles and difficult situations, you are making progress in many areas of your life. Let's keep that in mind as we come up with a plan for dealing with the challenges you just shared. You told me in one of our early sessions that Jeremy had broken your jaw one time and cracked your ribs another. A minute ago, when you lifted your arm I saw what looked like a large bruise, so even if the table caused it, you've told me more than once that Jeremy is bad news. While I'm concerned that you violated your commitment to distance yourself from your old crowd, especially those who are still using, I am most concerned for your safety."

The first words out of Carolyn's mouth are "You won't tell the treatment team, will you? I told you about Jeremy in confidence. You said that I could talk to you openly." She ignores Sophia's comment about being concerned about her safety. Despite her plea, Carolyn is well aware that, while as a drug court participant she can expect many things to be kept confidential, the breaking of the treatment plan contract is something Sophia must share with the court.

Rather than address the question Carolyn asked, Sophia again brings up the issue of Jeremy's violent outbursts and Carolyn's safety. Carolyn quickly says, "It's only really bad if he drinks. He doesn't want to hurt me; he just underestimates his strength. Still, I promise to honor my contract and stay away from Jeremy. Just don't say that I even mentioned seeing him to you. I'll do what I have to do. I'll even take Olivia up on her offer to stay with me for a while. If I didn't trust that I could tell you about Jeremy and the beer, you would have never known, but I want to be honest with you. But I can't have another strike against me, or I'll never get my kids back." Carolyn moves from being upset to being scared and almost combative, which is not what Sophia expected. She also knows that Olivia will do anything for Carolyn and, like herself, wants Carolyn to stay clean.

"What about the drinking, Carolyn? That violates your contract as well. You know it's dangerous to drink while on Suboxone," is the only thing Sophia can think of at the moment, so that's what she says. Sophia knows that she should have taken a minute to think before responding and that allowing her emotions to get in the way is a mistake. She is feeling frustrated because she already informed Carolyn that using any substance is something she must report.

Rather than responding angrily, Carolyn resorts to her hunched posture and says in a meek voice, "I know. I honestly only had a few drinks last night, and they didn't make me feel any different. In fact, they made me feel nauseous and gave me a horrible headache. I don't plan on drinking again, and if I make it another day or two without another drug screen, unless you say something, no one on the team will know I had a few drinks. It's not like I used again. Jeremy was over and kept on me to drink with him. I know I'm messing up in small ways, but like we said, I'm making progress, too. I'm really trying, but it's just so hard. You said you were on my side. Please, you've gotta give me one more chance. My kids aren't safe with my mom, and they need a mom who's not in prison. You and Olivia and almost everyone else can have a drink. That's not illegal. Please, Sophia, you know I can do it. You believe in me, right?"

QUESTIONS FOR DISCUSSION

1. Based on the background information provided, discuss the outcomes of the "war on drugs." Also, what are your thoughts about the relationship some claim there has always been between what is determined to be an illicit drug and race?

2. Drawing on information in the background section, respond to the following claim: "I used to be an addict, and I got clean on my own. Staying clean is a matter of will power, and those who keep using illicit drugs deserve to do jail time."

3. The current director of the Office of National Drug Control Policy is a recovering alcoholic. How might this be an advantage or a disadvantage to him in his position?

4. If you were to work with someone who had an addiction to a substance, what are some of the lessons set forth in the case that you would want to keep in mind?

5. If you were designing policy to increase the likelihood of recovery from addiction, what would you make sure to include in the policy?

6. The case only spoke briefly to the issue of the relationship between mental illness and substance abuse. Discuss why it is important that interventions take both into consideration. Which do you think should be primary, if either?

7. Along with a great deal of information on chemical dependency, this case presents challenges faced by social workers regarding setting appropriate boundaries, confidentiality, and self-determination. Does it appear that Sophia has appropriate boundaries with Carolyn? Explain your answer.

8. What options does Sophia have for responding to Carolyn? What is the best option, given what you know of the case? Put yourself in Sophia's shoes, and craft a response for her to Carolyn's last comments.

9. What challenges with boundaries can you see yourself having in the field?

10. In micropractice, what strategies might you use to make sure that the challenges clients are faced with don't eat away at you? Think about the population you want to work with at this time. Can you see yourself going home after your shift and not continuing to think about the hardships you heard about? What types of issues would you find most troubling? Least troubling?

11. Besides being a caring individual, what draws Olivia to Carolyn? Does it appear that Olivia is doing what a support person should, or is she possibly doing too much for her? Provide a rationale for your answer

12. Besides boundaries, are there other ethical issues involved in the case, specifically for Sophia?

13. Optional: Read the article at http://www.nytimes.com/2016/06/26/opinion/sunday/can-you-get-over-an-addiction.html. Discuss whether Szalavitz's perspective is consistent with the public health approach to substance abuse.

CASE ANALYSIS WRITING ASSIGNMENT

1. Read the assigned case study thoroughly prior to class in order to be fully prepared to join in the discussion.

2. Providing education to 7th and 8th graders is part of your job responsibilities as a social worker for a substance abuse treatment center. Drawing on content from this case study, "The Struggle to Stay Clean," write an essay that lays out what you think would be of key importance to include when you meet with this age group.

3. The essay should be approximately two pages, typed, and double spaced. Your essay should reflect the standards and expectations of college-level

writing: spelling, grammar, and appropriate use of paragraphs all matter. If you quote directly from the case study, use quotation marks, and at the end of the quote, indicate the page number the quote appeared on. For example, "Blacks are far more likely to be arrested for selling or possessing drugs than Whites" (Ingraham, 2014, p. 1, as cited in Lewis, 2016, p. 11).

4. Your case analysis is due _____ and worth a maximum of ____ points.

INTERNET SOURCES

Centers for Disease Control and Prevention (www.cdc.gov); Resources (http://search.cdc.gov/search?query=drug+abuse&utf8=%E2%9C%93&affiliate=cdc-main)

Drug Policy Alliance (www.drugpolicy.org)

Hazelton Addition Treatment Center (http://www.hazelden.org)

The National Council on Alcoholism and Drug Dependence (NCADD) (www.ncadd.org)

National Institute of Health: National Institute of Alcohol Abuse and Alcoholism (NIAAA) (http://www.niaaa.nih.gov)

National Institute of Health: National Institute of Drug Abuse (NIDA) (www.drugabuse.gov)

Substance Abuse and Mental Health Services Administration (SAMHSA) (www.samhsa.gov)

TED Talks: Why do our brains get addicted by Nora Volkow (http://www.tedmed.com/talks/show?id=309096)

TED Talks: Top 8 TED Talks to Inspire Recovery (http://www.reneveryday.com/top-8-ted-talks-to-inspire-the-recovery-journey)

REFERENCES

Botticelli, M. (2015, February 9). *The work before us: A message from Michael Botticelli.* Retrieved from https://www.whitehouse.gov/blog/2015/02/09/work-us-message-michael-botticelli-0

Centers for Disease Control and Prevention. (2012, December). *Evidence-based approaches to drug addiction treatment.* Retrieved from https://www.drugabuse.gov/publications/principles-drug-addiction-treatment-research-based-guide-third-edition/evidence-based-approaches-to-drug-addiction-treatment

Centers for Disease Control and Prevention. (2016a). *Fact sheet: Alcohol and your health.* Retrieved from http://www.cdc.gov/alcohol/fact-sheets/alcohol-use.htm

Centers for Disease Control and Prevention. (2016b). *Prescription drug overdose data.* Retrieved from http://www.cdc.gov/drugoverdose/data/overdose.html

Dufton, E. (2012, March 26). *The war on drugs: How President Nixon tied addiction to crime.* Retrieved from http://www.theatlantic.com/health/archive/2012/03/the-war-on-drugs-how-president-nixon-tied-addiction-to-crime/254319

Drug Policy Alliance. (2016). *A brief history of the war on drugs.* Retrieved from http://www.drug-policy.org/facts/new-solutions-drug-policy/brief-history-drug-war-0

Fuchs, E. (2013, August 19). HISTORIAN: Anti-drug laws have always been about race. *Business Insider.* Retrieved from http://www.businessinsider.com/richard-miller-on-anti-drug-laws-2013-8

Haberman, C. (2015, November 22). Heroin, survivor of war on drugs, returns with new face. *New York Times.* Retrieved from http://www.nytimes.com/2015/11/23/us/heroin-survivor-of-war-on-drugs-returns-with-new-face.html

Hedden, S., Kennet, J., Lipari, R., Medley, G., & Tic, P. (2014, September). Behavioral health trends in the United States: Results from the 2014 national survey on drug use and health. *Substance Abuse and Mental Health Services Administration.* Retrieved from http://www.samhsa.gov/data/sites/default/files/NSDUH-FRR1-2014/NSDUH-FRR1-2014.pdf

Ingraham, C. (2014, September 30). White people are more likely to deal drugs, but Black people are more likely to get arrested for it. *Washington Post.* Retrieved from https://www.washingtonpost.com/news/wonk/wp/2014/09/30/white-people-are-more-likely-to-deal-drugs-but-black-people-are-more-likely-to-get-arrested-for-it

Kerby, S. (2012, March 13). The top 10 most startling facts about people of color and criminal justice in the United States. *Center for American Progress.* Retrieved from https://www.americanprogress.org/issues/race/news/2012/03/13/11351/the-top-10-most-startling-facts-about-people-of-color-and-criminal-justice-in-the-united-states

Mental Health Wales. (n.d.). *What is serious mental illness?* Retrieved from http://www.mentalhealthwales.net/mhw/whatis.php

National Institute of Health: U.S. National Library of Medicine. (2016). *Naloxone Injection.* Medline Plus. Retrieved from https://www.nlm.nih.gov/medlineplus/druginfo/meds/a

National Institute on Drug Abuse. (2015a). *Costs of substance abuse.* Retrieved from https://www.drugabuse.gov/related-topics/trends-statistics

National Institute on Drug Abuse. (2015b). *Overdose death rates.* Retrieved from https://www.drugabuse.gov/related-topics/trends-statistics/overdose-death-rates

Nutt, D., & McLellan, A. (2014). Can neuroscience improve addiction treatment and policies? *Public Health Reviews, 35*(2). Retrieved from http://www.publichealthreviews.eu/upload/pdf_files/14/00_Nutt_McLellan.pdf

Obama drug control strategy marks policy shift. (2010, May 11). *CBS News.* Retrieved from http://www.cbsnews.com/news/obama-drug-control-strategy-marks-policy-shift

Rudd, R. A., Aleshire, N., Zibbell, J. E., & Gladden, M. (2016, January 1). Increases in drug and opioid overdose deaths—United States, 2000–2014. *Centers for Disease Control and Prevention.* Retrieved from http://www.cdc.gov/mmwr/preview/mmwrhtml/mm6450a3.htm?s_cid=mm6450a3_w

Schmidt, M. (Oct. 6, 2015). U.S. to release 6,000 inmates from prisons. *New York Times.* Retrieved from http://www.nytimes.com/2015/10/07/us/us-to-release-6000-inmates-under-new-sentencing-guidelines.html?_r=0

Seelye, K. Q. (2016, March 25). *Heroin epidemic is yielding to a deadlier cousin: Fentanyl.* Retrieved from http://www.nytimes.com/2016/03/26/us/heroin-fentanyl.html?emc=edit_th_20160326&nl =todaysheadlines&nlid=33216534Background&_r=0

Sledge, M. (2013, March 25). U.S. drug control strategy a bust, GAO report says. *Huffington Post.* Retrieved from http://www.huffingtonpost.com/2013/04/25/drug-control-strategy-gao_n_3158090.html

Smith, M. D. (2015, October 14). The senate's bipartisan criminal justice reform bill only tackles half the problem. *The Nation.* Retrieved from http://www.thenation.com/article/ the-senates-bipartisan-criminal-justice-reform-bill-only-tackles-half-the-problem

Society of Clinical Psychology. (2016). *Research supported psychological treatments.* Retrieved from http://www.div12.0rg/psychological-treatments/treatment

Substance Abuse and Mental Health Services Administration SAMHSA. (2011). *Scientific research has revolutionized our understanding of drug abuse and addiction.* Retrieved from https://www .samhsa.gov/medlineplus/magazine/issues/fa1111/articles/fa1111pg18.html

Substance Abuse and Mental Health Services Administration SAMHSA. (2015, July 25). *Understanding addiction.* Retrieved from https://www.samhsa.gov/about-addiction/drugs/understanding-addiction

Szalavitz, M. (2016, June 25). Can you get over an addiction? *New York Times.* Retrieved from http:// www.nytimes.com/2016/06/26/opinion/sunday/can-you-get-over-an-addiction.html

Top drug official: The old war on drugs is all wrong. (2015, December 11). *CBS News.* Retrieved from http://www.cbsnews.com/news/60-minutes-top-drug-official-says-the-old-war-on-drugs-is-all-wrong

Weiss, S. (2015, April 10). Major NIH study will examine the effects of drugs on the developing brain. *American Society of Addiction Medicine.* Retrieved from http://www.asam.org/magazine/ read/article/2015/04/10/major-nih-study-will-examine-the-effects-of-drugs-on-the-developing-brain

Wood, S. (2014, June 9). Heroin epidemic: Is it real? *The Inquirer Daily News.* Retrieved from philly .com/philly/news/Heroin_epidemic_Is_it_real.html

Chapter 8

Understanding the Draw of Gangs, Consequences for Neighborhoods, and Determining an Effective Response

The North Side Crew

Chandrika Greene dragged herself to the shower, drenched and exhausted after an extra grueling practice. As tired as she was, she loved those practices and felt like they gave her the stamina she needed during games. Plus, she had to admit, she enjoyed watching a couple of the players who smoked or had attitude have to suck for air. As she showered, she thought about the evening ahead. Her dad would have a hot meal ready when she got home that they would share before he headed off to finish his split shift as a janitor on the west side of Middleton. It would then be up to her to make sure her two younger siblings finished their homework and got to bed, and then there was the algebra test tomorrow that she had barely begun studying for.

Largely oblivious to the chatter in the locker room, Chandrika suddenly heard her name being called and knew, as usual, her two friends were ready and waiting for her. Silvia, Monique, and Chandrika lived in the same apartment complex, about a 12-minute walk from the school if they went the short way. They had walked to and from school together since kindergarten, both for camaraderie and, although they did not like to admit it, for safety.

The wind was biting as they headed down Young Street. They sometimes walked the long way home to avoid the Young/Whitman street intersection known for drug and gang activity. Often, a couple of members from one of the local street gangs, the North Side Crew (NSC), would be hanging out at the corner, regardless of how cold it was, in order to carry out their drug sales. Whether out of some sort of moral code or a pure business decision to avoid unwanted police attention, the NSC gang leader did not allow any sales right after school when a lot of young kids were passing through on their way home. But after four o'clock, business opened up again. Although the girls knew that the gang members would not approach them, they preferred to not hear the catcalls or witness the exchanges of drugs and money. But tonight they wanted to get home and out of the bitter cold as quickly as possible.

As they approached the intersection, they saw five guys gathered at the corner, then suddenly out of nowhere, a car came speeding by and shots rang out. Before the girls knew what happened, Chandrika was on the ground with blood all around her. As Silvia bent over Chandrika, the burning sensation in her arm grew hotter, and she realized she must have been hit by a bullet as well. Hollering and yelling from additional NSC members, who rushed out of a nearby building, went on for about 60 seconds. Then, within minutes, one of them returned with a car and took all three girls to the hospital. This mattered because everyone in the North Side area knew that Chandrika would bleed to death on the street waiting for an ambulance that would respond very slowly—if at all—to a call from that area of the city. An NSC member helped carry Chandrika into the emergency room area and then quickly disappeared.

The bullets that hit both girls had been intended as a payback to the NSC. The girls were, as too often is the case, innocent victims. The bullet that hit Silvia's arm ricocheted off a brick wall, and her wound fortunately was not serious. Two hours and 15 stitches later she was released from the hospital. Chandrika was not so lucky. She was rushed into surgery, and the doctors spent nearly 14 hours working to repair the extensive tissue damage in her abdomen caused by the black talon bullet that basically mushroomed after impact.

It was an NSC gang member who located Chandrika's father at his work to inform him of the incident. Otis Greene knew that leaving in the middle of his shift could easily result in the loss of his job. He had already missed a couple of shifts last month due to health problems of his own and had been warned by the supervisor "that there were plenty of people standing in line for his job." This possibility now concerned him not at all. His daughter was hurt. He was overcome with fear at the thought of not just losing yet another family member to violence but, of all people, Chandrika.

Chandrika and Otis's relationship was exceptionally strong. He did his best not to put too much responsibility on her for running the family, yet often felt guilty for how much he depended on her around the house, including taking care of her two younger twin brothers. Chandrika's mom died shortly after the twins were born, and this had served as a major wake-up call for Otis. Truthfully, up until then, he had largely been an absent parent. His days of drifting from job to job, selling drugs when money got tight, and carousing all night were long behind him. For the last 9 years, he had worked hard to be a responsible parent and protect his children the best that he could. More than anything, he wanted his children to have better opportunities available to them than he felt like he had growing up.

Chandrika, who was extremely agile and quick, had excelled in basketball since an early age and was depending on her hoops skills for her ticket out of the neighborhood. As a sophomore, she had already been contacted by a number of recruiters, including some Division I schools. With an education system inequitably funded by local property taxes and weakened by a magnet school that siphoned off lots of resources and many of the best teachers, her school rated poorly in terms of providing a good college preparatory education. But Chandrika sought out the best teachers in her school, and they gladly worked with her, doing their best to help her build a solid foundation so she would not be totally overwhelmed by the level of work that would be demanded in college courses. The school only had about three dozen outdated computers to be shared by almost 400 students, but one teacher made sure that Chandrika had access to a computer if she arrived at school a half hour early a few days a week so that she could complete a couple of online academic courses, too. Plus, due to her grades and work ethic, she was one of the dozen students at North Side High selected to take one class per semester at the junior college across town.

Otis could not believe that his only daughter, who held so much potential and who had avoided being lured into the sort of self-destructive behaviors he himself had got caught up in as a teen, might be robbed of her life. He loved all three of his kids, but she was the one he pinned his highest hopes on for really "going somewhere big." The thought of losing her was devastating.

Because she was a drive-by gunshot victim, Chandrika was provided with the best care that the Northgate Community Hospital could offer, which sadly was not always the case for low-income residents in the area. By day four, Chandrika was taken out of intensive care, and by the end of the week, she was joking and laughing with friends. Still, the doctors were unsure about the degree of permanent damage to the spinal cord and whether Chandrika would be able to regain full use of her legs. Chandrika, on the other hand, was determined to get back on the court and committed herself to doing everything she could to make it happen. She would not accept the idea of the possibility of life without being able to play basketball. And she knew her college career, and subsequently her future, would be severely jeopardized too if she could not overcome this adversity.

BACKGROUND INFORMATION

Crime, Delinquency, and Gang Involvement: Research, Theory, and Policy

Problem definitions determine policy solutions (Clemons & McBeth, 2009). In other words, regardless of the truth, if we believe that gang membership is simply a bad choice made by rational individuals who do not perceive the cost of that choice as outweighing the benefits, we will derive very different solutions (e.g., tough laws and even tougher penalties) than if we believe that gang membership is a direct reflection of poverty, leading to solutions such as jobs programs. Therefore, we need to explore the theory and research that attempts to explain crime, delinquency, and gang involvement. Theories backed by solid research are more likely to result in effective policies and programs. Before presenting some general theories that are used to explain involvement in gangs and crime and gang research, a definition, as well as the scope of the problem, is laid out.

Defining Gangs and the Scope of Gang Membership

There is no single universal definition of a gang, and there is a lot of variation in types of gangs. For our purposes, we use criteria that are widely accepted among many researchers to define a gang. A gang consists of three or more members, generally aged 12 to 24 (the majority being over 18 years of age), who share a view of themselves as a gang and who are viewed by others as a gang; there is some degree of structure and organization; and the group is involved in criminal activity (National Gang Center, 2016). The U.S. Department of Justice estimated that in 2011 there were approximately 782,500 gang members belonging to 29,900 gangs in the United States (Egley & Howell, 2013).

Between 6% and 8% of gang members are female, approximately 46% are Latino, 35% are African American/Black, and 11% are Caucasian/White (National Gang Center, 2016). We often think of gangs being a problem relegated to inner cities or prisons. Although 85% of gang activity does occur in metropolitan areas in the United States, Arlington County Regional Gang Task Force coordinator, Robert Vilchez, points out that "nobody is immune from this gang problem" (Axelrod, 2015, p. 1). He was making reference to gangs, such as the Bloods and MS-13, who have chapters located in suburbs in the United States.

Since the last major study in 2011, the number of gangs has continued to increase. A 2015 FBI report on gangs states that in half of the jurisdictions that responded to their survey, gang membership had increased in the last 2 years. And in half the jurisdictions, gang-related crimes increased as well (National Gang Intelligence Center, 2015). This latter statistic is not surprising if the findings by

Karl, Hill, Howell, Hawkins, & Battin-Pearson (1999) hold true today. They found that when compared to youth who are not in a gang, gang members are three times as likely to be engaged in selling drugs, twice as likely to carry a gun, and more likely to engage in violent crimes and property crime. A National Youth Gang Analysis reported that approximately 13% of all homicides in the United States in 2012 involved gangs. Moreover, the majority of gang violence is heavily concentrated in the largest cities in the United States (National Gang Center, 2016).

The increase in gang membership and violence has been paralleled with a significant increase in social media use by gangs in the very recent years. "Gangs use a number of sites, applications, and platforms to recruit prospects, facilitate communication, target rivals, and to thwart law enforcement efforts" (National Gang Intelligence Center, 2015, p. 10).

Why Do Youth Join Gangs? Theory and Research

Theory and research provide reasons youth join gangs and subsequently inform us of policy and prevention and remediation programs that can reduce gang involvement. Those who have researched gangs, interacted with gang members, or been part of a gang indicate that while each of the four key theories presented provide us with a partial explanation, an intersection of these theories, along with other factors, provides a more complete picture.

1. Strain theory, based on Emile Durkheim's anomie theory,[1] was developed by Robert Merton. The theory sets forth that people from all socioeconomic classes have similar desires and aspirations in terms of a good paying job, status, and material success. People in the lower socioeconomic classes have the fewest legitimate opportunities to achieve success, and thus experience pressure and *strain* to achieve economic success, often resorting to illegal means to do so. Merton stated, "It is the combination of the cultural emphasis and the social structure which produces intense pressure for deviation" (as cited in O'Connor, 2007, para. 5). *The Godfather* movies (based on Mario Puzo's novel) classically depicted this, as the protagonist was exceptionally bright and ambitious at a time when Italian Americans had very limited social mobility, so he found an arena where he could achieve status and gain power and wealth.

2. Social control theory speaks to the importance of social bonds (ties to the community and the people within it) that prevent individuals from engaging in crime and delinquency. People feel pressure to behave in socially acceptable ways (and criminal behavior is not acceptable) if they have strong bonds with community and family. As are bonds with community, social bonds with family are

---

[1] *Anomie,* a term used in sociology, refers to the personal sense that there is a lack of norms or standards, and it creates instability.

frayed in families that experience persistent poverty. The breaking down of bonds weakens the societal pressures that control our behavior and normally keep us from committing crimes.[2]

3. Differential association theory falls under cultural transmission theories, telling us that crime and delinquency are learned and culturally transmitted through socialization. Youth are socialized by the established norms in their environment regarding acceptable means of behaving. The messages from peers and role models, who for some are older gang members, are especially important as is the frequency, intensity, and duration of the messages. Gang membership, no less than fashion trends (such as baggy pants, tattoos, or gold grills in the mouth), is accordingly seen as learned behavior.[3]

4. Social disorganization theory posits that significant changes, in this case significant loss of decent paying manufacturing jobs that were once held by many inner-city residents, results in disorganization that leads to a breakdown in social rules and norms that inhibit engagement in crime and delinquency.[4]

Theory does drive policy, and too often monocausal explanations are adhered to when the reality is much more complex. Adherents to social control theory might advocate for a get tough approach, while differential association theory and strain theory supporters might argue that sentencing youths to a juvenile facility, or even an alternative school, as punishment may, in fact, increase the strain and anomie, provide them with terrible role models and lessons, and harm their employment chances significantly—all of which may make it more likely they end up in a criminal gang. Both social disorganization theory and strain theory point to the need to address structural issues rather than focusing on individuals as we seek solutions.

A less formal theory that adds a dimension to the four formal theories presented is that many poor youth initially turn to gangs as they feel alienated from society and find little sense of belonging, protection, or connection from the mainstream sources. Once a part of a gang, they are further stigmatized and ostracized (pushed out) by society and no longer seek achievement through, or find support from, acceptable channels. Gangs, needing new members regularly due to expansion, aging, death, and so on, reach out and offer protection, support, and a sort of family feeling (pulling them in). In some ways then, youth join gangs the same way anyone joins a group and for the same reasons (Aho, 2016).

---

[2] Rather than ask why people commit crime, social control theorists ask why people don't commit crime. Weiss and Hirchi are two theorists who are credited with developing social control theories.

[3] Edward Sutherland is the founding theorist for differential association theory, which posits that criminal behavior is learned.

[4] Social disorganization theory had its beginnings in the Chicago School of Sociologists and was first used to explain the relationship between an organism and its environment. In the 1990s, it was used to explain the relationship between what was perceived as failed social institutions and their relationship to the incidence of criminal activity.

Longitudinal studies provide insight into factors relating to gang involvement. Many of these factors tie directly into the four formal theories presented above. A sense of fellowship, needing a place to hang out, identity, self-expression, wanting to fit in, a need for protection from living in fear, prestige/social status, freedom, and the appeal of excitement, for example, sex and parties, are factors that come into play. There is often a great deal of peer pressure, including intimidation, threats, and harassment. If children live in a neighborhood with lots of negative influences such as peers often getting into trouble, lots of drug activity, high crime, and violence, they are likely to be more prone to gang involvement, especially if added to those factors are lack of supervision, structure, and guardian concern, for example, excessive permissiveness, parent engaged in drug activity or other criminal behaviors, and lack of success at school.

Whereas poverty itself is not necessarily a risk factor, the gross disparity between what others have and what youth see as available for them to attain leads to feeling alienated and disenfranchised. This, coupled with the allure of making money through gang involvement when no satisfying jobs are perceived to be available, is a key reason for many youth to join a gang (Esbensen, Peterson, Taylor, & Freng, 2009; Gangfree, 2008; Karl et al., 1999; Vigil, 2003; Violence Prevention Institute, n.d.; Wood & Huffman, 1999). The higher the number of risk factors, the higher the likelihood a youth will choose to join a gang.

Stanley Tookie Williams, cofounder and leader of the Crips until his imprisonment for murder, shed light on his reasons for gang involvement in an interview with Amy Goodman of *Democracy Now* while he was on death row. "Thuggery was all I knew. I lived it. I breathed it. Being a Crip was all I knew. I thought there was nothing else. I dreaded life after Cripping. I dreaded that." (*Democracy Now,* 2005, para. 51).[5] Many of the above-mentioned risk factors are ones Williams experienced. His mom, 17 years old when she gave birth to him, had to go it alone after his father abandoned them when Tookie was 1 year old. She moved from New Orleans to California when he was 6 in hopes of providing a better life. Despite his mom's efforts, aspects of the environment Tookie was exposed to were toxic. Starting at a fairly young age, he hung out on the streets with delinquent peers, often skipped school, and regularly observed criminal activity. It was the norm to see adults using drugs and engaging in all types of gambling, including dogfighting and betting on the young boys they made fight each other. "I learned from the street culture that criminal activity was an economic necessity and violence a means to a desired end. Plain and simple, in my neighborhood, if you wanted something, you had to take it—and then fight to keep it" (Williams, 2007, pp. 4–5).

---

[5] Williams was executed in the State of California in December 2005. He had committed many crimes during his life but to the end maintained his innocence for the murders he was executed for.

In prison, Tookie Williams had a major change of heart and mind. He became a voice for trying to keep youth from getting involved in gangs. He wrote books that spoke out against violence and gangs. In the 2005 *Democracy Now* interview, shortly before he was executed, he concluded with "I say to any individual who is in a gang that if you have enough courage to get into a gang, you should have equally enough or even more to get out of it" (*Democracy Now,* 2005, para. 51).

Ethnographic studies (observing first hand and asking questions directly) of gangs also reinforce and add to some of the factors noted thus far on why youth join gangs. Two such studies are *Code of the Street* by Elijah Anderson (1999) and *Gang Leader for a Day* by Sudhir Venkatesh (2008). Both spent a great deal of time over an extended period getting to know and interacting with people in high poverty inner-city neighborhoods, including gang members.

Venkatesh and especially Anderson speak of the draw of joining gangs as, in part, being a consequence of persistent urban poverty and joblessness, which results in some people in high-poverty environments feeling an intense sense of alienation from mainstream society; they have no legitimate means to acquire goals highly regarded in our society—success, money, and material possessions. Not having the opportunity to function and achieve societal goals through mainstream norms may cause some individuals to adapt by living by what Anderson (1999) refers to as the "code of the street." In other words, a street culture emerges as a result of the street realities. Mainstream institutions, such as family, school, and the judicial system, that help ensure social control (resulting in individuals abiding by mainstream rules) have failed to some degree in some neighborhoods. In such neighborhoods, poverty makes families less stable, schools do not meet student needs, and police are not trusted.[6] Some youth spend a great deal of time on the streets learning from what they witness. They are socialized on the street, and some adopt behavioral and attitudinal traits needed to survive on those streets.[7] Survival requires living by the code of the street. Even if this is just a perception (i.e., that safety and success are not possible via so-called legitimate routes), it is a logical perception, and we act on the basis of our perceptions. After all, it is the only way we know the world.

Moreover, this code is marked by the importance of gaining respect on the streets, which consequently results in social capital, recognition, approval, and protection—all

---

[6] Social control theory speaks to the importance of social bonds that prevent individuals from engaging in crime and delinquency. Social bonds with family are also frayed in families that experience persistent poverty.

[7] Differential association theory falls under cultural transmission theories that tell us that crime and delinquency are learned and culturally transmitted through socialization. Youth are socialized by the established norms in their environment regarding acceptable means of behaving. The messages from peers and role models, who for some are older gang members, are especially important as are the frequency, intensity, and duration of the messages.

basic needs sought by all human beings. The code entails unwritten rules that govern how people behave and interact, including how to respond if challenged. In this world, engaging in illegal means to survive economically through the selling of drugs, prostitution, working the books, and other cottage industries, legal and illegal, is acceptable. Violence is permissible, and the code actually provides a rationale for those who instigate violent encounters; however, the code also governs the use of violence. Both fear of retaliation for snitching and a lack of faith that police will engage in a helpful manner lead residents to choose not to even notify police and to refuse to testify at hearings. Crimes go unreported and unsolved, enabling gang members to get away with crimes, turning this aspect of the code into a sort of self-fulfilling prophecy. On the other hand, it may actually be gang leaders who are looked to for things such as keeping some order, ensuring the safety of some of the people in the neighborhood, or giving money to a youth center (Venkatesh, 2008).

It is important to keep in mind that the majority of youth who live in inner-city, low-income areas do not engage in delinquency or join gangs, but instead they attempt to live by general society's dominant societal values. Still, in many areas where gangs are prevalent, nongang members are well aware of the code of the street and at times must live by it to avoid physical harm.

Assessment, Prevention, Intervention, and Suppression

The National Gang Center (2016) states that "gangs and gang violence has become increasingly complex, lethal, and resistant to prevention and control over the years." The Office of Juvenile Justice, which created the National Gang Center, supports the Community Based Violence Prevention Initiative that draws from evidence-based practices across the United States as well as public health research findings. The four-pronged community-based approach of effective antigang strategies include

> targeted suppression of youth who commit the most serious and chronic offenses; intervention with youthful gang members; prevention efforts for youth identified as being at high risk of entering a gang; and implementation of programs that address risk and protective factors and targets the entire population in high-crime, high-risk areas. Additional public health research conducted over the last decade shows success in those programs, which have focused on not only managing incidents of serious youth violence and gang violence, but also those that include proactive interventions to prevent further retaliatory acts of youth or gang violence. (U.S. Department of Justice, n.d., para. 5)

In regard to an overall approach, interventions need to be community specific and involve youth (Karl et al., 1999; Malec, 2003). Theory, logic, and experience suggest that a collaborative, multifaceted approach that entails a coordinated effort, including businesses, schools, community groups, religious institutions, health care, family, social services, and volunteers, is needed to successfully address the issue. Schools, community members, and other groups need to work as a united front (Pace, 2010).

CHANDRIKA AND OTIS: MOVING FORWARD

During the first few months after leaving the hospital, Chandrika's focus was on getting her life back to normal or, more accurately, finding her new normal. There was physical therapy twice a week, and not only was progress painstakingly slow, but some of the sessions were more demanding than the basketball practices she thought were killers. She still needed a crutch 12 weeks after the shooting, but her range of motion and strength were returning, and her doctors now believed that a basketball scholarship to a Division I university was once again a possibility.

Added to the physical challenges were the psychological issues Chandrika was struggling with. The second night home from the hospital Chandrika started having nightmares, and many nights she would wake up screaming. Fears about her own personal safety and that of her twin brothers had greatly intensified. She often wondered if she would ever be able to leave the house again without feeling extremely scared and anxious. The medical social worker at the hospital had mentioned to Chandrika that she might want to consider seeking counseling to deal with the trauma she had experienced. While in the hospital, Chandrika shrugged off the suggestion, but after 2 weeks of nightmares decided it was time to pull out the list of social workers and counselors she had been provided with.

Two weeks after calling Stellar and Associates, a local clinical social work agency, Chandrika showed up for her first appointment. She felt comfortable with Jeremiah within a few minutes of meeting him. His greeting was warm and friendly, and he followed it up with "So, it sounds like you're just hoping you'll luck out and get a good social worker. The receptionist told me you were willing to go with whoever had the first opening."

Chandrika was surprised to hear herself joke back, saying, "I figure I just won't return if I don't like you."

"Definitely your call. This is about you, and my role is to assist you," Jeremiah said in a more serious tone before telling Chandrika just enough about his professional experience to put her further at ease. Jeremiah paused for a second, and without being asked, Chandrika launched into one of the primary reasons she was seeking help. Twenty-five minutes later, Chandrika realized she had surprised herself for the second time this session with how open she was being. She appreciated that Jeremiah just listened. She was tired of people trying to console her or feeling bad for her. Plus, she figured sharing her fears with Jeremiah wasn't going to increase his fears as she thought might be the case with her friends. She said for a second time, "Violence has been all around me my whole life. In the past year alone there have been four deaths in my neighborhood. Besides the murders, there have been at least a dozen injuries from gunshots, mostly rival gangs shooting at each other. Then there are the brutal beatings I hear about. And I've seen more than a few girls about my age who have been beaten up by boyfriends who are in gangs. Although gunfire is a regular occurrence, until I got shot I would have said that neither I nor my family or my friends were going to be killed by gunfire. Now I live in constant fear, asking myself who among us will be next."

Chandrika didn't get why she had opened up so readily or why she felt understood, but Jeremiah's nonverbal communication left her feeling reassured that he got it, at least to some degree. Before the session ended, Jeremiah talked with her about trauma and posttraumatic stress and ways that they would work on countering her paralyzing feelings. She left thinking that at least she was not totally losing it. Once home, she made a list of other issues she wanted to talk to Jeremiah about that she hadn't gotten to. High on the list was the anger she felt as well as the sense of loss. Also, she was now very worried her younger brothers would consider joining a gang for protection. There were so many thoughts swirling around in her head, and Chandrika had a hunch they would interfere with her being able to play Division I ball more than any physical limitation. She knew how to work hard to improve physically, but she wasn't sure how to get her head on straight.

Sessions with Jeremiah continued to be helpful, and Chandrika particularly liked the variation of cognitive behavior therapy he used. The nightmares were still there but not as constant. The exercises Jeremiah gave her, and journaling, seemed to be helping. She felt less angry. The anxiety was still fairly intense at times but overall better.

About a month and a half into working with Jeremiah, Chandrika shared her desire to get involved in making changes so that residents in her neighborhood would feel safer. "Dad and I have been talking, and we both want to do something. I know I still need to work on my own anxiety and fears, but I feel I need to think bigger than myself. My neighborhood has a lot of problems, but it's still my neighborhood, and the families who live here, including mine, can't just pack up and move to a safer neighborhood. I want to do something. I just am not sure what that is."

They processed her desire to get involved for a bit, then moved on to other issues. The next session when Chandrika brought up getting involved again, Jeremiah's response caught her a little off guard, as he had never talked about himself. "I lost my little brother to gangs about 10 years ago and went through a pretty dark period.

I came from a pretty rough neighborhood, too, and was fed up with the attitude of too many that 'this is just the way it is here.' I found some folks who wanted to make a difference, and ended up immersing myself for 5 years in gang prevention efforts. I quit only when I moved to Middleton 3 years ago. I know there are a couple of groups in Middleton working on violence prevention. A key focus of one group is on mentoring. When, and if, you want, I can connect you with the leaders of the groups if you want to find out more about what they're doing. I didn't bring this up sooner as I needed to make sure I wasn't encouraging you to seek out something that was just a passing thought, but clearly you want to get engaged. The groups might not focus on exactly what you want to do, but the people I'll connect you with can likely help you figure out exactly what you're interested in and what is feasible given your already full schedule."

"That would be awesome, Jeremiah. I have no grand illusions that we'll eliminate gangs and violence in my neighborhood, but I do think we can make a positive difference and make the neighborhood a little safer. My dad, Monique, and Sylvia are all committed to getting involved, too, and I want to figure out what will help keep the twins from joining a gang. What's great is that my dad is respected by the average law-abiding neighbor, as well as by many of the NSC members. I don't quite get how he walks that line, but he does. Anyway, how can I get in touch with these groups?"

QUESTIONS FOR DISCUSSION

1. Provide a definition for the term *gang,* and provide statistics on the number of youth involved in gangs.

2. Discuss four theoretical explanations for why youth join gangs. Provide your perspective on which theory, or what aspects from different theories, are most useful in explaining this phenomenon.

3. Discuss the "code of the street" and its implications for the behavior of individuals involved in gangs.

4. What insights do theory and research shed on understanding why youth become involved in gangs? How do these insights help inform you in determining how to address the issue?

5. If you were to develop a program to address youth violence in your community, how would you go about it? You are not being asked for a detailed plan, but you should provide an overall approach and strategy as well as a few tactics. What additional information do you need to fully develop an effective

program? What social work skills are needed to both develop the program and implement the program?

6. What are the key challenges communities face when attempting to address gang violence?

7. As a way to reduce gang violence, there is federal and some state legislation that allows for tougher penalties for criminal acts committed by gang members. More states are considering such measures (http://www.nij.gov/topics/crime/gangs/pages/prosecution.aspx). Given that the difficulty is knowing with certainty whether the offender is connected to a gang, how effective do you think this legislation might be in reducing gang violence?

8. Might legislation that enhances the penalty for violent crimes be effective in reducing gang related crime? Explain your answer.

9. What other types of legislation might result in fewer youth joining gangs in the future?

CASE ANALYSIS WRITING ASSIGNMENT

1. Read the assigned case study thoroughly prior to class in order to be fully prepared to join in the discussion.

2. Write an analysis in which you set forth what you believe is the best course of action for Middleton regarding addressing gang violence. Your analysis should clearly indicate which theoretical explanation(s), set forth in the case, informs your approach. Also, make sure that the course of action reflects research findings on why youth become involved in gangs and ideas from the intervention plans in other communities that are highlighted in the case.

3. The analysis should be an approximately two- to two-and-a-half-page, typed, double-spaced essay. Your essay should reflect the standards and expectations of college-level writing: spelling, grammar, and appropriate use of paragraphs all matter. If you quote directly from the case study, use quotation marks, and at the end of the quote, indicate the page number the quote appeared on. For example, "The U.S. Department of Justice estimated that in 2011 there were approximately 782,500 gang members belonging to 29,900 in the United States" (Egley & Howell, 2013, as cited in Lewis, 2015, p. 6).

4. Your case analysis is due _____ and worth a maximum of ____ points.

INTERNET SOURCES

Department of Justice, Office of Juvenile Justice and Delinquency Prevention (http://www.ojjdp.gov/programs/antigang)

Federal Bureau of Investigation: National Gang Intelligence Center (https://www.fbi.gov/about-us/investigate/vc_majorthefts/gangs/ngic)

National Gang Center (www.nationalgangcenter.gov)

National Institute of Justice (https://www.crimesolutions.gov/OJPResearch .aspx?Research_id=6)

Prevention Institute (http://www.preventioninstitute.org/focus)

Youth.gov (http://youth.gov/feature-article/gang-prevention-overview-research-and-programs)

REFERENCES

Aho, J. (2016). *Far-right fantasy: A sociology of American religion and politics.* New York, NY: Routledge.

Anderson, E. (1999). *Code of the street: Decency, violence and the moral life of the inner city.* New York, NY: W. W. Norton.

Axelrod, T. (2015, March 6). Gang violence is on the rise, even as overall violence declines. *U.S. News and World Report.* Retrieved from http://www.usnews.com/news/articles/2015/03/06/gang-violence-is-on-the-rise-even-as-overall-violence-declines

Clemons, R., & McBeth, M. (2009). *Public policy praxis: A case approach for understanding policy and analysis* (2nd ed.). New York, NY: Pearson, Longman.

Democracy Now. (2005, November 30). *A conversation with death row prisoner Stanley Tookie Williams from his San Quentin cell.* Retrieved from http://www.democracynow .org/2005/11/30/a_conversation_with_death_row_prisoner

Egley, A., Jr., & Howell J. C. (2013, September). Juvenile justice fact sheet. *U.S. Department of Justice.* Retrieved from http://www.ojjdp.gov/pubs/242884.pdf

Esbensen, F., Peterson, D., Taylor, T., & Freng, A. (2009). Similarities and differences in risk factors for violent offending and gang membership. *The Australian and New Zealand Journal of Criminology, 42*(3), 310–335.

Gangfree. (2008). *Why people join gangs.* Retrieved from http://www.gangfree.org/gangs_why.html

Karl, G., Hill, J., Howell, J., Hawkins, D., & Battin-Pearson, S. (1999). Childhood risk factors for adolescent gang membership. *Journal of Research in Crime and Delinquency, 36*(300).

Malec, D. (2003). Transforming Latino gang violence in the United States peace review. *A Journal of Social Justice, 18,* 81–89.

National Gang Center. (2016). *National youth gang survey analysis.* Retrieved from https://www.nationalgangcenter.gov/Survey-Analysis/Measuring-the-Extent-of-Gang-Problems# homicidesnumber

National Gang Intelligence Center. (2015). *FBI 2015 national gang report.* Retrieved from https://www.fbi.gov/stats-services/publications/national-gang-report-2015.pdf

O'Connor, T. (2007). *Strain theories of crime.* Retrieved from http://www.drtomoconnor.com/1060/10601ect06.htm

Pace, P. (2010). Workshops tackle gang recruitment. *NASW News, 55*(7), 1, 8.

U.S. Department of Justice. (n.d.). *Comprehensive anti-gang initiative.* Retrieved from http://www.ojjdp.gov/programs/antigang

Venkatesh, S. (2008). *Gang leader for a day: A rogue sociologist takes to the streets.* New York, NY: Penguin Press.

Vigil, J. (2003). Urban violence and street gangs. *Annual Review of Anthropology, 32,* 225–242.

Violence Prevention Institute. (n.d.). *General reasons for gang membership.* Retrieved from http://www.violencepreventioninstitute.com/youngpeople

Williams, S. (2007). *Black rage, black redemption: A memoir.* New York, NY: Touchstone

Wood, S., & Huffman, J. (1999). Preventing gang activity and violence in schools. *Contemporary Education, 71*(1).

Chapter 9

Eminent Domain, Urban Renewal, and NIMBY

Is There a Win-Win Solution?

Ty and Gabrielle Stevens plopped down in the swinging chair on their back porch, emotionally exhausted after yet another gathering with some of their neighbors on Ellwood Avenue in the Bethel Park neighborhood of Middleton. It had been very muggy and hot for the past several weeks so the cool breeze that came up that evening was especially refreshing. The porch had always been one of their favorite places to relax at the end of the day. Yet this relaxed setting masked an underlying source of tension for the couple. One month earlier, the Stevenses had received word that the city wanted to purchase their property and the properties of 24 other homeowners on the north side of Ellwood Avenue. The problem was that the Stevenses, and some of their neighbors, had no interest in selling. While their house was modest and not worth a lot monetarily, Ty and Gabi had grown to love the area, and they could not imagine leaving a home so filled with memories of life with their children and friends.

The Stevenses had grown up in different sections of Middleton, and although they had heard of each other, since the high schools they each ran cross-country for were archrivals, they did not meet until they landed at Newburg College in 1982, where they also ran cross-country. This time, instead of running for competing teams, they were on the same side. The men's and women's cross-country teams often trained together, and many of the runners, including Ty and Gabrielle, hung out together outside of practice. Their junior year they started officially dating. Following graduation, Gabrielle left for a 2-year stint in the Peace Corps while Ty, a journalism major, was hired by the *Mid-Times* newspaper.

Gabrielle did not know if she ever wanted to settle down and raise a family, whereas Ty had more conventional plans for their life together. She envisioned putting her public health degree to use working abroad for some nongovernmental organization (NGO) that addressed women's health issues. Ty had been devastated when Gabrielle left for Zambia and could not imagine or appreciate the life for which Gabi yearned. Still, he was not about to give up on the relationship, and decided to visit her in the village of Golvina, Zambia, where she was working. Through Gabi, Ty had been able to connect with an NGO in the area and signed up to volunteer for a month, during which time he wrote several human-interest stories for the *Mid-Times*. He was overwhelmed by the hospitality and warmth of the villagers. They possessed little in terms of material goods but seemed genuinely happy, and the value they placed on human relationships and community impressed Ty. To his own surprise, he found himself wanting to do some international service work. And he figured he could put his journalism skills to further use by writing about some of his experiences in developing areas of the world.

Over the next 6 years, Gabi and Ty worked for three organizations in two different countries. Surprisingly to both of them, it was Gabi who started talking about returning to Middleton to settle down and raise a family. Of course, the job offer by Olapha strongly influenced this decision. Olapha was an international women's health organization whose headquarters were in Middleton. Gabi could spend most of her time in Middleton and also travel periodically to Olapha's health clinics located abroad. Ty was ready to be back in the United States close to his family and figured he would travel with Gabi when circumstances allowed but looked forward to returning to a part-time position at the newspaper and continuing his freelance work.

Taking advantage of a first-time homeowner's loan, and the generosity of Ty's mom, who helped with the down payment, they purchased a somewhat rundown house on Ellwood Avenue. Little by little, they molded it into a comfortable home. They had resided there for 18 years and raised three children in that home. They loved the strong sense of community within the Bethel Park neighborhood and were really saddened when they received notice that the city wanted to acquire their property.

"Damn developers," Gabi muttered as Ty sat beside her sipping a beer. "How many more specialty shops and eateries can this area support anyway?"

Ty had heard these frustrations voiced by Gabi and his neighbors repeatedly over the past few weeks. Their home was situated near Market Avenue, which in recent years had become the favorite site for experimental urban renewal by ambitious Middleton business and political leaders. The progress associated with these redevelopment efforts, including the start-up of some unique local businesses, had produced both benefits and costs to local residents. Market Avenue was slowly becoming one of the hip areas of the city. But now the process of urban renewal had landed, quite literally, in the Stevenses' backyard.

"I don't believe that taking out more homes for the expansion of yet more retail shops is going to pay off," she continued. "The city backers of this plan have fallen for their own slick propaganda campaign. As far as I'm concerned, they've provided no convincing arguments."

After years of being happily married to a rabble rouser, Ty knew better than to interrupt Gabi when she got on one of these rants. Gabi's passion for big causes had always fascinated and attracted Ty, who tended to maintain a slight detachment about such issues, perhaps based on his observational instincts as a journalist. Now their home and their neighborhood was the cause. He could tell Gabi was steeling herself for battle.

"And the upscale condominiums Hartford Developers want to build are not going to fit into the neighborhood, or what's going to be left of it anyway," Gabi said. "Hartford Developers only care about making a buck for themselves, and that is all. They don't care one iota about what is good for Middleton and its residents."

Similar sentiments had been expressed over and over in the past few weeks, as Gabi had become the unofficial leader of the neighborhood opposition to the latest renewal initiative. More and more evenings were being devoted to community gatherings, where beer and backyard barbeques provided the backdrop for Gabi to mobilize her forces in preparation to defend the neighborhood from the impersonal forces of change. Yet Ty wondered, privately, if the proverbial effort to "fight City Hall" would end in inevitable defeat.

BACKGROUND INFORMATION

The framers of the U.S. Constitution viewed eminent domain, the power of the state to acquire private property for "public use" without the consent of the property owner, an inherent power that did not need to be explicitly stated in the Constitution (Jost, 2005). "The government recognized that, on occasion, private interests must give way where the greater good is concerned, even when this means compromising one party's private property interests so that another's may dominate" (Main, 2005, para. 4). Also recognized was the need to pay for the property seized. A key provision for the use of eminent domain is set forth in the Fifth Amendment of the Bill of Rights, which states, "Nor shall private property be taken for public use, without just compensation" (clear evidence that the Framers wanted government to have this power). In circumstances where the federal, state, or local government uses its authority to acquire private property for "public use," fair market value of the property (just compensation) must be paid. Another limitation on the state's right of eminent domain is that land cannot be seized for the sole purpose of transferring it from one private citizen to another for a private purpose. Instead, it is to be for the "public good."

In this section we look at how eminent domain was used in earlier times in the United States and how it is being used today, as well persistent opposition to its use. There has been no shortage of lawsuits, and some of the major court decisions, along with the current debate surrounding the use of eminent domain, are touched upon. This will lead to some insights as to the possible future of eminent domain.

Historical Overview of Use of Eminent Domain and Court Cases in the "Early" Years

The traditional use of eminent domain in the 1800s and early 1900s was largely, but not totally, the taking of private land for facilitating transportation (railroads, roads, canals, and bridges), public utilities, the supply of water, national defense/security projects, building schools and other public buildings, preserving historical sites, and establishing parks. Once land was acquired by the state, private developers often carried out the projects deemed to be for public use. It appears quite evident that eminent domain allowed the state to provide for the public use of land in a wide array of activities, including safeguarding national interests and furthering the existence of the state. Yet public use is a contested value, and opposition to eminent domain spurred many lawsuits, some of which made it to the U.S. Supreme Court.

In these cases, the Supreme Court had to determine if the authority of the state met constitutional muster. That is, did the taking of private land meet the public use and just compensation requirements? The *Kohl v. United States* (1875) ruling found the state within the bounds of the Constitution in supporting the condemning of property in order to build a post office, customs house, and other public buildings. In *Sharp v. United States* (1903), the court ruled in favor of the state in their acquisition of land for "fortifications and works of defense"; and in *United States v. Great Falls Manufacturing Company* (1884), the court ruled in favor of the state's constitutional right to use eminent domain to secure land to build aqueducts needed for safe drinking water (Legal Information Institute, n.d.).

These are just a few examples of key U.S. Supreme Court cases where public use may appear clear-cut, but there were always various degrees of ambiguity. In fact, in the 1905 *Clark v. Nash* case, the U.S. Supreme Court ruled that varying circumstances throughout the country would affect the definition of public use. The specific case they were ruling on had to do with the constitutionality of a farmer expanding an irrigation ditch across the property of another farmer, as it was the only way for him to be able to water his crops. This use of eminent domain was ruled to be constitutional in this circumstance. Similarly, in the state-level court decision in the *Boston and Roxbury Mill Corporation v. Newman* case (Main, 2005), the court ruled it was constitutional for a landowner to build a dam that flooded upstream neighbors as long as the neighbors were justly compensated. The rationale for this was that landowners needed the dams to generate power at their mills to grist their corn, which was then put on the market for public use. Furthermore, while the grist mills were privately owned, there were government oversight and fees (Main, 2005).

Eminent Domain and Urban Renewal

Although in earlier times eminent domain did indeed transfer private property to private ownership and benefited some property owners over others, it was the 1954 *Berman v. Parker* Supreme Court case that led some critics to conclude that the power of the state to use eminent domain was being taken beyond the scope of the intent of the framers of the Constitution. In this case, the U.S. Supreme Court upheld the constitutionality of The District of Columbia Redevelopment Act of 1945, which used eminent domain. A comprehensive plan had been developed to clean up and revitalize a "blighted" area of Washington, DC. The property acquired through eminent domain was to be used for commercial purposes with private developers constructing condominiums, private office buildings, and a shopping center. Thousands of homes and businesses were demolished, and while some of the housing destroyed included substandard housing, some questioned just how blighted all of the bulldozed property actually was (Jost, 2005). More important, it displaced residents who were mainly renters, so they got no compensation, had limited financial means, and were left to fend for themselves.

Also of significance in the *Berman v. Parker* (1954) case was the Supreme Court ruling that properties that were not blighted could be taken for redevelopment efforts if necessary. Moreover, the definition of "blight" in many state laws is extremely vague and subjective. Property does not need to be dilapidated, boarded up, in crime-ridden neighborhoods, or not up to building codes to be deemed blighted. In fact, a nice middle-class dwelling can fall under the label of blighted (Kokot, 2011). For example, in the past decade in Lakewood, Ohio, in an area the city sought for redevelopment homes, not having a two-car attached garage, having less than two full bathrooms, or less than three full bedrooms fell under the legal definition of blighted (Leung, 2009).

On the heels of the DC Redevelopment Act was the federal Housing Act of 1949, which, in a similar fashion, led the way to the widespread use of eminent domain during the urban renewal period of the 1950s and 1960s. While the stated goal of the Housing Act was "a decent home and suitable living environment for every American," the reality was far different (Leung, 2009). The Housing Act led to large-scale government-funded demolishing of blighted urban areas, displacing tens of thousands of residents, mainly poor and ethnic/racial minorities. Eminent domain was used as needed to secure properties; then redevelopment companies went to work.

Entire neighborhoods were bulldozed in the name of renewing cities by making room for upscale shops, eateries, entertainment establishments, ballparks, mixed office buildings, and new housing. The vast majority of the new condominiums and upscale housing were far out of the reach of those with low incomes who had their living quarters destroyed. Residents not only lost their homes but also the support they got from neighbors. As Jane Jacobs so persuasively pointed out, whole neighborhoods were destroyed, and in doing so, the very fabric of what is important for a vibrant society was ripped apart (Jacobs, 1961). On the other hand, many amenities such as San Francisco's Yerba Buena Park, Skyland Shopping Center in Washington, DC, Dudley Street Neighborhood Initiative in Boston, and the Kansas City Speedway have led to hundreds of millions of dollars' worth of commercial and retail investment, as well as mixed private-public developments such as Baltimore's Inner Harbor (Dreher & Echeverria, 2006). This smattering of examples demonstrates the positive results from the uses of eminent domain as a tool for urban renewal. Eminent domain has provided cities with a means to attract businesses, residents, and tourists to their communities, helping their cities and their residents survive economically.

Current Controversy Over Eminent Domain

As always, the devil is in the details, which, in the case of eminent domain, rests in large part on the interpretation of public use. There are those who claim that over time the definition has broadened while others claim that public use has always entailed a broad range of "public purposes" and "public benefits." As noted, critics argue that with a few key rulings in the second half of the 20th century, the U.S. Supreme Court went beyond the intent of the Founding Fathers. Today, the controversy remains as to the circumstances where the use of eminent domain can be considered constitutional. The two broad views are that (1) eminent domain "requires either public ownership or public access such as a post office, airport, or highway," or that (2) "eminent domain can be justified for any private use so long as the taking ostensibly produces a general public benefit" (Kelly, 2005, p. 2). The latter view allows for the land taken to be used by private developers to build stadiums, shopping centers, luxury condominiums, factories, and other private sector uses.

These differing perspectives are evident in recent court cases. In 2004, Wayne County, Michigan, attempted to use eminent domain for the development of a business, technology, and industrial park and services for the park such as a conference center. Although most of the property owners whose land was sought voluntarily sold their property, there were a few holdouts who sued. Despite the county's argument that the new facilities would be significant in terms of job creation generating revenue, thus providing a public benefit, the Supreme Court of Michigan ruled that in this case, *County of Wayne v. Hatchcock* (Somin, 2004), the proposed taking of private property for private economic development did not meet the criteria of public use and was therefore not constitutional (Somin, 2004). This decision overturned the infamous Michigan Supreme Court ruling in the 1981 *Poletown Neighborhood Council v. City of Detroit* case in which the court deemed the use of eminent domain constitutional (Michigan Municipal League, 2004).

The *Poletown* decision has been called infamous because it allowed for the uprooting of over 3,000 residents and the destruction of churches and businesses, in what was considered a stable and diverse neighborhood, so that the city could sell to General Motors city property General Motors wanted to build on. Given that there were eight other potential undeveloped sites in Poletown that the city had identified as potential land for the General Motors site that would not have led to large-scale displacement, the court ruling resulted in significant criticism. Namely, the concern was that private parties were the beneficiaries of eminent domain, and this was an abuse of state power (Bird, 2010). Moreover, some critics concluded that the *Poletown* decision resulted in more economic harm than good given that less than half of the 6,000 promised jobs by GM came to fruition (Somin, 2004).

Another court case worthy of mention is *Kelo v. City of New London* (2005). This case put a high-powered spotlight on the issue of eminent domain, and a growing number of citizens in the general public became aware of its use. In 2005, the U.S. Supreme Court ruled in the *Kelo* case that private property could be condemned and given to private developers for the purpose of economic development. The city of New London, Connecticut, had established a comprehensive redevelopment plan that entailed the taking of private property and transferring it to Pfizer Pharmaceutical. Pfizer promised to build a plant projected to create over 3,000 jobs and bring in well over a million dollars per year in tax revenues, both of which were much needed (Jost, 2005). Thus, eminent domain was interpreted as meeting the public use clause. In this 5–4 decision, John Paul Stevens, voting with the majority, wrote that promoting economic development is a traditional and long-accepted function of government, while Sandra Day O'Connor voiced in her dissent that the beneficiaries are those with power and money, and the small property owner really has no options (John Paul Stevens on Environment, 2012; Lane, 2005). The end of this story is that Kelo, the plaintiff for whom the case was named, had her home picked up and relocated, and she and the other plaintiffs received generous compensation packages, but for some that was not their preference. In addition, the area that was to be the Pfizer plant is an empty lot, as the developer never came through with the necessary funding.

Many viewed the *Kelo* decision as a misinterpretation of the Fifth Amendment, far exceeding the Founders' intent when it comes to the power of eminent domain. And this led to significant backlash. Property rights advocates, who had picked up support in the 1990s, gained momentum, and within about 5 years, 43 states had taken constitutional or legislative action intended to limit the use of eminent domain. The laws varied greatly from state to state, with some states having much stronger property rights protections and some states implementing only small reforms (Institute of Justice, 2010).

In the last decade, there has been no shortage of cases where property owners believe their rights are being violated or they are not being granted fair compensation. In 2014, the Casino Reinvestment Development Authority (CRDA) wanted to acquire private property for development. They had a holdout, an older gentleman who used part of his home for a workshop and rented out the top two stories. He argued that the CRDA didn't even have a detailed plan for how they would use his property, and therefore he should not have to sell what had been his parents' home. A New Jersey judge ruled that the CRDA, "charged with developing the gambling and tourism industries in Atlantic City, had broad leeway to exercise eminent domain and could take the property if it felt there would be a better use that would enhance the city" (Berger, 2014, para. 2). The owner didn't give up, and in 2015 the same judge, who nine months earlier had voted in favor of the CRDA, reversed his ruling and determined the authority could not use eminent domain to take possession of the property. The ruling resulted from reviewing the situation and discovering that two casinos nearby had closed and that there were no immediate plans for the property the CRDA was trying to secure through eminent domain (Hollingsworth, 2015).

Another New Jersey case dragged on for over 10 years before a settlement was finally reached in 2013. In 2002, the Mount Holly Township declared a 30-acre area, Mount Holly Gardens neighborhood, blighted. There were issues of crowding, vacant homes, and crime (Oyez Project, 2015). The area contained 329 row houses, most of which were owned by low-income and minority residents. The developer was planning to replace the row houses with far more housing than currently existed. Only 56 of the units were to be low-income housing, leaving the price for the majority of new units way out of the price range of most who wanted to remain in the area (Wang, 2012). The holdouts filed a suit in 2003 that they lost and then another in 2008 claiming violation of the Fair Housing Act (FHA). A lower court ruled for the township, stating discrimination under the FHA was not shown. A higher court then ruled in favor of the plaintiffs, but plaintiffs were prepared to appeal to the Supreme Court (Oyez Project, 2015). In 2008, Mount Holly started playing hardball to get the remaining residents to leave, including ripping up sidewalks; cutting electricity to street lights, leaving the streets dark at night; reducing public services such as trash collection; and even demolishing row homes that still had occupants living in the houses connected to them, causing damage to the occupied homes (Wang, 2012). The case was dismissed when the parties settled out of court in 2013 (Oyez Project, 2015). Before the settlement costs were figured in, Mount Holly Township was in debt $18 million for development that had not yet started (Wang, 2012).

Where Do We Go From Here?

Reaching agreement on the central point of contention with eminent domain—the correct interpretation of public use—is likely to continue to elude policy makers. The *Kelo* case and other high-profile examples of property owners being left with no option but to sell have fueled the anger of property rights advocates and influenced policy makers. One can understand the opposition to the use of eminent domain for economic development. Certainly, there are cases where it appears the state could have more aggressively pursued alternative options or made certain the promised benefits would be significant and come to fruition.

On the other hand, what is often overlooked are the many examples, such as those listed previously, demonstrating the significant economic gains (the public good or public benefit) that cities have achieved through the use of eminent domain (Dreher & Echeverria, 2006). Based on their research of the use of eminent domain for economic development, Robert Dreher and John Echeverria (2006), writing for Georgetown Environmental Law and Policy Institute and Georgetown University Law Center, provide some conclusions for consideration that pose a challenge to the critics of the use of eminent domain.

In addition to providing examples of how eminent domain and public-private partnerships have led to urban redevelopment goals, they point out the following:

> Not enough is known about the use of eminent domain for economic develop-ment to fully evaluate its benefits and impacts, or to assess the potential conse-quences of eliminating or restricting eminent domain for communities' ability to pursue successful economic development. . . . Evidence suggests the property owners are frequently given compensation well above fair market value. . . . There is little evidence that eminent domain authority is often abused to serve purely private interests, although "one-to-one" transfers outside the context of comprehensive planning pose risks. . . . Legal and cultural changes make it less likely that eminent domain will be used to target sensitive populations or reli-gious properties. . . . Particularly in view of our uncertainty about the poten-tial consequences of radical surgery to local governments' traditional eminent domain powers, reform efforts should focus on establishing procedural mecha-nisms that will assist government and the public in making more discriminate use of the eminent domain power. (Dreher & Echeverria, 2006, pp. 2–3)

As with most public policy decisions, gathering all the objective data necessary to be certain about outcomes and then objectively weighing the pros and cons is not feasible, in part because eminent domain is a value-laden issue. Property rights advocates and city officials seeking urban redevelopment have very different agen-das and perspectives, which is why eminent domain is likely to remain a contentious issue. Where there might be agreement is on policy that leads to, as Dreher and Ech-everria (2006) suggest, more discriminate use of eminent domain.

When Eminent Domain Hits Home

Over the past decade, Ty, Gabi, and many of their neighbors had been involved in some of the community's revitalization efforts. The city had asked for citizen input and participation in remaking Market Avenue, which stands just one block north of the Stevenses' home and had housed a five-block-long section of older run-down businesses and offices, along with some vacant buildings. The city, using eminent domain and federal grants, had been successful in refurbishing many of the buildings on Market Avenue and had beautifully landscaped the area, giving it a welcoming and attractive appearance. The city had partnered with the Middleton Economic Development Corporation to entice new businesses to locate on Market Avenue. In the brief span of a decade, Market Avenue had turned into a hub of civic and business activity and drew tourists and their much-needed dollars as well as local patrons. There were a couple of brew pubs, a bakery, gelato shop, sports store, antique store, music store, pipe store, and other specialty shops. Interspersed with the new development were some of the older businesses that had received a facelift. There was a tailor and shoe repair store, as well as offices belonging to professionals who had moved to Market Avenue after the makeover.

Ty reflected on the backyard discussions from years past when the first phase of the Market Avenue transformation was under way. At the time, the potential changes were mostly a matter of speculation and did not literally involve any changes in their own backyards. He remembered hearing a range of hopes and fears expressed about the future. Jocelyn, always the optimist, had commented, "Could we get any luckier? I now not only have great neighbors, but I can walk a couple of blocks and experience some of the city's best shopping."

Leslie responded, "I just hope Market Avenue doesn't impact the peace and quiet of our neighborhood. I don't want a whole bunch of people who aren't from the neighborhood hanging around. I know Market Avenue was getting too run down, but I don't want it to turn into Grand Central Station either."

Carla jumped in, "If it's just neighborhood folks who take advantage of Market Avenue, many of the businesses that are opening or getting a facelift won't survive, and yet I don't want people parking in front of my house to walk to Market Avenue."

"I heard," said Cyndi, "that three parking lots will go up right on Market Avenue once they take down the old Frasier, Gaff, and Kamp buildings. Those buildings were condemned and an eyesore, so I for one will be glad to see them go even if it's for parking lots. And that'll keep traffic off of our street." Darla, who often saw the glass as half empty, surprisingly added, "I imagine there is likely to be some negative consequences from the remaking of Market Avenue, but it was carefully planned, and with our input, the benefits will likely outweigh any costs. All in all, I think it will be a boost to the image of the Bethel Park area."

"You know," Gabi said to Ty as he opened a second beer, "in all the conversations we've had with friends about Market Avenue and in all the planning we were involved in, I can't believe none of us saw the possibility that Market Avenue would really take off. How could what seemed to be such a good thing have gone so awry?"

"I don't know, Gabi. Remember how it was back then? More and more professionals were moving their offices from Market Avenue to nicer areas, old outdated

Market Avenue businesses were closing down, and the real possibility existed that the whole area would spiral downward and crime rates spiral upward. We were pretty desperate to turn the tide."

"Exactly," said Gabi, clearly exasperated. "Even though I've spent my career helping organizations and communities think about the long-term impact of decisions on women's health, when faced with a crisis, I fell into the trap of focusing only on the short term."

"Whoa, Gabi, I agree; too often decisions are made that only focus on the short term, but I don't think the city was focused on the short term when they determined they would need to employ eminent domain to acquire the land of the few business owners who didn't want to sell. You have to admit, there has been significant long-term gain for the community as a whole. Where would this neighborhood be today without the revenue generated by the development of Market Avenue?

Now Ty, somewhat to his own surprise, was doing a little ranting himself. "That revenue is funding critical services we all expect, like police and firefighters. And the revitalization efforts helped the city secure federal matching money to fund the Community Arts House. So many low-income children from the city have been given an opportunity to experience dance, theatre, and painting."

"I didn't know you were so torn, Ty," Gabi responded, sounding a little hurt. "Good thing you didn't try to defend the city at the meeting today."

"Gabi, I'm not defending the city. I'm just pointing out there is not a simple solution for the city."

"If there is going to be more short-term profit-driven development," Gabi said, sounding somewhat defiant, "it's not going to be in my neighborhood."

Knowing Gabi was exhausted and in no mood to talk about the needs of the city that they both cared about, Ty tried to change the focus of the conversation. "I don't want to buy and start over somewhere else either, but I'm feeling like David up against Goliath and lacking a slingshot."

Sounding perturbed, Gabi said, "Well, I have no intention of just selling like the Bentleys and Fairbanks plan to do. They might end up with enough money to buy in the new housing development in the Beacon Hills area, but they're giving up too much."

"You know, I didn't want to say this at our meeting, but staging a protest at city hall is not likely going to be an effective tactic," Ty said. "Our private meeting with the mayor didn't exactly bring her over to our side. We didn't get much closer to a clear plan of action, which we clearly need if we have any chance of hanging onto our home and maintaining the community we worked so hard to create."

"Absolutely, Ty. I wasn't much help at the meeting today either since I was just angry at myself for being so naïve last week when we met with the mayor. I bet there's not another block in the city that is as diverse as ours and where neighbors really look out for each other like we do. I really thought that explaining to Mayor

Elton and her staff all that would be lost through using eminent domain to acquire properties on Ellwood Avenue would be enough to get them to at least have more discussions about it."

"Well, I was afraid it was a mistake not to first gather together with elected officials and influential city leaders before we met with the mayor. We know that council members Shatoia Dixon and Adrian Griffin are definitely in our corner, and I've heard through the grapevine that a couple of other council members, including Cally Hunter, are sympathetic to our cause." Gabi chimed in, "And there is Mike Elliot from Metro-Magnetics and Sandy Taylor from Taylor Construction who have said they would do whatever they can for our cause."

"Uh huh," Ty responded. "If we could just make some inroads with the editors at the *Mid-Times*. They haven't been very sympathetic to us. Of course they weren't sympathetic when some property owners didn't want to sell 10 years ago when Market Avenue underwent its transformation, and truthfully, neither were we."

"So I need to know something, Ty," Gabi said, softly. "Are you 100% with me in this fight?"

Ty paused before responding and realized immediately he was signaling his own lack of certainty about the battle that lay ahead of them. "At the end of the day, you know I want to stand shoulder to shoulder with you and fight to save our home," he said. "But maybe I don't see the issue being so clear-cut."

"Why not?" asked Gabi.

"I do love our neighborhood and our home, Gabi, you know that," Ty said. "But what if everybody took our same stance—progress is fine but not in my backyard? Could any change really ever happen?"

Gabri yawned. "I better get to bed. I just hope I don't have more nightmares of our family and the seven other families who don't want to sell standing out on the street and watching our homes demolished."

Challenges at City Hall

While the Stevenses and their neighbors struggled to figure out how to convince the city that they should not be forced to sell their homes, Mayor Elton was dealing with a plethora of challenges. During her time on city council for 8 years, and then as mayor for the past 3, much progress had been made in reviving areas of the city. Still, economically, Middleton is on the cusp. The late 1970s and 1980s had not been kind to Middleton, and the consequences of the loss of four large employers during that era and subsequent population loss significantly impacted its tax base. The city is faced with an aging infrastructure, high unemployment, pockets of extreme poverty, and increased demands for services.

Mayor Elton was all too well aware that the city needed to figure out more ways of drawing people into the city to purchase goods and to make sure people who live in the city do not have to leave the city to buy goods and services or feel safe. The development of Market Avenue had resulted in generating more revenue than had been expected. A cost-benefit analysis, paid for by the city, indicated that further development in the Bethel Park area would also prove fruitful financially for the city, which ultimately, the mayor reasoned, was promoting the public good. By no means a fan of using eminent domain in order to turn over land to private developers, her staff and office of economic development could not come up with a better alternative. She felt caught between a rock and a hard place.

"How can I not take steps that will improve the tax base, help us bring in federal dollars, and provide much needed jobs," the mayor said as she argued with City Council President Cally Hunter. Cally had supported the use of eminent domain on Ellwood Avenue until she became aware of just how many residents were adamant that they did not want to sell regardless of just compensation.

She reminded the mayor that "we badly underestimated how much opposition we would face. I knew that the Stevenses and many of their neighbors had built a close-knit community, but I didn't realize how tight they are. I had actually talked to a few of the homeowners who said they would be okay with selling, and then after they met with their neighbors, these homeowners quickly changed their minds."

"Cally, you remember there was opposition to using eminent domain to secure Market Avenue property, but we rode out that storm and look how it turned out," responded the mayor.

"Sure, but this is different. Only a couple of the homes are what I would consider truly blighted. The majority of homes on the section of Ellwood Avenue we're interested in are not rundown, vacant, or boarded up, and while we can technically call some of them blighted properties, you know as well as I do that that is a stretch."

"What I know is that this development will be one more much-needed economic boost to the entire city, and while it may pain me personally, the needs of the few do not outweigh the needs of the whole city."

Cally left city hall frustrated and at a loss. She could understand the positions of both the residents on Ellwood Avenue and the mayor. What she could not figure out was how to create a win-win situation.

QUESTIONS FOR DISCUSSION

1. Explain how, according to the author, the Framers of the U.S. Constitution conceived and viewed eminent domain.

2. How did the use of eminent domain in the 1800s and early 1900s differ from its use in the past 60 to 70 years? Provide some case examples to demonstrate the difference. Make sure to discuss why the 1954 *Berman v. Parker* case

was viewed as a turning point by some critics of how the states were using eminent domain.

3. Discuss the relationship between urban renewal and eminent domain. What are the benefits and consequences of urban renewal?

4. In the past 40 to 50 years, the author sets forth that there have been two opposing perspectives on what the Framers of the Constitution meant by the term "public use." Present these perspectives along with examples of Supreme Court cases, since the 1980s, where these counter perspectives are at the heart of the case.

5. Provide a solid rationale that supports using the power of the state to use eminent domain to acquire properties on Ellwood Avenue.

6. In addition to your answer for #5, discuss any other positive impact eminent domain can have on a community.

7. Provide a solid rationale for opposing the use of eminent domain on Ellwood Avenue.

8. You and your family own property that you very strongly do not want to sell. Under what circumstances is the use of eminent domain to acquire your property justifiable?

9. As a society how do we balance the needs of the community with the needs of the individual?

10. If you were developing public policy, what criteria would you use for drafting legislation regarding eminent domain? What research is still needed to determine the criteria?

CASE ANALYSIS WRITING ASSIGNMENT

1. Read the assigned case study thoroughly prior to class in order to be fully prepared to join in the discussion.

2. Write a case study analysis responding to the following statement: Mayor Elton should use the power of the state to acquire properties on Ellwood Avenue, as it would lead to public good. Make sure to use specific content from the case study to provide a sound rationale for supporting the use of eminent domain in this circumstance, opposing it, or proposing a compromise that can be defended using content from the case.

3. The analysis should be an approximately two- to two-and-a-half page, typed, double-spaced essay. Your essay should reflect the standards and expectations

of college-level writing: spelling, grammar, and appropriate use of paragraphs all matter. If you quote directly from the case study, use quotation marks, and at the end of the quote, indicate the page number the quote appeared on. For example, "The city is faced with an aging infrastructure, high unemployment, pockets of extreme poverty, and increased demands for services" (Lewis, 2017, p. 80).

4. Your case analysis is due _____ and worth a maximum of ____ points.

INTERNET SOURCES

Georgetown Environmental Law & Policy Institute, Georgetown University Law Center (www.law.georgetown.edu/academics/centers-institutes/gelpp)

Hoover Institution Stanford University (http://www.hoover.org/publications/policy-review/article/7292)

Legal Information Institute (https://www.law.cornell.edu/wex/eminent_domain)

Michigan Municipal League (http://www.mml.org)

U.S. Department of Housing and Urban Development (http://portal.hud.gov/hudportal/HUD?src=/program_offices/public_indian_housing/centers/sac/eminent)

U.S. Department of Justice (https://www.justice.gov/enrd/history-federal-use-eminent-domain)

REFERENCES

Berger, J. (2014, November 17). Setback in Atlantic City for man hoping to save parents' home. *New York Times.* Retrieved from http://www.nytimes.com/2014/11/18/nyregion/setback-in-atlantic-city-for-man-hoping-to-save-parents-home.html

Berman v. Parker, 348 U.S. 26 (1954).

Bird, R. (2010). Reviving necessity in eminent domain. *Harvard Journal of Law & Public Policy, 33*(1), 239–281.

Clark v. Nash, 198 U.S. 361 (1905).

Dreher, R., & Echeverria, J. D. (2006). *Kelo's* unanswered questions: The policy debate over the use of eminent domain for economic development. *Georgetown Environmental Law & Policy Institute, Georgetown University Law Center.* Retrieved from http://www.gelpi.org/gelpi/current_research/documents/GELPIReport_Kelo.pdf

Hollingsworth, B. (2015, August, 31). NJ judge reverses self on eminent domain, sides with piano tuner, *CNSNEWS.* Retrieved from http://www.cnsnews.com/news/article/barbara-hollingsworth/nj-judge-reverses-himself-sides-piano-tuner-eminent-domain-case

Institute of Justice. (2010). *Five years after* Kelo: *The sweeping backlash against one of the Supreme Court's most-despised decisions.* Retrieved from http://ij.org/wp-content/uploads/2015/08/kel05year_ann-white_paper.pdf

Jacobs, J. (1961). *The death and life of great American cities.* New York, NY: Random House.

John Paul Stevens on Environment. (2012, May 27). *On the issues.* Retrieved from http://www.ontheissues.org/Court/John_Paul_Stevens_Environment.htm

Jost, K. (2005). *Urban issues: Selections from Congressional Quarterly Researcher: Property rights: Should the use of eminent domain be limited? 15*(9). Thousand Oaks, CA: CQ Press.

Kelly, D. B. (2005). The "public use" requirement in eminent domain law: A rationale based on secret purchases and private influence. *Harvard Law School.* John M. Olin Center for Law, Economics, and Business Fellows' Discussion Papers Series.

Kelo v. City of New London, 545 U.S. 469 (2005).

Kohl v. United States, 91 U.S. 367 (1875).

Kokot, M. J. (2011). Balancing blight: Using the rules versus standards debate to construct a workable definition of blight. *Columbia Journal of Law and Social Problems,* 46–82.

Lane, C. (2005, June 24). Justices affirm property seizures. *Washington Post.* Retrieved from http://www.washingtonpost.com/wpdyn/content/article/2005/06/23/AR2005062300783.html

Legal Information Institute. (n.d.). *United States v. Great Falls Manuf'g Co.* Cornell University Law School. Retrieved from https://www.law.cornell.edu/supremecourt/text/112/645

Leung, R. (2009, February 11). Eminent domain: Being abused? *CBS News.* Retrieved from http://www.cbsnews.com/2100–18560_162–575343.html

Main, C. T. (2005, October 1). How eminent domain ran amok. *Hoover Institution, Stanford University.* Retrieved from http://www.hoover.org/research/how-eminent-domain-ran-amok

Michigan Municipal League. (2004). *Eminent domain: County of Wayne v. Hathcock.* Retrieved from http://www.mml.org/legal/ldf_top25/ldf_2.htm

Oyez Project at IIT Chicago-Kent College of Law. (2015). *Mount Holly v. Holly Gardens Citizens, (2015).* Retrieved from https://www.oyez.org/search/Mount%20Holly%20v.%20Holly%20Gardens%20Citizens%20Inc.%20%282013%29

Sharp v. United States, 191 U.S. 341 (1903).

Somin, I. (2004). Overcoming *Poletown: County of Wayne v. Hathcock,* economic development takings, and the future of public use. *Michigan State Law Review, 4,* 1005–1039.

Wang, D. (2012, August 1). New Jersey town rips up working-class neighborhood for private developers. *Huffington Post.* Retrieved from http://www.huffingtonpost.com/2012/08/01/new-jersey-development-mount-holly-gardens_n_1723746.html

Chapter 10

Homelessness and the Housing First Debate

Wrestling With the Issues

It takes Middleton City Council President Cally Hunter a few minutes to quiet the packed room at city hall where 200 residents are gathered for a public forum concerning homelessness. A first-time visitor to this solid, comfortable city of 700,000 would not suspect that Middleton is facing a significant homeless problem, yet the facts are undeniable. Shoppers or professionals who work downtown occasionally complain about being approached by shabbily dressed panhandlers asking for spare change, but few people other than homeless advocates, a couple of congregations, and social workers are focused on this growing problem. In reality, homelessness in Middleton has grown far beyond the modest resources currently devoted to addressing this problem. The shelters are often overflowing, and people are being turned away most nights. They join others who have resorted to living on the streets, in alleyways, or under bridges, all of whom are largely hidden from the public eye and consciousness.

A recent tragedy has greatly raised awareness. In January 2014, Middleton was hit with a record-breaking cold snap. While most residents bundled up, and the media warned citizens to protect their pets from single-digit temperatures, two homeless men died from exposure after being turned away from an overcrowded shelter. It was discovered that one of the men had served honorably in Iraq before his life took a series of unfortunate twists and turns. The other man had spent the last several years homeless after losing his job at a plastics company. This tragedy was an embarrassment to city leaders, who had ignored pleas from housing advocates to more effectively address the growing number of homeless persons in Middleton. It also served as a surprising wake-up call to many citizens as the media provided details about the magnitude of the city's problem. The fact that a couple of churches had already opened up their buildings to provide beds for the home-less, and that one agency had warming hours on especially frigid nights, became well known. The media attention was short-lived but sufficient to push the home-less agenda forward among some city officials, though how long it will remain on the front burner is uncertain.

On tonight's council agenda is a proposal to use city dollars to help finance (and expand) a local project called A Brighter Tomorrow (ABT). The project has a simple goal: build more permanent housing for the chronically homeless citizens of Middleton. Proposal advocates are demanding that the city provide, at a minimum, the funding needed to maintain the current program that houses 100 individuals. Given the scope of the problem, this group has its sights set a little higher. They are seeking funding to increase the number served to 170 by the end of next year. To serve 100 people for a year, the city would have to budget $750,000. The amount the city would have to contribute to serve 170 for one year is $1.25 million.

ABT was initiated 4 years ago by a subcommittee of an antipoverty movement that had been spearheaded in 2010 by leaders from various nonprofits, including a local social work professor, Moe Coleman. The antipoverty movement was community driven and aimed to have an inclusive and open process in all of its work. Guided by a strategic plan, all committees and subcommittees are made up of volunteers tasked with continually reporting to the larger group on their efforts toward achieving agreed-upon goals. This particular subcommittee had quickly, and rather quietly, developed a complete plan for ABT before reporting back to the larger committee. Two of the subcommittee members were very familiar with programs in the United States similar to what they were proposing with ABT. A few of those who had spearheaded the antipoverty movement, including Moe Coleman, voiced concerns first to each other and then to the subcommittee regarding the fact that key stakeholders from agencies serving the homeless had not been part of the discussion and drafting of the proposal. The subcommittee was a little taken aback and indicated that service providers in the area could have participated if they had chosen to. They stated that their work had not been done in secret and that their plan was well researched. What remained to be done was the lengthy grant application. Subcommittee members assured the movement leaders that they would fill homeless service providers in on their plan, which could potentially benefit 100 chronically homeless individuals. Moreover, sub-committee members pointed out, the deadline for the Department of Housing and Urban Development (HUD) grant was fast approaching, and they needed to move quickly in order to get a proposal in.

The leaders of the antipoverty group still had reservations about the process. Moe Coleman, in particular, was worried about a backlash and not having enough buy-in, but he also believed that the work furthered the movement's purpose.

They settled on an agreement that the one staff person for the antipoverty movement (all the others were volunteers, often on company/organizational time) would attend the meetings with the other homeless service providers. The leaders believed this would at least serve the purpose of updating other key stakeholders who were unhappy not to have been included earlier in the process. Moe, who often voiced concerns about process and inclusion, had already let his position be known and decided to quit pressing the issue.

The notice that ABT had received federal funding through HUD came as a big surprise. The private sector (foundations, charitable organizations, corporations) had promised dollars if the HUD money came through, in large part due to pressure on the federal bureaucracy by a couple of regional members of Congress. In addition to private sector dollars being needed to supplement federal dollars, after 4 years, the federal government contributions would have to be matched by money from the state and local levels. Predictably, state officials would only consider providing a share of program funding if the city kicked in its portion, and still there was no guarantee they'd ante up. All donors think the project is promising in general, but nobody wants to be left holding the bag as the exclusive source of funding. Thus, whatever the city decides will help determine if the program continues or if the entire complex web of shared funding unravels.

Cally can feel the tension in the room and knows this discussion is likely to get heated as a wide variety of stakeholders weigh in. In contrast to the myth of town meetings in the popular lore of American democracy, very few "average citizens" attend a forum of this kind. More often, the room is packed with representatives of various advocacy organizations: well-informed, articulate, and passionate speakers convinced of the justice of their respective causes. Cally recognizes the antitax group representatives who often voice opposition to any type of social service spending. Then there are the social justice advocates who have been to city hall on a number of occasions over the past few years to voice alarm at the growing number of visibly homeless people and what they see as the city's callous lack of response. She further notes the presence of representatives from housing agencies that work with the homeless. Spokespersons for these agencies have repeatedly tried to get across the message that the growing number of cardboard box homes and lean-tos under the bridges is a sign of a much larger homelessness problem.

Also in attendance is a group of individuals who protested in front of the ABT housing complex when it first opened. Cally is familiar with the raw emotions—sometimes erupting in anger—inspired by any discussion about spending city money to house the chronically homeless. She checks to make sure she has her official gavel nearby, ready to summon the meeting back to order if things get unruly. Sometimes in situations like this, Cally feels like a baseball umpire making an unpopular call in front of screaming fans in a packed, noisy stadium. She's gotta "call 'em like she sees 'em," but things could get uncomfortable as she presides over this discussion. Cally just hopes that the evening will remain civil. She lays out the ground rules and then opens up the floor for comments.

BACKGROUND INFORMATION

Scope of the Problem

How many Americans are homeless? It is difficult to get a simple, unambiguous answer to this question. For example, some studies count the homeless who are staying in shelters and on the streets. Yet we know that many people are turned away from shelters due to lack of space, and for others, the streets are not their only option. They may stay in their car, on the floor of a friend's home for a few nights or weeks before moving on, or they may ask a family member for the couch. Access to all who are homeless is just one reason to view official counts of people who are homeless with caution. Nonetheless, the counts do provide an idea of the magnitude of the problem, who makes up this population, and provides a baseline from which to monitor progress.

Three main approaches to counting those who are homeless include (1) determining how many people are homeless within a year, (2) a snapshot that entails counting the homeless at a single point in time, and (3) studying trends over time. The National Law Center on Homelessness and Poverty (NLCHP, 2015) estimates that each year "between 2.5 and 3.5 million Americans sleep in shelters, transitional housing, and public places not meant for human habitation. At least an additional 7.4 million have lost their own homes and are doubled up with others due to economic necessity" (p. 1). A 2015 study conducted by HUD attempted to capture (as best they could) people who were homeless—either sheltered or unsheltered at a single point in time. They found that on a given night in January, approximately 358,422 individuals and 206,286 persons in families (a total of 564,708 people) in the United States were homeless. The same HUD report gives a picture of trends. It reports that there has been "an overall 11 percent reduction [in homelessness] since 2010 (Henry, Shivji, de Sousa, Cohen, & Abt Associates Inc., 2015, p. 5). *Opening Doors,* the nation's first comprehensive strategy to prevent and end homelessness, launched under the Obama administration, is credited with this decrease. The 2015 report also states that the number of families with children experiencing homelessness declined 15% since 2010. This is on the tail of an increase of 20% in the number of homeless families from 2007 to 2010 (Henry et al., 2015).

Getting a reliable count of the number of homeless people in suburban areas is also difficult, but according to Megan Hustings, director of the National Coalition for the Homeless, it is on the rise but is also hard to track. While it is anecdotal, there is evidence to indicate homelessness has increased just as poverty has increased

(*Guardian*, 2015). Another population where there has been an increase in homelessness is children under 18. Close to a quarter of all homeless individuals are children under 18 years of age. The U.S. Department of Education[1] reported that in the 2013–2014 school year there were approximately 1.36 million preschool–Grade 12 children and youth who were homeless. This is the highest number ever recorded (Dohler, 2015).

The latest U.S. Conference of Mayors survey conducted between September 2014 and August 2015 indicates that of the 22 participating cities, there was an overall increase of 1.6% in the number of people who experienced homelessness. This breaks down to 58% of the cities indicating an increase and 42% of the cities a decrease in the number of people who were homeless. Across cities overall there was a 5.2% decrease in the number of families experiencing homelessness. This breaks down to 53% of cities experiencing a decrease, 42% an increase, and 5% no change in the number of families experiencing homelessness (U.S. Conference of Mayors, 2015).

An example of one of the many cities that have faced an increase in homelessness is Seattle. At the single point-in-time count in 2015, a 19% increase was found in the number of people sleeping on the street. The Seattle mayor and the King County executive declared a state of emergency over the housing crisis (Woodard, 2015). They are not alone. Portland, Oregon, Los Angeles, California, and the State of Hawaii also declared states of emergency in 2015. In Columbus, Ohio, the Community Shelter Board indicates that over the last 2 years, their community has experienced a 16% increase in single men and women and a 63% increase in families (Community Shelter Board, 2016). To prepare for the winter of 2015–2016, New York City had plans to add 500 shelter beds, and Washington, DC, was housing homeless families in hotel rooms (Beitsch, 2015). These examples illustrate that despite decreases in some cities, the issue of homelessness is still extremely prevalent and growing within certain subgroups and in certain communities.

The 100 tent cities that have sprung up between 2008 and 2013 across 46 states also speak to the scope of homelessness and the lack of affordable housing and shelter services available in many communities (Hunter, Linden-Retek, Shebaya, & Halper, 2014). Hunter et al. (2014) note that tent cities are sometimes preferred over shelters even when there is enough bed or floor space, as shelters don't always meet the needs of the homeless. Not all shelters accommodate couples or different family types. There are also safety concerns, restrictions about storing belongings, conflict with work hours and shelter hours, and rules that are sometimes resented.

---

[1] The U.S. Department of Education includes having to double-up and live with other individuals or families in their definition of homelessness. The U.S. Department of Housing does not include those who have moved in with others in their homeless count.

Veterans are an important subgroup to mention when discussing the scope of homelessness. Estimates by both HUD and the Department of Veterans Affairs put the number of veterans who are homeless on a given night in 2015 at about 47,728. The departments note that veterans make up a disproportionate number of the homeless population given that only 8% of the U.S. population are veterans, and yet 12% of all people who are homeless have veteran status (Henry et al., 2015).

Reasons for Homelessness

To determine effective policies, we must keep in mind that there are multiple reasons, some of which are overlapping, for the high rates of homelessness. As alluded to above, the primary reason for homelessness is lack of affordable housing. Stagnant wages and increasing rent prices significantly impact access to adequate housing. Almost half of those who are homeless work, but they cannot afford to pay housing expenses on top of all other expenses (Mazzara, Sard, & Rice, 2016). Today, more than one in four renters have rent and utility expenses that equal at least 50% of their family income (CBS Money Watch, 2015). And 80% of the lowest income families pay more than one third of their income in rent (MacArthur Foundation, 2016). If a family's housing costs exceed 30% of their income, it is determined burdensome by government standards.

Figure 10.1   Renters' Incomes Haven't Kept Pace With Housing Costs

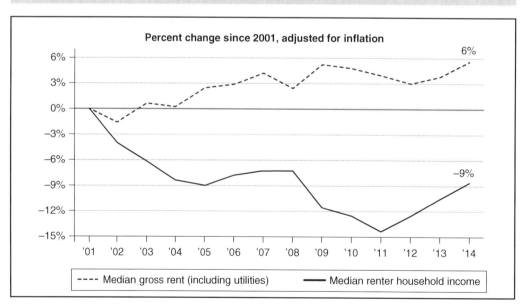

Note: Includes households with zero rent who pay utilities.

Source: Center for Budget and Policy Priorities. (April 12, 2016). Renters' Incomes Haven't Kept Pace With Housing Costs. Retrieved from http://www.cbpp.org/renters-incomes-havent-kept-pace-with-housing-costs

Homelessness among some groups has decreased despite cuts in government funding for rent assistance in 2011. Some of this money has since been restored, and total housing assistance has slightly increased since 2004. However, a 2016 report indicates that overall rental assistance for families (other than those in the child welfare system) has dropped 13% since then, serving 250,000 fewer families.

Targeted subgroups such as veterans and nonelderly people with disabilities have seen an increase in vouchers available. Still, the demand for housing assistance far outweighs the supply of funding, with only one in four eligible families receiving assistance. The remaining families end up on what are most often long waiting lists (Mazzara et al., 2016).

Along with low wages and underemployment, unemployment is a significant contributing factor to homelessness, as were foreclosures during the housing crisis and decreasing public assistance. Other factors that *increase* the risk of homelessness, but should not be said to *cause* homelessness, are domestic violence, mental illness, and substance abuse (National Coalition for the Homeless, 2011; U.S. Conference of Mayors, 2015). Because there are multiple reasons why people end up homeless, and because the makeup of the homeless population is so diverse, there is a need for varied approaches to addressing this problem.

Figure 10.2   Federal Rental Assistance Helping Fewer Families With Children

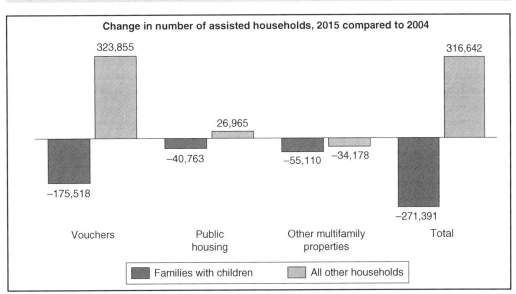

Note: Families with children have at least one member who is under 18 at home. Includes all Department of Housing and Urban Development (HUD) programs with subsidies whose value varies based on the tenant's income except Housing Opportunities for People with AIDS/HIV and McKinney-Vento permanent housing, which assist few families with children.

Source: Mazzara, A., Sard, B., & Rice, D. (May 24, 2016). Rental assistance to families with children at lowest point in decade. *Center for Budget and Policy Priorities*. Retrieved from http://www.cbpp.org/research/housing/rental-assistance-to-families-with-children-at-lowest-point-in-decade

Another important variable regarding the makeup of individuals who are home-less is the length of time one is homeless. Of the thousands of homeless individuals and families in any given year, approximately 80% are transitionally and episodi-cally homeless. The *transitionally homeless* are, in essence, people who are down on their luck for a host of reasons. Some have been living close to the edge financially. A sudden, unexpected change (e.g., loss of a job, break-up with a spouse) has them scrambling for shelter. Typically, members of this category are homeless for a short period of time and then are able to return to conventional housing (Caton, Wilkins, & Anderson, 2007; Kertesz et al., 2007). The episodically homeless people cycle in and out of homelessness, falling somewhere between temporary and chronic homeless-ness. The remaining 20% are chronically homeless, defined by the U.S. Department of Health and Human Services (2007), as "an unaccompanied homeless individual with a disabling condition who has either a) been continuously homeless for a year or more or b) has had at least four episodes of homelessness in the past three years" (para. 2).

Homelessness—What Should We Do About It?

In the past decade, plans to end homelessness, and in particular chronic homelessness, have been developed in well over 300 cities in the United States. In 2003, the Bush administration pledged to work to end chronic homelessness, with the goal of doing so in 10 years. Clearly we have fallen short, but progress has been made, and current legislation remains focused on ending chronic homelessness and homelessness among veterans, as well as preventing homelessness in the first place. An example of federal commitment is the 2009 American Revitalization and Recovery Act, which provided funds for the Homelessness Prevention and Rapid Re-Housing Program. This program, in its first year of implementation, resulted in close to 700,000 people either moving from homelessness to permanent housing or avoiding becoming homeless by providing assistance to current tenants who had fallen behind on rent and preventing homeowners from becoming homeless due to foreclosure (Smith, 2010). In 2010, the first federal strategic plan regarding homelessness was laid out by the U.S. Interagency Council on Homelessness (USICH). The plan, *Opening Doors,* set the goal of ending chronic homelessness and homelessness among veterans by 2015. Furthermore, the goal for ending homelessness among families, youth, and children was set for 2020. In its 2013 update, USICH was pleased with the progress made over the last 3 years. Despite the struggling economy, the number of people experiencing homelessness on any given night has decreased by 6%, and the number of people experiencing chronic homelessness has decreased by 15.7% since 2010 (U.S. Interagency Council on Homelessness, 2013). In the 2017 budget, the Obama administration included funding targeted to homelessness among families with the goal of ending homelessness among families by 2020 (Mazzara et al., 2016).

Throughout the country, initiatives are under way to increase the availability of affordable housing. The demand still far exceeds supply, but the efforts under way are making a difference for many. Just a few of the plethora of examples will be mentioned here. In Orlando, Florida, the state is providing a nonprofit with $26.1 million in tax credits and loans to build 166 units in place of what is now dilapidated, boarded-up apartments. To be able to qualify to rent, a family or individual can't make more the 60% of the median income for the areas (Santich, 2016). In Los Angeles, an initiative on the November 2016 ballot to incentivize and impose requirements regarding the construction of affordable housing was approved (BALLOTPEDIA, 2016). New York City Mayor de Blasio announced in January 2016 that a record number of affordable housing units, over 21,000, had been built or renovated and made available for use in 2015. During his tenure, his affordable housing plan had resulted in over 40,000 new units available for housing over 1,000 people. Mayor de Blasio is not claiming lack of affordable housing is still not a major issue but points to the progress being made. Seattle has plans in place to build 20,000 more affordable housing units by 2025 (NYC, 2016). Smaller cities have projects underway as well. The MacArthur Foundation (2016) is just one of the foundations investing in affordable housing development.

Tiny houses, often 100 to 200 square feet in size, are one option being used to provide housing for people who are homeless. These small, simple units, which provide formerly homeless individuals with a small home complete with electricity and sleeping, cooking, and bathroom areas, vary in cost and can be built for as little as $2,200 (not including the property they are built on). Although there is not universal support of tiny-house villages as part of the solution to homelessness, there is a good deal of support, and tiny-house villages are being built in a growing number of cities in the United States. Advocates point out that along with shelter, tiny-house villages offer residents dignity, privacy, safety, and often community (Haq, 2016).

A Paradigm Shift in Addressing Chronic Homelessness (Traditional Continuum of Care Versus Housing First)

The needs of those who are transitionally homeless must be addressed, but the focus of the remainder of this section, and the case study as a whole, is on chronic homelessness. While those who are chronically homeless make up 20% of the homeless, they are by far the most expensive and present the greatest barriers to economic stability.

In recent years, we have seen growing support for an alternative to the dominant approach to addressing homelessness, which for over 25 years has been the traditional continuum of care approach (Morgenstern, 2010). The traditional continuum of care approach includes using government and private funding to help people who are homeless through a range of services and interventions such as emergency shelters, transitional housing, assistance in accessing treatment for substance abuse and mental health issues, job counseling, training programs, and basic education. In the best of all worlds, the traditional continuum of care approach is designed as a step-by-step process to transform a homeless person with an array of problems into a self-sustaining, stable member of society. While programs vary, the traditional continuum of care approach requires that certain conditions, such as sobriety, be met before permanent housing is even considered. Ending up in an apartment or housing unit of one's own is viewed as the final step for the homeless person under the traditional continuum of care approach. Modest housing is the richly deserved reward for a difficult journey of self-improvement. While this approach works for some, it has not been effective for all, especially those in the chronically homeless category. People who fit the chronically homeless category face significant barriers to escaping homelessness due to some form of disability, most often substance abuse or mental health issues.

The idea behind the Housing First approach—in contrast to the traditional continuum of care approach—is that first, and foremost, stable housing must be provided in order to put the formerly homeless person in a position to address other problems. (The term *Housing First* is sometimes used interchangeably with *permanent supportive housing* or *rapid rehousing*.) For example, if Jerry is panhandling for his next meal (or drink) and doesn't know where he might find a place out of the elements to sleep tonight, it is unlikely he can look beyond his immediate needs for staying alive. Under these conditions, Jerry is a poor prospect for a successful alcohol treatment program and, consequently, is likely to remain homeless, since his drinking problem gets in the way of taking positive steps in other aspects of life. Under the Housing First model, once housed, an array of services is provided (but not mandated) to help the new resident succeed in life. People are not just left on their own after being afforded housing; instead, supports are wrapped around them. They have access to services such as medical care, drug and alcohol counseling, mental health professionals, caseworkers, and job placement services. There are Housing First programs designed to help the transitionally homeless, but they were originally targeted at the chronically homeless.

Housing First—Assessing Its Effectiveness

While there are critics of the Housing First approach, there is also a great deal of support among policy makers, advocates, and academics. Proponents of Housing First point to evidence-based programs that indicate the cost effectiveness of this approach. These findings have resulted in significantly more investment by government and nonprofits in this approach and fewer dollars for longer-term (more than 6 months) transitional housing.

As noted, the Housing First approach puts formerly chronically homeless individuals into stable housing as a first step rather than having them go through a series of services first. One such private initiative, Pathways to Housing, in New York, was founded in 1992. Pathways is credited with giving birth to the Housing First approach that moves people who are homeless and mentally ill into places of their own, straight from the streets. Then it wraps various services (e.g., health, clinical, and vocational) around them, providing a multidisciplinary clinical team available 7 days a week, 24 hours a day. By 2012, Pathways had housed over 3,000 individuals, with a retention rate of 85% to 90%. This rate includes people who did not fare well in other housing programs (Pathways to Housing, 2012). Retention rates are based on the percentage of formerly homeless residents who remain in stable housing for 2 or more years. The bottom line is that the Housing First approach has a higher retention rate than the traditional continuum of care alternative, even among the most difficult, least likely to succeed, target population. An evaluation of the 128 chronically homeless people with serious mental illnesses that Pathways worked with from October 2008 to April 2010 in Philadelphia indicated that the success rate during the period was 92% (Fairmount Ventures, Inc., 2011). Currently Pathways to Housing is being replicated in other countries as well as in over 40 cities across the United States.

Before heralding Housing First as the optimal approach for all subgroups, specifically those with active and severe addiction, a group of researchers who have assessed current outcomes of Housing First suggest that more data are needed. Still, they point out that studies thus far indicate Housing First results in excellent housing retention. These same researchers point out studies of linear (traditional continuum of care) approaches that cite "reductions in addiction severity but have shortcomings in long-term housing success and retention shortcomings in long-term housing success and retention" (Kertesz, Crouch, Milby, Cusimano, & Schumacher, 2009).

Columbus, Ohio, has a nationally recognized model for addressing homelessness. The foundation for this model is the Community Shelter Board, which oversees a network of service providers who provide services such as prevention, shelter, case workers, and affordable housing. (Community Shelter Board, 2016). When in 1999 the Community Shelter Board, which adopted a Housing First approach, set forth the goal of building 800 Housing First units, they faced numerous challenges. These challenges included lack of sufficient funds, a not-in-my-backyard mentality, skepticism about the effectiveness of such an approach, and some emergency shelters that opposed the plan out of fear they would lose resources. Despite obstacles, the Community Shelter Board and city forged ahead and opened their first supportive housing unit in 1999. As of March 2016, 1,951 permanent housing units have been established. On average, formerly homeless individuals and families stay in permanent supportive housing for 3 years. The successful housing outcome or successful housing exit[2] is currently at 98% (L. Barbu, personal communication, July 1, 2016).

---

[2] Successful housing outcome for permanent supportive housing is defined as continued stay in permanent supportive housing or exit to other permanent housing environments.

In Washington, DC, the District of Columbia's Department of Human Services (DHS) partnered with the Veterans Affairs Medical Center (VAMC) in 2010 to address the high rates of homelessness among veterans. Partnering the VAMC with the local DHS enables them to provide case management services for veterans housed through Veterans Affairs Supportive Housing (VASH) vouchers. This new program was called VASH Plus, and both the case management and housing were rooted in Housing First principles. The program aimed to help the most vulnerable veterans who were chronically homeless, dealing with serious health conditions, and either living on the streets or in emergency shelters. At the end of 2010, all 105 veterans who were housed through the program remained in housing and engaged in services (U.S. Department of Housing and Urban Development, n.d., p. 5).

Another of the many and growing number of cities adopting the Housing First approach is Seattle, Washington. Findings from their Housing First Program indicate that the provision of stable housing, even without first requiring abstinence, results in reduced drinking among homeless alcoholics. In fact, the longer the participants stay in the housing program, the less they drink. Reduced drinking results in these individuals staying out of jails and emergency rooms, which means it costs the taxpayer a lot less money (Larimer et al., 2009).

Moving beyond a focus on specific programs, evaluations of permanent supportive housing in general indicate a retention rate of 75% at 2 years and 50% at 3 to 5 years (Caton et al., 2007). In other words, this approach is effective at keeping this population off the streets, out of jail and hospital emergency rooms, and from tying up shelter beds. Housing First gives the chronically homeless a sense of hope. In a series of qualitative interviews conducted with 31 people beginning the transition from homelessness to permanent housing, one person described homelessness as "the worst of the worst, the bottom of the bottom that it can get. It can't get no worse. The next thing to this is death" (Carranza et al., 2013, p. 53). When asked how they felt about transitioning to housing, participants responded, "Well, I feel great. . . . I'm excited, optimistic and I'm encouraged and inspired by it [moving into housing]" and "Right now I feel like happy and because of the hardship I been through out there in the street . . . what's making me happy about moving in my place, I have time enough to . . . just focus on me and, and get myself more in order. . . . I'll be able to have a roof over my head. Now that's very important too . . . really this is the first apartment I ever received that, that's really mine" (Carranza et al., 2013, p. 53).

These programs are said to make people feel as if, despite their past, success is attainable. Although not required to do so, the majority of Housing First participants do engage in services provided such as health care services, mental health treatment, substance abuse treatment, and money management (Caton et al., 2007).

A 2008 *Wall Street Journal* article discusses a 4-year study of 407 homeless people with chronic medical problems. They were randomly assigned to either get immediate housing or to get the "usual care." The findings indicate those participants who ended up getting housing fared much better in terms of improved health. What's more, about 60% were still in stable housing at the end of an 18-month period compared to 15% of the usual care participants (Barrett, 2008).

Cost-effectiveness is a key reason for the fairly widespread support of the Housing First approach. Studies of Housing First programs in Seattle, Denver, and Portland all indicate significant cost savings in the social and health expenses of a chronically homeless person provided with stable housing as compared to those who do not have stable housing. For example, a study referenced above in the *Journal of the American Medical Association* found that during the first year of operation in the Seattle Housing First program, taxpayers were saved over $4 million dollars (Kertesz & Weiner, 2009). An evaluation by the Colorado Coalition for the Homeless (2012) of the Denver Housing First Collaborative found that the costs of services for the chronically homeless such as emergency care, inpatient medical and psychiatric care, emergency shelter, and incarceration were significantly reduced. Emergency room cost savings alone averaged $31,545 per participant. The success rate for those still in housing after 2 years was 77%, with participants indicating marked improvements on a wide variety of health and wellness issues. In addition, reductions of 66% in inpatient costs and 76% in incarceration costs were found. The cost savings of the statewide Massachusetts Housing First program was calculated to be $9,507 per year per participant (Massachusetts Housing and Shelter Alliance, 2011). Net savings per participant in the Pathways program in New York City are also thousands of dollars per year. While not all studies indicate savings as significant as the above, Kertesz and Weiner (2009) note that studies by Larimer et al. (2009) and Sadowski, Kee, VanderWeele, & Buchana (2009) indicate "that overall it appears that there is increasing evidence that indicates that at least some large cities cannot afford *not* to house some who live on their streets" (p. 1823).

THE SITUATION IN MIDDLETON

As the public hearing unfolds, Cally reflects on how Middleton has reached this point in the city's history of dealing with the homeless. The debate over A Brighter Tomorrow in Middleton is, in essence, a debate about extending an existing Housing First program. Three years ago, the Middleton Coalition for A Brighter Tomorrow (MCBT) received a grant from the federal government to implement a Housing First program in Middleton. The State Coalition for the Homeless, the Middleton

Department of Human Services, the Middleton Department of Mental Health, the VA Hospital, and Middleton Community Services made up the coalition. MCBT members' relationships with city and county officials were no doubt important in gaining the necessary buy-in from city and county officials. The grant request required letters of support from the mayor and county council that, when received, resulted in federal funding to provide integrated housing and services to 100 chronically homeless individuals.

Given the broad-based coalition behind Housing First, Cally recalls her surprise at the anger expressed about the city's letters of support for the initial ABT funding. Instead of a pat on the back for doing a good deed and exercising fiscal responsibility, city council members received a scolding—some of it from advocates for the homeless! It quickly became evident that both Cally and city council members had underestimated how much opposition there might be to this approach. Part of the opposition stemmed from the nature of the program and the other part from the decision-making process. The decision to support ABT had taken place through private conversations and behind closed doors rather than through an open discussion during a city council meeting or consultation with all providers of services to the homeless population. Cally knew Moe Coleman was too nice to say, "I told you so," but, as Cally had learned the hard way years ago, the policy process is not only political, it is a social process involving human beings who have feelings, pride, and issues in terms of values, ownership, territoriality, self-interest, and conflicts of interest.

Some organizations that provided direct and indirect services for the homeless, like the Middleton Council of Churches and their soup kitchen program, were dismayed that they had not been at the table discussing whether Housing First was the best approach and, if so, the role that they might play in the program. Reverend Ricardo Jones of the inner-city Full Gospel Assembly expressed the sentiments of many of his fellow clergy. "We care about the homeless, but we are interested in more than just building houses. The typical homeless person needs more than just a roof over his head." Reverend Jones has a reputation for wanting to "save the souls" of "his" homeless clients in exchange for a hot meal and a warm bed.

Insecurity about limited resources and envy at the favored treatment for ABT rankled several local organizations. "Even in the best scenario," said Jack Sanders, "city funds for homelessness are limited. We have real needs and a proven track record. ABT does not." Sanders, head of a nonprofit homeless agency, had heard plenty of rumors about the "new direction" Middleton was taking in homelessness policy and was aware of the greatly reduced federal funding for anything but rapid rehousing and Housing First. His experience assisting the homeless with the step-by-step process of rehabilitation made Sanders skeptical about such a full-scale commitment to the Housing First philosophy in Middleton.

Cally, whose day job was social worker at a mental health agency, used her mediation skills in an effort to patch up relations with the disgruntled agencies and to assure them that city funding available for homeless shelter services was not in jeopardy as a result of ABT. Still, in the few years since ABT opened its doors, the Middleton housing agencies involved have been viewed by some as more competitive than collaborative. Further federal cutbacks are making it increasingly hard for all of the agencies to keep their doors open and their programs staffed. Cally knows they are here tonight to voice concerns that emergency shelters and transitional housing are ending up with fewer federal dollars as HUD continues to increase funding for Housing First programs such as ABT.

Staying informed about how ABT is faring has been a priority of Cally's, and she's been thankful for that as she anticipated debate about its effectiveness during tonight's discussion. She knows that the first 2 years of ABT have not been without challenges, but that overall those in charge feel good about the program's progress. Referrals to the program greatly exceed slots available. Priority is given to individuals who've been homeless for more than 4 years and who have one or more serious disabilities. Fifty of the residents are housed in private sector apartments, all within one building, and the other fifty participants are provided apartments in a public housing complex purchased and refurbished with grant money. The buildings are side by side. While not luxurious, the apartments in each are typically one-bedroom (with a small number of two-bedroom apartments), equipped with basic furnishings, and attended to by a full-time maintenance supervisor. All participants pay 30% of their income for rent, with the program picking up the remaining balance. Twelve of the original 100 participants have either left on their own or been discharged during the first 2 years. The reasons for leaving vary greatly. For example, one resident was asked to leave because of aggressive behavior toward other residents, which is not tolerated, one resident moved back in with a family member after reconciling, and one gentleman claimed he did not want to use any of his social security insurance check for housing. This type of discharge is expected by those overseeing the program. The ABT administrator and staff members strongly believe that, on balance, ABT is meeting its goal of providing stable housing and appropriate support services to participants. The evaluation of the program's cost effectiveness is under way and soon to be released, but not before the forum.

PUBLIC FORUM

Cally forces herself to stop letting her thoughts drift to what has transpired with ABT since she signed the support letter 3 years ago. Debate at the forum is beginning to heat up. As expected, many attendees are voicing fervent support for expanding ABT, but the vocal opposition is what captures Cally's attention. Jay Harper, owner of one of the last old-fashioned barber shops, located a block away from the ABT residential buildings, states that "having ABT so close to my business has kept customers away. I plain don't like the thought that almost next door tax dollars are being spent so people can sleep off a hangover." On the other hand, Cindy Trassle responds, "Having ABT just across the street from my watch repair business has actually been good for business as the buildings were in disrepair and an eyesore before ABT refurbished them, improving the aesthetics of the whole block." Martin King, another area business owner, concludes, "It's a mixed bag. For the most part, the ABT residents are considerate and well behaved, but there have been a couple of times that a resident has really gotten out of hand just outside my coffee shop. Of course, it's not like there weren't obnoxious people hanging around outside before ABT took over the building. Still, I just don't think allowing 'those people' to live in this neighborhood will be good in the long run."

Though he's already had a turn, Jay Harper grabs the microphone from King and adds, "Why do they dump a bunch of lowlifes in our neighborhood anyway?" Next up, Monique Williams, who lives in an apartment over the laundromat just kitty-corner to the ABT buildings, emphatically states, "No one ever gave me a place to live before I cleaned up my act, and if they had, I would still be actively using. It is simply a bad idea to reward bad behavior." Monique's friend, Kevin, also a recovering addict who was formerly homeless, stresses that "while for some addicts providing stable housing might work, others will just end up trashing whatever housing they are in." Other speakers also express support for the idea that hard work and accountability ought to come first.

Interspersed with comments opposing maintaining what ABT already has in place, as well as the proposed expansion, is input from advocates of Housing First who point to studies demonstrating millions of dollars in savings as well as the effectiveness of Housing First in keeping people off the streets and out of hospitals and jails. They also highlight the fact that so many formerly homeless people do make positive life changes after being provided with stable housing. Sam Gavins, an Iraq vet, talks passionately about how Housing First "saved my life, and now I am working to help other veterans."

The time for comments from the public is drawing to an end, and there are still many hoping to speak. Cally recognizes Liz Setter and is not surprised by Liz's well-thought-out comments. She's the spokesperson for a local group that works with many low-income people. She states emphatically, "We're not against the federal government's support for Housing First as a means to end chronic homelessness. Our concern is that too many families and children, who make up as much as 41% of the homeless population,[3] are not getting the help they need. There are families that fall under the definition of chronically homeless, but many do not, and too often Housing First units are not set up to house families. We cannot target a certain segment of the homeless for stable housing and relegate others to emergency shelters. This is simply not fair. Moreover, funding dollars to other services for low-income people cannot withstand further cutbacks. Given the city's financial situation, how are you going to fund an expansion of ABT and maintain the current level of funding for other services for those who are poor?" One person in the audience yells out, "Fix the potholes on the street in front of my house before you give some panhandler a free apartment!" For the second time that evening, Cally has to use her gavel.

Cally indicates that there is time for one more speaker. Moe Coleman has been waiting patiently to contribute but instead points Cally's attention to a woman neither of them knows. The final citizen to hold the microphone is a single mom with two children. Jennifer has left an abusive relationship and is working two part-time jobs and living in a two-bedroom home with her brother, his wife, and their child. On the waiting list for Section 8 housing for the last 10 months, Jennifer voices frustration about her situation: "I am playing by the rules and working hard. It seems like I would get into housing faster if I were an addict. This is messed up."

CONCLUSION

The morning after the public forum, Councilwoman Maxine Alverson, one of Cally's golf partners and political allies, sent Cally an e-mail that read, in part, "Hey, nice gavel swinging last night, Cal. That could have ended up a disaster, but you managed to give people a chance to blow off a little steam. From what I gathered from the comments, we're looking at the following options regarding ABT:

"1. Support the ABT proposal with the city contributing its full share of funding to maintain a Housing First program in Middleton.

"2. Oppose the ABT expansion proposal and, instead, use the equivalent amount of city dollars to ensure there are no cuts to the more traditional continuum of care approach to the city's homeless problem.

---

[3] According to Henry et al. (2015), authors of the 2015 Annual Homeless Assessment Report published by the Department of Housing and Urban Development, 36% of the homeless, on a single night in January of 2015, were families with children.

"3. Encourage religious groups and charitable organizations to develop their own response to the city's homelessness issue. The city will not contribute public funding for addressing this issue. Instead, the city will use the funds for other services such as police, fire, or street repair.

"4. Support an alternative Housing First proposal that has different criteria for who is provided with housing. It should not just be the chronically homeless. Priority should go to people who are playing by the rules, not those who have serious drug and alcohol problems.

"Where do we go from here, Madame President?"

QUESTIONS FOR DISCUSSION

1. Based on the content in the case, discuss the prevalence of homelessness in the United States and who makes up the homeless population. Include in this discussion the differences between the transitionally, episodically, and chronically homeless.

2. What are the reasons that people find themselves homeless?

3. Explain both the traditional approach for addressing chronic homelessness and the Housing First approach.

4. Who are the stakeholders involved? (Stakeholders include all those who have an interest either directly or indirectly in the issue. Stakeholders are those who can affect or be affected by the issue/situation at hand.)

5. What do you see as some of the major advantages of the city increasing funding for A Brighter Tomorrow? What are the major disadvantages? Draw from specific examples provided in the case.

6. What are the value issues at stake in regard to determining which subpopulations of homeless should have highest priority in receiving Housing First apartments? Should priority be given to the chronically homeless?

7. Who should be responsible for addressing homelessness? Explain your reasoning.

8. Samantha is a worker at a transitional housing facility for homeless women who have had a lot of trauma in their lives. Many of the women have a history of substance abuse, mental health challenges, and/or are involved with the child welfare system. The program provides an array of services aimed at helping the women with all facets of life, including such things as decision making,

problem solving, building self-worth, developing financial literacy, securing employment, and positive relationships. Substance abuse and mental health services are offered to the women but not on-site. The typical length of stay for the women is 18 months. They are assisted with securing long-term housing. Samantha strongly believes that many of these women, if provided with Housing First or rapid rehousing, and are not required to attend classes and support groups, would fall back into old habits. Their time at the agency provides structure and order and a chance to change behaviors that the women themselves say have not helped them accomplish goals or even set goals. Does the social worker have valid concerns? If the federal government is greatly decreasing funding for transitional housing, what are the options for the agency?

9. The issue of the value of process and inclusion comes up in the case. What might have been different if more stakeholders had been included in the initial discussion about providing housing for those who are homeless?

10. As long as more homeless individuals are served effectively, how important is the process in how that end is reached?

CASE ANALYSIS WRITING ASSIGNMENT

1. Read the assigned case study thoroughly prior to class in order to be fully prepared to join in the discussion.

2. Write an analysis in which you set forth what you believe is the best course of action for Middleton regarding the issue at hand. You may choose one of the options provided, or set forth an alternative option. Make sure to provide arguments and evidence from the case to support the position you take.

Options

a. Support the ABT proposal with the city contributing its full share of funding to expand the Housing First approach as it is in Middleton.

b. Oppose the ABT proposal and, instead, use the equivalent amount of city funding to ensure that the agencies providing the continuum of care approach do not get a reduction in funding.

c. Encourage religious groups and charitable organizations to develop their own response to the city's homelessness issue with no contributions from the city. Instead, the city will use the funds for other services such as police, fire, or street repair.

    d. Support an alternative Housing First proposal that has different criteria for who is provided with housing. It should not just be the chronically homeless. Priority should go to people who are playing by the rules, not those who have serious drug and alcohol problems.

3. The analysis should be an approximately two-page, typed, double-spaced essay. Your essay should reflect the standards and expectations of college-level writing: spelling, grammar, and appropriate use of paragraphs all matter. If you quote directly from the case study, use quotation marks, and at the end of the quote, indicate the page number the quote appeared on. For example, "The amount the city would have to contribute to serve 170 for 1 year would be $1.25 million" (Lewis, 2016, p. 2).

4. Your case analysis is due _____ and worth a maximum of ____ points.

NOTE: Before you start your essay, make sure you have a very clear understanding of what Housing First entails, as well as what continuum of care entails. Your essay must include an introduction with a thesis statement, a body, and a conclusion. An effective way to approach the essay is to determine a position and jot down three to five key points that you can find *evidence for in the case* to support your stance. You are graded on effectively supporting your position using evidence from the case.

For this essay, assume the reader (teacher) has a general understanding of concepts used in the case, for example, continuum of care, Housing First, episodically homeless, chronically homeless. Therefore, you do not need to provide definitions of concepts in the case. Also, do not retell the story. Again, your goal is to take a position and provide evidence, with examples, that convinces the reader your position is the one that should be taken.

INTERNET SOURCES

Center for Budget and Policy Priority (http://www.cbpp.org)

Community Tool Box (http://ctb.ku.edu/en/table-of-contents/implement/physical-social-environment/affordable-housing/main)

The Cooperative Movement (http://www.umich.edu/~nasco/OrgHand/movement.html)

National Low Income Housing Coalition (http://nlihc.org)

Tiny-House Movement for Homeless (http://www.csmonitor.com/USA/USA-Update/2016/0121/Tiny-house-villages-An-innovative-solution-to-homelessness)

U.S. Department of Housing and Development (https://www.usa.gov/federal-agencies/department-of-housing-and-urban-development)

U.S. Interagency Council on Ending Homelessness (https://www.usich.gov/opening-doors)

REFERENCES

Barrett, J. (2008, March 6). Homeless study looks at 'Housing First': Shifting policies to get chronically ill in homes may save lives, money. *Wall Street Journal,* A10.

Beitsch, R. (2015, November 11). Cities, states turn to emergency declarations to tackle homeless crisis. *Pew Charitable Trusts.* Retrieved from http://www.pewtrusts.org/en/research-and-analysis/blogs/stateline/2015/11/11/cities-states-turn-to-emergency-declarations-to-tackle-homeless-crisis

Carranza, A., Dent, D., Henwood, B. F., Hsu, H., Wenzel, S., & Winetrobe, H. (2013). Transitioning from homelessness: A "fresh-start" event. *Journal of the Society for Social Work and Research, 4*(1), 47–57. http://doi.org/10.5243/jsswr.2013.4

Caton, C., Wilkins, C., & Anderson, J. (2007). *People who experience long-term homelessness: Characteristics and interventions.* Paper presented at the 2007 National Symposium on Homelessness Research. Retrieved from http://aspe.hhs.gov/hsp/homelessness/symposium07/caton/index.htm#Research

CBS Money Watch. (2015, May 1). When your rent costs more than half your income. *CBS News.* Retrieved from http://www.cbsnews.com/news/when-your-rent-costs-more-than-half-your-income

Colorado Coalition for the Homeless. (2012, March). *Housing first works.* Retrieved from http://www.coloradocoalition.org/!userfiles/Library/HousingFirstFinal.pdf

Community Shelter Board. (2016). Retrieved from http://www.csb.org

Dohler, E. (2015, September 15). The alarming rise in homeless students. *Center for Budget and Policy Priorities.* Retrieved from http://www.cbpp.org/blog/the-alarming-rise-in-homeless-students

Guardian. (2015, October 14*). Suburbanites are becoming the new face of homelessness in the United States.* Retrieved from http://www.rawstory.com/2015/10/suburbanites-are-becoming-the-new-face-of-homelessness-in-america

Fairmount Ventures, Inc. (2011, January). *Evaluation of Pathways to Housing PA.* Retrieved from http://www.dvg.org/resource/resmgr/research_reports/pathways_to_housing_report.pdf

Haq, H. (2016, January 2016). Tiny-house villages: An innovative solution to homelessness? *Christian Science Monitor.* Retrieved from http://www.csmonitor.com/USA/USA-Update/2016/0121/Tiny-house-villages-An-innovative-solution-to-homelessness

Henry, M., Shivji, A., de Sousa, T., Cohen, R., & Abt Associates (2015, November). The 2015 Annual Homeless Assessment Report (AHAR) to Congress. *The U.S. Department of Housing and Urban Development, Office of Community Planning and Development.* Retrieved from https://www.hudexchange.info/resources/documents/2015-AHAR-Part-1.pdf

Hunter, J., Linden-Retek, P., Shebaya, S., & Halper, S. (2014, March). Welcome home: The rise of tent cities in the United States. *National Law Center on Homelessness & Poverty & Yale*

University Law School Allard K. Lowenstein Human Rights Clinic. Retrieved from https://www.nlchp.org/documents/WelcomeHome_TentCities

Kertesz, S., Crouch, K., Milby, J., Cusimano, R., & Schumacher, J. (2009). Housing first for homeless persons with active addiction: Are we overreaching? *Milbank Quarterly 87*(2) pp. 495–534.

Kertesz, S., Mullins, A., Schumacher, J., Wallace, D., Kirk, K., & Milby, J. (2007). Long-term housing and work outcomes among treated cocaine-dependent homeless persons. *Journal of Behavioral Health Services & Research 34*(1).

Kertesz, S., & Weiner, S. (2009, May). Housing the chronically homeless: High hopes, complex realities. *Journal of the American Medical Association, 301*(17), 1822–1824.

Larimer, M., Malone, D., Garner. M., Atkins, D. C., Burlingham, B., Lonczak, H. S., . . . Marlatt, A. (April, 2009). Health care and public services use and costs before and after provision of housing of chronically homeless persons with severe alcohol problems. *Journal of the American Medical Association, 301*(13), 1349–1357.

MacArthur Foundation. (2016). *Housing grant guidelines.* Retrieved from https://www.macfound.org/info-grantseekers/grantmaking-guidelines/housing-grant-guidelines

Massachusetts Housing and Shelter Alliance. (2011, March). *Home and healthy for good: A statewide Housing First program—progress report: March 2011.* Retrieved from http://www.mhsa.net/matriarch/documents/HHG%20March%202011%20report-Final.pdf

Mazzara, A., Sard, B., & Rice, D. (2016). Rental assistance to families with children at lowest point in decade. *Center for Budget and Policy Priorities.* Retrieved from http://www.cbpp.org/research/housing/rental-assistance-to-families-with-children-at-lowest-point-in-decade

Morgenstern, J. (2010, August 15). 'Housing first' and helping the homeless. *Los Angeles Times.* Retrieved from http://articles.latimes.com/2010/aug/15/opinion/la-oe-morgenstern-homeless-20100815

National Coalition for the Homeless. (2011). *Why are people homeless.* Retrieved from http://www.nationalhomeless.org/factsheets/why.html

National Law Center on Homelessness and Poverty. (January, 2015). *Reports: Homelessness in America, overview of data and causes.* Retrieved from http://www.nlchp.org

NYC. (2016, January 11). Breaking records: Mayor de Blasio's affordable housing plan has financed 40,000 apartments so far, enough for 100,000 New Yorkers. *Office of the Mayor.* Retrieved from http://www1.nyc.gov/office-of-the-mayor/news/040–16/breaking-records-mayor-de-blasio-s-affordable-housing-plan-has-financed-40-000-apartments-so-far

Pathways to Housing. (2012). *Annual report.* Retrieved from http://pathways.feralagency.com/wpcontent/themes/pathways/assets/files/2012_Annual_Report.pdf

Sadowski, L., Kee, R., VanderWeele, T., & Buchana, D. (2009, May 6). Effect of a housing and case management program on emergency department visits and hospitalizations among chronically ill homeless adults: a randomized trial. *Journal of the American Medical Association, 301*(17):1771–1778. doi: 10.1001/jama.2009.561

Santich, K. (2016, June 28). Orlando gets affordable housing boost with new project. *Orlando Sentinel.* Retrieved from http://www.orlandosentinel.com/news/breaking-news/os-homeless-housing-mercy-drive-20160628-story.html

Smith, T. (2010, June 22). Obama Administration unveils national strategic plan to prevent and end homelessness. *U.S. Department of Housing and Development.* Retrieved from http://portal.hud.gov/hudportal/HUD?src=/press/press_releases_media_advisories/2010/HUDN0.10–132

U.S. Conference of Mayors. (2015, December). *Hunger and homelessness survey: A status report on hunger and homelessness in America's cities.* Retrieved from https://www.usmayors.org/pressreleases/uploads/2015/1221-report-hhreport.pdf

U.S. Department of Health and Human Services. (2007, March). *Strategic action plan on homelessness.* Retrieved from http://www.hhs.gov/homeless/research/endhomelessness.html

U.S. Department of Housing and Urban Development: Office of Community Planning and Development. (2015, October). *The 2015 annual homeless assessment report to Congress.* Retrieved from https://www.hudexchange.info/resources/documents/2015-AHAR-Part-1.pdf

U.S. Department of Housing and Urban Development: Office of Community Planning and Development. (n.d.). *"VASH Plus": A brief review of a successful strategy for implementing the HUD-VASH program in Washington, D.C.* Retrieved from https://www.hudexchange.info/resources/documents/vashplus.pdf

U.S. Interagency Council on Homelessness. (2013). *Annual update 2013: Opening doors.* Retrieved from http://usich.gov/opening_doors/annual-update-2013

Woodard, B. (2015, June 29). What you need to know about Seattle's homeless crisis. *Seattle Times.* Retrieved from http://www.seattletimes.com/seattle-news/seahomeless-what-you-need-to-know-about-seattles-homeless-crisis/?utm_source=news.google.com&utm_medium=Referral&utm_campaign=rss_editors_picks_feed_homepage&google_editors_picks=true

Chapter 11

Examining the Elementary and Secondary Education System in the United States and One Family's Dilemma

Fight or Flight

When the letter addressed to "The Parents of Julius Wilson" arrived, Lavonda knew it might contain great news or just more disappointing news for her 9-year-old son and his future. Even without opening the envelope, Lavonda could see from the return address that it contained results of the annual lottery for admission to Oakesdale Charter School. Each year, hopeful parents from across Middleton School District enter the lottery, pinning the hopes and dreams of their children on a winning ticket offering the chance at an excellent education and all that comes with it. The waiting list for Oakesdale is long; no amount of pressure, lobbying, or special pleading by parents would give their children a better chance of enrollment. Many believe that the lottery, with all of its impersonal, impartial randomness, determines a child's future. Or so it seems. At the very least, it is a ticket out of some of the elementary schools in Middleton that many people consider inferior.

Lavonda Wilson had been down this road twice and twice opened the letter only to be very disappointed. For the first lottery, she and Julius had gone in person to witness the drawing of names, holding their breath each time a name was read aloud with a sobering formality by a Oakesdale Charter School administrator. Each time a name was read, the lucky family members celebrated with clapping, whistles, high fives, or shouts of "Hallelujah," expressing excitement and gratitude that their child had been selected. Julius, a 7-year-old optimist at the time, remained steadfast and hopeful to the very end; he was certain his dream of going to Oakesdale with its friendly teachers, brightly painted walls, and a treasure trove of library books was within his grasp. When, given the odds, the nearly inevitable happened and Julius was not selected, Lavonda expected him to tear up and mope. Instead, Julius calmly said, "Let's go home, Mom." Perhaps he was attempting to support his mother in their time of mutual disappointment. Lavonda feared, instead, that Julius was recognizing the facts about his world: the roll of the dice doesn't always, or even usually, go your way when you are poor. It's a good lesson about gambling but sad when seen in such a young child.

Lavonda vowed never to put herself or Julius through that experience again. Last year, like this year, she simply waited at home for the formal letter announcing the results. Julius was aware he had been entered in the lottery, but he did not understand the process or the time frame for selection. When last year's bad news arrived in the mail, Lavonda opened it immediately. The ever-curious Julius stood by her side, and she was forced to reveal the results while still reeling from her own disappointment. This year, she chose to wait for an opportunity when Julius had his nose in a book and when she had a rare moment of privacy from her extended family in the crowded apartment before nervously opening the envelope. Lavonda did not want anybody, especially Julius, to witness her tears this time.

She ripped open the envelope and read the first sentence. *"Congratulations! Your son Julius Lamar Wilson has been selected for admission to the fourth grade class of Oakesdale Charter School, to be enrolled in August of . . ."* Lavonda read the letter twice before fully absorbing the good news. Fortune was smiling on her. Julius had a winning ticket and an opportunity for a potentially better future. Lavonda also realized, though, that the choices she faced were more complicated than before, and the decision to transfer Julius to Oakesdale was a little less cut-and-dried. Here is a look back at why.

LAVONDA'S LIFE

Only 3 weeks before, Lavonda had received a different life-changing envelope. "At last!" shouted Lavonda as she read the letter from the housing department. She and her son were actually going to be able to move into an apartment of their own. It seemed too good to be true. During the 3 years she had been on a waiting list for Section 8 housing, the two of them lived with her sister, Nettie, Nettie's partner, Karl, and their three young children. Seven people in a two-bedroom apartment meant tight quarters. Lavonda and Julius slept on the living room floor and shoved their bedding into the hall closet during the day. While Nettie and Karl tolerated the arrangement, Lavonda knew that she had long worn out her welcome. Until then, however, she had no other viable option.

Lavonda felt that she and Julius were finally going to get a break. Life had been hard since she left home at 18 to marry, much to the disappointment of her parents. They had encouraged her to follow in the footsteps of her college-educated brother, Devon, rather than her sister, Nettie, who chose to start a family rather than continue her education. Lavonda's marriage quickly turned sour, ending before Julius was born. Always struggling just to survive, Lavonda held a series of low-wage, part-time jobs—often more than one at a time—and took classes when she could toward an associate degree. "If only I had listened to my parents," she often told herself, but then always concluded the thought with "Well, then I wouldn't have Julius in my life." She was determined to do everything in her power to ensure that Julius chose his uncle Devon's path. Devon now lived abroad, and while she rarely saw him, they remained close. Her brother's generous gifts of money helped Lavonda get by; in fact, that extra cash was the only way she would be able to get the electricity turned on in her new apartment and maybe have enough to buy a few modest furnishings.

The routine of their life would not change much after they moved into the new apartment, but Lavonda felt lighter and more relaxed. She was optimistic that things would keep getting better. Lavonda and Julius would be a family living on their own, not in her parents' home, which had been the case for a few years, or with her sister. She envisioned quiet evenings with just the two of them doing homework together and taking turns reading to each other from books Julius checked out from the library. They did this now, but the constant racket and interruptions of three noisy young children and two additional adults made privacy a rare privilege. Their weekend rituals would certainly not change. When Lavonda had a rare Saturday off, she would check out free cultural events or find out if the Boys and Girls Club that Julius attended had discount tickets to any events. One outing that they would never miss, regardless of where they lived, entailed their weekly visit to Lavonda's mom, who had early onset Alzheimer's and now resided in a nursing home. Seeing Julius, even if she could not always remember his name, brought a smile to her mom, and Julius's patience with Gram always made Lavonda proud.

It had been during one of those bus rides to the nursing home that Julius had noticed a billboard advertising the exhibit scheduled for the next month at the nearby Fairview Zoo called "Turtles: Coming Out of Their Shell." He rarely asked to do anything that cost money, but he pleaded with his mom to take him, which she promised to do. Working three double shifts meant having to miss class, which she hated to do, but Lavonda managed to pay for tickets and was even able to get off work for the opening day of the exhibit. During the month of waiting, Julius talked constantly about the exhibit and checked out all the books he could find about turtles. On the opening day of the exhibit, he made sure they arrived at the zoo long before the exhibit actually opened so he could be the first to witness what he was sure would be a magnificent sight. He was not disappointed and would have remained at the exhibit all day had Lavonda not coaxed him away to go look at the rest of the zoo inhabitants. During the next couple of days, Julius's delight from their zoo excursion left Lavonda feeling truly satisfied.

SCHOOL DAZE

The feeling of satisfaction only lasted until Julius returned home after school on Monday reporting the reaction he received from his teacher and schoolmates when he talked about the turtle exhibit. He could not hide his disappointment as he recounted that in science class he had raised his hand during show and tell. He had been looking forward to sharing about the turtle exhibit. He told his mom, "I barely got started explaining the unusual properties of ectotherms when Mrs. Galston interrupted and said they are called reptiles." Julius continued, "I responded, 'Actually, reptiles are also known as ectotherms,' and Mrs. Galston said that I should not be so sassy." Julius fell quiet, so Lavonda asked if that was it. Julius, practically in tears, continued the story saying that "Mrs. Galston also said I wasn't following the classroom citizenship rules, and that my name would be put in the warning box. Mrs. Galston said I was to put my head on the desk until I had an attitude adjustment." Lavonda could feel herself fuming but made sure she kept quiet as Julius continued. Tears were rolling down his cheeks by the time he told his mom about how the other kids started giggling, and the giggles got louder when one classmate whispered he was an "ecto-nerd."

This was not the first time that her son had encountered responses from teachers, other staff at the school, or students that Lavonda worried would stifle his enthusiasm for learning. For example, Julius got in trouble on a previous occasion because he was caught reading a book when he was supposed to be reviewing a worksheet of basic addition and subtraction questions.

"I've known addition and subtraction since last year," Julius told his mom after the incident. "My teacher said we need to keep going over them so our school will pass a test. But I already know them, and it's boring."

When Lavonda spoke to his teacher, she affirmed Julius's claim that they were going over some fairly simple review material. "We've got both state and federal standardized tests, Ms. Wilson," said Mrs. Galston. "Frankly, I would enjoy doing something more creative, but we simply don't have that luxury at Worthington Elementary." She added, "And besides, I want these young people to learn to follow my directions. If they're lucky enough to get jobs someday, they'll need to listen to the boss." Lavonda noted that Mrs. Galston assumed kids like Julius would never themselves be qualified enough to be "the boss," but she let it pass.

The ectotherm episode was Lavonda's tipping point. Julius had always been an inquisitive child, and Lavonda marveled at his curiosity and knowledge about plant and animal life. It also reminded her of an incident when a teacher threw away a report Julius had spent hours on because the newspaper article he used was longer than the page, while the instructions said it had to fit on the page (he had folded it neatly up). "Damnit," said Lavonda under her breath, "this is the last straw; I have to do something. It's important for Julius to be in a school that helps him reach his full potential." But what should I do, and realistically, what can I do? I haven't gotten very far before in trying to get Julius into a better school. *I have to do something,* she thought

This incident confirmed her decision to, for the third time, sign Julius up for the lottery at the much-heralded Oakesdale Charter School. She knew that given the limited number of slots, there was not a high probability of his name being selected. Stellar Start, a private Lutheran school, a half-hour bus ride away, was a long shot as well. Unless they had increased the maximum scholarship available since the last time she inquired, even with her brother's help she would need to make almost double her current wage to pay the tuition. Lavonda understood why those who could afford to do so had chosen to leave the poorer neighborhoods in the city for better schools. Yet it still left her angry. Most people simply did not have the option to pick up and relocate. Stuck in one place, they were too often assigned to schools seemingly incapable of providing students with a success-oriented education, and every time someone with a job and parents who cared about education left the area, it made it tougher for those left behind.

Lavonda also was kicking herself for being so excited about finally receiving the notice that she could move into a subsidized apartment. While it would be a much better living situation for Julius, the new apartment would be smack dab in the middle of one of the poorer areas in the Middleton school district. Lavonda believed that, in the long run, the focus should be on improving all the mediocre public schools in low-income areas. However, for the short run, her primary concern was for Julius to get a good education.

Lavonda knew it was not an all-or-nothing situation. There were some high-quality, dedicated teachers at Worthington-Elementary who work hard to overcome the lack of adequate facilities and resources. Over the years, the Middleton City Public School District had graduated some students who went on to be doctors, authors, a U.S. congressman, and even a Nobel Prize-winning scientist. Still, there were lower test scores and higher drop-out rates than in other surrounding school districts where there was more wealth and less poverty. It seemed that many of the best teachers ended up leaving once they could secure a teaching job in one of the nearby districts.

Sometimes Lavonda thought the lottery at Oakesdale Charter School was less random than the unequal allocation of public school funds. She feared that Julius might get a subpar education if he remained in the Middleton Public School District but didn't know for sure that would be the case. She did know that discipline, or lack thereof, is a huge issue in many of the classrooms and is getting progressively worse as the children get older. Violent outbursts were not a daily occurrence, but Julius had shared plenty of stories about fights that had gone on for quite a while before any adult intervened. There had even been a couple of cases in the past year of aggressive acts against teachers. And although he was only 9, Julius had told his mom that he knew kids at the schools who used drugs.

Knowing of no other immediate solution, Lavonda made an appointment with Dr. Clara James, the new principal at Worthington Elementary. A week after the incident in Mrs. Galston's class, Julius and Lavonda were sitting in a sparsely decorated but welcoming office ("Home of the Worthington Eagles"), where they were greeted warmly by Dr. James. Lavonda found herself impressed with the way Dr. James interacted with Julius. After a few minutes together, Dr. James suggested Julius wait back in the outer office where he could look through some new puzzles and creative games while she had a private talk with his mom. Dr. James listened intently to Lavonda's concerns, but when Lavonda raised the topic of Mrs. Galston, Dr. James sighed and lowered her voice.

"Ms. Wilson," said Dr. James, "I understand your concerns, but I must tell you, Mrs. Galston is one of our most experienced teachers. I might have handled the situation with Julius somewhat differently, but Mrs. Galston knows how to keep discipline in her classroom, which is half the battle around here. She has outlasted some of the young idealistic teachers. They show up here with a bag full of new methods and techniques but find that their classrooms descend into complete chaos. They are gone, but Mrs. Galston is still here. I assure you, Ms. Wilson, I have much bigger headaches than Mrs. Galston."

"You're the principal," Lavonda said. "Why don't you get rid of the bad teachers?"

"Lavonda—may I call you Lavonda? Are you familiar with tenure?" asked Dr. James. "Isn't it like job security or something?" answered Lavonda, with some uncertainty. "Pretty much job security for life," said Dr. James, adding, "While there are arguments for and against it, it does have some drawbacks at a place such as Worthington Elementary. I cannot remove a tenured faculty member without cause. And, I'm sorry to say, lack of creativity in the classroom is not one of those causes." "Then why should I keep Julius at Worthington?" asked Lavonda, surprised at her own bluntness.

Dr. James smiled at Lavonda. "Thank you for that excellent question. Let me tell you." Much of the remainder of the 20-minute meeting was an overview of changes being implemented at the school, one being a committee of teachers and parents appointed to work on improving the school atmosphere. Another idea being pursued was the introduction of an advanced placement for students like Julius. Before she knew it, Lavonda agreed to be on the committee, surprised to be asked, somewhat flattered but also inspired. The winning argument by Dr. James had been this challenge: "If you dream of a better school, Lavonda, why not work at improving the one right here in your community? This is your school. It belongs to you and Julius. Help me make it work so that every child in the area can get a quality education, not just those who can access already outstanding schools or hit the lottery. Don't take that the wrong way. I certainly understand why some children from this area attempt to get into Oakesdale or cross boundaries and attend a school outside of the district.

"As far as Oakesdale, the principal from there and I actually went to school together and are friends. We share similar philosophies about education. I just want you to know that, under my direction, this school is headed in the right direction. Test scores are improving, bad behavior is less frequent, and more children believe that they can succeed. In the last few years, inner-city schools in many large cities in the United States have been making substantial gains in student outcomes. Inner-city schools in poor areas are not doomed, and I intend to make sure Worthington continues to make the changes needed for our students to thrive academically and socially."

Dr. James was honest when explaining that Worthington Elementary had a long way to go and that it was an uphill battle: "We are making progress and have seen some small victories. Big changes will happen as well, but it is going to take several years to remake a school like Worthington Elementary." Lavonda nodded, but inside she had some nagging questions about the slow pace of reform. And, of course, what about the future for Julius, not just for other kids, in the years to come?

Lavonda left Dr. James's office feeling somewhat better but knew Julius would still be in a classroom with a less than stellar teacher. Dr. James had mentioned her plans for more teacher training and working with teachers so they would do a better job of engaging all students, the slower ones and the brighter ones, as well as those in the middle. Lavonda had her doubts that a training session would be enough for Mrs. Galston to change her ways. On the other hand, although Julius had been very upset about the ectotherm incident, he enjoyed school, fit in well, was getting good grades, and he took initiative on his own to challenge himself and learn, so she didn't feel he was way behind where he should be academically. Lavonda also believed if she worked within the system, supporting Dr. James in the school reform efforts, Julius might get a little favored treatment when it came to future classroom assignments. One good turn deserves another or so she hoped.

The best thing she could do in the immediate future, Lavonda concluded, was to become more informed about the education system in general and how to be an active member of the committee that she had been invited to join. Not quite sure where to start, Lavonda decided to check into how public education was funded; she often wondered why public schools in wealthier areas seemed newer and had more state-of-the-art equipment. She also did not really know the difference between public schools, private schools, magnet schools, and charter schools. She decided to check out home schooling as well, although this was not a viable option for her. From a class she had taken at the junior college, she knew it was important to look at the reported outcomes of the different types of schools. Middleton did not have a voucher system, but Lavonda thought it was still worth knowing what they were. Finally, she was most curious about what the practices of the "best" schools were as she felt that she could not really contribute to the committee if she did not look into what appeared to be working.

BACKGROUND INFORMATION

There are approximately 57 million elementary and secondary students in schools in the United States. In 2016, it was estimated that approximately 87% of these students would attend public school, and 10% would attend private schools (National Center for Education Statistics, 2016a). The remaining approximately 3% of children are home-schooled (National Center for Education Statistics, 2014). In early 2008, the national average graduation rate[1] was 73%, but in the 50 largest cities, the graduation rate was 52% (Grey, 2008). Just a couple of years before that, in some schools in Detroit, Baltimore, and New York City, the graduation rate was less than 40% (Toppo, 2006).

Many schools across the nation have increased their graduation rates in recent years with students of color showing greater gains than Whites. In the 2013–2014 school year, the national graduation rate was up to 82%. As Figure 11.1 indicates, there is a difference in graduation rates when broken down by race/ethnicity with students of color having lower graduation rates than White students. When narrowing the lens to just public schools in large metropolitan areas with high concentrations of poverty, the graduation rates are even lower at 65.4% for Blacks and 64% for Hispanics in 2015 (National Center for Education Statistics, 2016b). That same year, the overall graduation rate in Washington, DC, was 64% (Chandler & Balingit, 2015). While low, these numbers still showed a marked improvement, suggesting that some of the

---

[1] The method used to arrive at this number was to determine the percentage of ninth graders who graduated within 4 years.

Figure 11.1   Adjusted Cohort Graduation Rate (ACGR) for Public High School Students by Race/Ethnicity: School Year 2013–2014

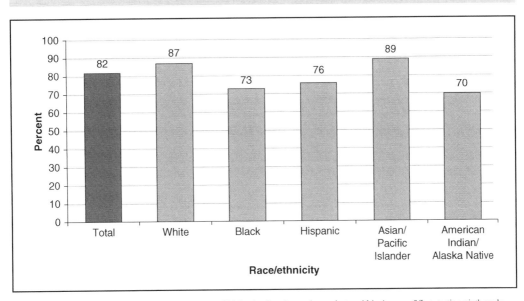

Note: The AFGR provides an estimate of the percentage of high school students who graduate within 4 years of first starting ninth grade. The rate uses aggregate student enrollment data to estimate the size of an incoming freshman class and aggregate counts of diplomas awarded 4 years later.
Source: U.S. Department of Education, Office of Elementary and Secondary Education, Consolidated State Performance Report, 2013–14. See *Digest of Education Statistics 2015.*

changes being implemented have paid off. A factor to keep in mind when looking at graduation rates is that they do not necessarily mean students are ready for college. For example, in New York City, fewer than half those graduating from high school tested as being prepared for academic success in college (Harris, 2016).

Funding Sources for Public Education

Though it might come as a surprise to many citizens, the U.S. Constitution does not guarantee its citizens the right to a free education. That decision was left to the states. In fact, in 1973, a U.S. Supreme Court case, *San Antonio Independent School District v. Rodriquez,* ruled that education is not a "fundamental right" under the federal Constitution. However, each state's constitution does guarantee that free public education is a right that will be afforded by the state. Many states have been sued by claimants who do not believe this right is being upheld. In most states there has been some form of legal action taken to address education-funding disparities or what plaintiffs have framed as educational adequacy. As of 2010, plaintiffs had won 26 cases in which they claimed a lack of educational adequacy (New America, n.d.).

The latest year that the National Center for Education Statistics (2013a) provided costs for K–12 education in the United States was 2012–2013. The total from all levels of government was approximately $620 billion. Currently, approximately 12% of funding for public schools comes from the federal government with state and local governments picking up the remaining 88%. There is great variability between states regarding the percentage of funds that comes from the state and the percentage that derives from local taxes. Moreover, this percentage has changed over time. Some states have chosen to contribute a percentage much higher than the average 44% state contribution in order to deal with the disparity that results from depending heavily on local taxes (New America, n.d.). When local property taxes are depended on, school districts in wealthier districts generate a lot more revenue from taxes than do poorer districts even if the tax rate is the same.

An Education Law Center study on the disparity for funding public education concludes that "only six states are positioned relatively well on all four measures[2] [of equity] to provide equality of educational opportunity for all children regardless of background, family income, where they live or where they go to school" (Strauss, 2010, p. 1). In discussing their findings and the need for more equitable funding, the authors of the report state that

> funding alone will not lead to better academic performance and outcomes for students. . . . High poverty schools need sufficient funds, effectively and efficiently used, to achieve established outcome goals and prepare students for high school graduation and for post-secondary education or the workforce. (Baker, Sciarra, & Farrie, 2010, p.1)

There are four states[3] that provide more funding to districts with a high number of students living in poverty than to wealthier districts. On the other hand, there are states where just the opposite takes place. Districts with high poverty rates are provided with less state funding than districts with low poverty rates (Strauss, 2010). Added to the existing disparity are the budget problems that states across the nation are facing. In 2014, 35 states were providing less funding for education than they had before the recession, and 14 of the 35 were spending 10% less per pupil. Moreover, in states that increased funding in 2013–2014, the increase was not enough to make up for the cuts that had been made in the preceding years (Leachman & Mai, 2014).

---

[2] The four measures are interrelated and include funding level, funding distribution, ratio of state spending to state per capita gross domestic product, and proportion of children attending public school to those attending private schools (Baker, Sciarra, & Farrie, 2010). The states include Connecticut, Iowa, Massachusetts, New Jersey, Vermont, and Wyoming.

[3] Utah, New Jersey, Minnesota, and Ohio.

Disparities in Public Education

The Government Accountability Office (GAO)[4] (2016) released findings of their investigation into disparities and discrimination in K–12 public education in the United States. Their findings support other research indicating that today segregation is widespread in U.S. schools and has grown since the turn of the 21st century. Research by Orfield, Frankenberg, Ee, & Kuscera (2014) informs us that changing demographics are part of the picture, with a drop of close to 30% of White students and close to five times as many Latino students.

In some parts of the country, schools are more segregated than others. More and more Black and Latino students are attending suburban schools with low enrollment of White students. In New York, California, and Texas, over half of Latino students attend schools that are 90% or more minority children. In New York, Illinois, Maryland, and Michigan, over half of students who are Black go to schools that are 90% or more minority (Lee, 2014, p. 1). The concern is the quality of education received by students who attend highly segregated schools that most often overlap with high levels of poverty. The GAO report (2016) notes that these schools offer fewer resources and disproportionately fewer courses in science, math, and college prep. Both the GAO report and Civil Rights Project reports call for actions that will lead to more effectively addressing racial disparity that exists and limits children of color from obtaining a quality education. Orfield et al. (2014) conclude that "desegregation is not a panacea and it is not feasible in some situations. Where it is possible, . . . desegregation properly implemented can make a very real contribution to equalizing educational opportunities and preparing young Americans to live, work and govern together in our extremely diverse society" (executive summary).

Charter Schools

Charter schools are part of the public education system but provide an alternative to the traditional public school. There are a wide variety of types of charter schools: some charter schools have no one area of specialization but just seek to provide a high-quality education, while others specialize in areas such as science, technology, or the arts. Charter schools are exempt from some of the rules and regulations of traditional public schools, but there are other rules, such as length of school year and testing requirements, that they must abide by. More important, as part of the public school system, they must be approved by the local school board.

---

[4] The General Accountability Office is a nonpartisan government watchdog agency that works for Congress. Given the research on school segregation, it was charged with completing an independent study.

Charter schools typically receive less government funding per student than do traditional public schools, though that too varies.

While charter schools have been growing in number since their inception in 1991, they still only enroll a small percentage of our nation's 57 million public school students. As of the 2014–2015 school year, there were 6,700 charter schools nationwide enrolling over 2.9 million students (National Alliance for Public Charter Schools, 2015). Too often there are more students than openings for enrollment at charter schools because many parents, especially those in low-income areas, see them as a way to escape urban public schools where test scores are low and failing grades are common for students. The National Alliance for Public Charter Schools estimates that there are over 1 million students nationwide on the waiting list to get into charter schools (National Alliance for Public Charter Schools, 2014). A lottery system is relied upon for the available spots, leaving parents whose children are not selected disheartened. President Obama and his initial Secretary of Education, Arne Duncan, were strong proponents of increasing the number of charter schools and have made more federal dollars available for high-quality charter schools, especially in areas where existing public schools have been marked as needing improvements (Federal Register, 2010).

Comparing learning at urban charter schools to traditional public schools is challenging, and there are limitations to the research, so results should be considered with caution. Moreover, general conclusions and averages can be misleading. There is great variability among charter schools just as there is great variability among traditional public schools. In 2013, the Center for Research on Education Outcomes at Stanford University (CREDO) released its research findings of charter schools in 26 states and New York City. The findings indicated a small positive overall difference on reading scores when comparing charter school students' test scores to traditional public school students. No overall difference was found on math scores. Some charter school children scored better on reading and math scores, but in some schools, they also scored worse than their traditional public school counterparts. The researchers concluded that while a statistically significant difference was found in reading scores, the difference in practical terms was "trivial" (CREDO, 2013). Moreover, they advised caution in drawing any conclusions from the findings due to limitations of the research (Maul & McClelland, 2013). There was a relative improvement in average charter school quality since CREDO's 2009 study, but it may be largely attributed to the closing of some poorer performing charter schools.

The most recent study by CREDO in 2015 indicates that in the 41 regions (in 22 states) assessed, on average, "urban charter school children showed significantly greater success in both math and reading than their tradition public school counterparts" (CREDO, 2015, p. 1). A more detailed look informs us that math scores in 26 of the regions and reading scores in 23 of the regions were higher for urban charter school students than students in traditional public schools. In 11 regions in math and in 10 regions in reading, the test scores for those in urban charter schools were worse than those of their counterparts in traditional public schools. There was no difference in the scores for math in four regions, and in reading, there was no difference in scores in eight regions. Moreover, despite the overall positive learning impacts of urban charter schools, especially among Black, Hispanic, and special education students, in some cities the majority of charter schools show worse learning outcomes, and in some cities, over half the charter schools show significantly worse outcomes than traditional public school alternatives (Wihbey, 2015).

Magnet Schools

Magnet schools, like charter schools, are not private schools but are part of the public school system. Also, like many charter schools, they have a special focus area or mode of instruction. There are Montessori magnet schools (and Montessori charter schools), and there are magnet schools that might focus on the performing arts or math and science just as is the case with charter schools. A key difference is that charter schools have a contract that is established (a charter) that allows them to operate on their own and not under the public school bureaucracy; magnet schools have no such separate contract and operate under the local public school administration. Another difference is that approximately one third of magnet schools have selection criteria in place. That criterion might, for example, require that students have a particular talent, or fall into the "gifted" category, in order to gain acceptance. The name "magnet schools" comes from the fact that students who attend them are pulled from different areas of the community and leave the zone in which the public school they would otherwise attend is located. Magnet schools often receive "extra" funding from the government for the supplies they need to implement their focus. While there are great benefits for the 3.2 million[5] students who attend magnet schools, they are criticized for pulling the brightest students from neighboring public schools and also taking needed funds from regular public schools. Moreover, those who could benefit from them often are not selected to attend them (Chen, 2015).

Private Schools

Private schools vary greatly in terms of mission, focus, cost, resources, and quality. Of the total number of K-12 students in the United States who attend private schools (approximately 9% of all students), 81% of them attend religiously

---

[5] Data provided by the National Center for Education Statistics (2015).

affiliated schools. One factor that makes comparisons of school types difficult is the fact that the household income of private school students is two thirds higher than the household income of public school students (Strauss, 2010). In households with income under $50,000, 6% attend private schools, whereas the percent is 26% in households with incomes of $200,000 or more (Kolko, 2014).

Parents choose private schools for many reasons. A study by the Friedman Foundation found that for low- and middle-income families receiving scholarships, the top reasons included better student discipline, small class size, learning environment, student safety, and the individual attention their child receives (Bedrick, 2013). Some parents like the focus on religious values. While there is research that supports the belief that private schools provide a better education, not all private schools measure up, and a study by Lubienski and Lubienski calls into question some of the previous research. The Lubienskis claim that traditional public school students actually score better in math than do private school students when demographic differences are accounted for (Snyder, 2013). Still, studies do show that private school students, when compared to similar public school students, are more likely to both graduate and continue on to college (Dynarski, 2014). Dynarski (2014) goes on to say that it is more helpful to determine ways to improve education in general than debate if public or private is better.

Private School Choice: Vouchers, Scholarship Tax Credits, Personal Tax Credits, and Deductions

Today there are 27 states, and the District of Columbia, who offer vouchers, scholarship tax credits, or personal tax credits and deductions as a means to increase the opportunity for children to access a private education (Cunningham, 2013). These policies have been put in place despite a great deal of opposition by the public. A 2013 Gallop Poll indicated that 70% of Americans oppose private school vouchers (Bushaw & Lopez, 2013). Proponents of private school choice claim that choice serves as incentive to the public schools to improve. School choice, proponents argue, introduces competition, and if poor-performing public schools want to retain their students, they will improve. Some parents in areas with poor-performing schools support private school choice knowing that it is their only chance of enrolling their child in a school with a record of good outcomes.

Opponents of private school choice, and vouchers in particular, voice a variety of concerns. Many believe that vouchers simply siphon off money from public schools that 88% of all students still attend. They claim that the money used for vouchers will impact more children if used to improve the public school system rather than help a small number of students escape the system. Opponents also argue that students already in private schools should not be given government dollars to subsidize their private education. Vouchers often do not provide enough of a subsidy for a low-income child to attend an expensive private school.

Opponents, claiming that vouchers are a violation of the Constitution, have taken cases to state supreme courts as well as one being heard by the U.S. Supreme Court. In 2002, the U.S. Supreme Court upheld the Cleveland school voucher program. In 2006, the Florida Supreme Court ruled that a voucher program "violated the state constitution by shifting money from public education to the support of private and religious schools." And a Maine law banning state funding of religious schools has twice been upheld by the state supreme court. In March of 2013, the Indiana Supreme Court ruled that vouchers were not a violation of church and state (Religion News Foundation, 2014).

Home Schooling

Home schooling has grown significantly over the past decade. While the overall numbers are low, relative to the number in public schools, they continue to climb. The National Home Education Research Institute estimates that, in 2015, there were approximately 2.2 million children in grades K–12 who were home schooled. Of these children, there is a wide demographic mix in terms of parents' educational status, ethnicity, religion, and socioeconomic class. There are also a wide variety of reasons parents give for choosing to home school. Ray (2015) found common reasons for home schooling included teaching a certain set of values and beliefs; wanting to be able to individualize the curriculum; enhancing family relationships; providing a safe environment; and limiting exposure to physical violence, drugs and alcohol, psychological abuse, and inappropriate messages about sex.

In his 3-year study on home schooling, Vanderbilt professor Joseph Murphy found that values and religion were the key reasons parents chose to homeschool, and parents believed they could provide their children with a higher quality education. Murphy also found that most home-schooled children have strong social networks, which has been a concern voiced by skeptics of home schooling. Measuring academic outcomes is challenging, but Murphy did find that the same percentage of home-schooled children attend college as do children who attend traditional public schools (Wetzel, 2012).

The Need for an Improved Education System
With Effective Teaching Models and Practices

The landmark Elementary and Secondary Education Act of 1965 has been revised and amended countless times, always with the hope of improving our educational system to better prepare our children for their future and for the future of the nation. At the dawn of this century, No Child Left Behind (NCLB) legislation promised better academic outcomes, yet it has fallen far short of its goal of 100% proficiency in math and reading. While there has been improvement in performance since NCLB became law in 2001, the 2013 National Report Card indicated that "forty-one percent of public school students at grade 4 and 34 percent at grade 8 performed at or above Proficient in mathematics in 2013" (National Center for Education Statistics, 2013b, p. 8). And "thirty-four percent of public school students performed at or above Proficient in reading in 2013 at both grades 4 and 8, with the percentages in the states ranging from 17 to 48 percent" (National Center for Education Statistics, 2013b, p. 9).

President Obama's long-serving secretary of education, Arne Duncan, viewed NCLB as "out-of-date, and tired and prescriptive" (Duncan, 2013, p. 1). Then Secretary Duncan also stated that "I believe we can replace it with a law that recognizes that schools need more support—and more money, more resources—than they receive today" (Duncan, 2013, p. 1). Due to the many unintended consequences of NCLB, such as lowering standards so it appears the students appeared proficient, many states have received waivers from having to follow all aspects of NCLB. These states are implementing their own educational reforms aimed at truly increasing proficiency. There are also federal dollars through the federal Race to the Top initiative that states can apply for. And more reform is always on the horizon.

While there are no magic bullets, there appear to be some common ingredients in private, traditional public, charter, and magnet schools where children are meeting and exceeding academic expectations. Schools currently being praised for providing students with the opportunity to succeed and thrive include but are not limited to the following: strong leadership; structure; high expectations; allowing no excuses from teachers or students; highly motivated and good-quality teachers who care deeply about the students and are committed and willing to put in whatever it takes; teachers who are knowledgeable about how to engage students where they are, in order to bring them to the next level (teachers who are skilled at using a variety of innovative methodologies); using a team approach; and safety. Longer school days, longer school years, tutoring before and after school, and incentives such as a "paycheck" or trips are also ingredients found in some of the schools such as Harlem Success Academy and KIPP, which are known for quality outcomes. A number of schools are attempting to bring in citizen teachers that would not replace the regular teachers but will provide lessons based on their profession. For example, a biologist might bring in water samples that the students can help test and determine levels of bacteria. Citizen teachers are also used to assist with tutoring. Attempting to involve parents more creatively is another approach being taken.

LAVONDA'S CURRENT DILEMMA

In addition to the knowledge that Lavonda acquired from her research, another factor that complicated matters was what she learned when she shared the good news about the letter from Oakesdale with Nettie. "This is what we have hoped and prayed for and now it can become a reality," she told her sister. Her sister's response took Lavonda by surprise. Instead of being overjoyed, Nettie's face expressed concern as she told Lavonda a little news of her own. Nettie had been assigned the early morning shift at work. "I'm sorry, but I wasn't given a choice other than to quit my job. I won't be able to drive Julius to Oakesdale like we planned when we discussed it in the past."

Lavonda's heart dropped. Their new apartment was across town from Oakesdale, and she had no one to get him there. Public transportation was an option, but he would have to make a transfer in a rough area of town, and it was a 20-minute wait at the transfer point. The letter had made it clear that transportation was the responsibility of the parent. "What am I going to do?" Lavonda said, half out loud. "I can't quit work to get him to school. I could pick him up from school since they have extended day, but that means he won't be spending time at the Boys and Girls Club." Nettie just looked sadly at Lavonda, as she had no good solution.

At first, Lavonda had thought the Boys and Girls Club was an okay place for Julius but nothing special. In the past 6 months, however, Lavonda noticed that a couple of the male staff members had become heroes in Julius's eyes. One of them gave him challenging, but fun, extra problems to solve in math, and they served as positive role models. Thinking about what he might miss out on if he stopped going to the Boys and Girls Club was also a factor Lavonda had to consider.

While Oakesdale had a great reputation, she realized she was depending exclusively on the information they provided about themselves in their glossy brochures; she needed to dig deeper. Lavonda did know a couple of parents with kids who attended Oakesdale, and they always spoke very highly about the school. They say their children feel both safe and cared for, and they like the cheerful, safe environment. Yet, when she compared state standardized test scores, Lavonda found that third graders at Oakesdale had achieved nearly the same results as Worthington Elementary third graders. Oakesdale had not "blown away" the competition as Lavonda would have expected (or as the school's press releases implied). However, Lavonda also knew test scores were not everything; Oakesdale had greater resources and the atmosphere there was clearly more welcoming than at Worthington Elementary. Maybe Oakesdale was not as exceptional as Lavonda had originally thought, but people were lining up to get into it. Once enrolled, a higher percentage of Oakesdale students stayed in school and graduated compared to Worthington.

No one was lining up to get into Worthington Elementary, yet Principal James was clearly bringing about changes. Although Lavonda had only been to a couple of committee meetings at the school, she was convinced that the leadership of Dr. James would turn the school around eventually. She had met parents and school staff, including the school social worker, who she was impressed by. And Ms. Posey, the teacher Julius would have next year at Worthington, was a favorite of the children. Lavonda doubted there was a more top-notch teacher, but what about after next year? Plus, in the back of her mind, Lavonda knew that even if Julius went to Oakesdale through middle school, she would want him to apply to Collegiate Prep, the area's high school for students who had good academic performance. It was a public school, so there were no tuition costs and there was no lottery. The only criterion was a very good academic record. Lavonda was confident that Julius could and would be able to qualify if his elementary and middle school opportunities were enhanced.

One more factor gnawed at Lavonda's conscience: Nettie's children would likely be going to Worthington Elementary unless each of them, too, beat the odds and hit the lottery for a future slot at the charter school. And even if they did get in, who knew if their parents could transport them. They were headed to the local public school like the majority of kids in her neighborhood, and their future depended on the willingness of parents, administrators, and teachers to stick around and fix the problems. Lavonda wanted to do everything in her power to make sure Julius got a good education, but her nephews and niece were like her own children. Why do you have to win a lottery to get into a charter school? Does it provide that much better an education after all? Lavonda's thoughts were scattered, and she knew she needed to sit down and reflect on her priorities and her options.

QUESTIONS FOR DISCUSSION

1. How are public schools funded? What are options for ensuring more equitable funding of public education?

2. What are some of the common ingredients of schools that have positive outcomes? Do these ingredients suggest that there are structural problems in our education system, that children are simply not putting in enough effort (personal attribution), or that parents are not being responsible enough and making sure their children do well (personal attribution)?

3. Which, if any, statistics stand out to you as alarming in regard to education in the United States?

4. Discuss the relationship between education and social justice.

5. What are the pros and cons of vouchers, charter schools, and magnet schools?

6. Provide three to five reasons that Lavonda should send Julius to Oakesdale Charter School.

7. Provide three to five reasons that Lavonda should keep Julius at Worthington Elementary.

8. Discuss how the characters in this chapter fit, or do not fit, with common stereotypes. What messages about the characters do you think the author was trying to convey?

9. What were the strengths and weaknesses of your K–12 educational experience? Based on your experience, do you have ideas about what should be considered when trying to improve poor-performing schools?

CASE ANALYSIS WRITING ASSIGNMENT

1. Read the assigned case study thoroughly prior to class in order to be fully prepared to join in the discussion.

2. Write a case study analysis in which you address the following question: Should Lavonda Wilson transfer her son, Julius, to the Oakesdale Charter School? Why, or why not? Make sure to provide a strong rationale for your choice, drawing specifically from the information presented in the case study.

3. The analysis should be an approximately two-page, typed, double-spaced essay. Your essay should reflect the standards and expectations of college-level writing: spelling, grammar, and appropriate use of paragraphs all matter. If you quote directly from the case study, use quotation marks, and at the end of the quote, indicate the page number the quote appeared on. For example, "The jury is still out as to whether the trend toward more charter schools will bring about the desired outcomes" (Lewis, 2017, p. 97).

4. Your case analysis is due _____ and worth a maximum of _____ points.

INTERNET SOURCES

Brookings Institute (http://www.brookings.edu/research/topics/education)

Center for Budget and Policy Priorities (http://www.cbpp.org)

Harlem Children's Zone–Jeffrey Canada (http://hcz.org)

The Harlem Children's Zone (https://www.youtube.com/watch?v=Di0-xN6xc_w)

Mathmatica Policy Research (https://www.mathematica-mpr.com/our-focus-areas/education)

National Center for Education Statistics (https://nces.ed.gov)

The Civil Rights Project at UCLA (https://www.civilrightsproject.ucla.edu)

The Center for Research on Education Outcomes (https://credo.stanford.edu)

U.S. Department of Education (http://www.ed.gov)

REFERENCES

Baker, B., Sciarra, D., & Farrie, D. (2010). Is school funding fair? A national report card. *Education Law Center.* Retrieved from http://www.schoolfundingfairness.org/National_Report_Card.pdf

Ballotpedia. (November, 2016). Los Angeles, California, affordable housing and labor standards initiative, measure JJJ. *The Encyclopedia of American Politics.* Retrieved from https://ballotpedia.org/Los_Angeles,_California,_Affordable_Housing_and_Labor_Standards_Initiative,_Measure_JJJ_(November_2016)

Bedrick, J. (2013, November 13). New study explains how and why parents choose private schools. *CATO Institute.* Retrieved from http://www.cato.org/blog/new-study-explains-how-why-parents-choose-private-schools

Bushaw, W., & Lopez, S. (2013, January). The 45th PDK/Gallop poll of the public's attitude toward the public schools: Which way do we go? *PDK/Gallop Poll.* Retrieved from https://www.au.org/files/pdf_documents/2013_PDKGallup.pdf

Center for Research on Education Outcomes (CREDO). (2013). *National charter school study.* Retrieved from https://credo.stanford.edu/documents/NCSS%202013%20Final%20Draft.pdf

Center for Research on Education Outcomes (CREDO). (2015). *Urban charter school study.* Retrieved from http://urbancharters.stanford.edu/index.php

Chandler, M., & Balingit, M. (2015, September, 29). Graduation rates surge for Washington, DC public schools, reaching 64% in 2015. *Washington Post.* Retrieved from https://www.washingtonpost.com/local/education/graduation-rates-surge-for-dc-public-schools-reaching-64-percent-in-2015/2015/09/29/57f53cbe-66c9-11e5-9ef3-fde182507eac_story.htm

Chen, G. (2015, May 28). What is a magnet school? *Public School Review.* Retrieved from http://www.publicschoolreview.com/articles/2

Cunningham, J. (2013). Comprehensive school choice policy: A guide for legislators. *The Conference of State Legislators.* Retrieved from http://www.ncsl.org/documents/educ/ComprehensiveSchoolChoicePolicy.pdf

Duncan, A. (2013, February 7). *No child left behind: Early lessons from state flexibility waivers.* Retrieved from http://www.ed.gov/news/speeches/no-child-left-behind-early-lessons-state-flexibility-waivers

Dynarski, M. (2014, June 12). Public or private school? It shouldn't matter. *Brookings Institute.* Retrieved from http://www.brookings.edu/research/papers/2014/06/12-public-vs-private-school-dynarski

Federal Register. (2010). *U.S. Department of Education report on charter schools.* Retrieved from http://www2.ed.gov/legislation/FedRegister/announcements/2010-3/072610b.html

Government Accountability Office. (2016). *K-12 education: Better use of information could help agencies identify disparities and address racial discrimination.* Retrieved from http://www.gao .gov/products/GAO-16–345

Grey, B. (2008, April 3). High school drop-out rate in major US cities at nearly 50 percent. *International Committee of the Fourth International.* Retrieved from http://www.wsws.org/articles/2008/ apr2008/scho-a03.shtml

Harris, E. (2016, January, 11). New York City's high school graduation rates top 70%. *New York Times.* Retrieved from http://www.nytimes.com/2016/01/12/nyregion/new-york-citys-high-school-graduation-rate-tops-70.html=0

Kolko, J. (2014, August 13). Where "back to school" means private school. *Trulia.* Retrieved from http://www.trulia.com/blog/trends/private-vs-public-school

Lee, J. (2014, May 15). Still apart: Map show states with most segregated schools. *USA Today.* Retrieved from http://www.usatoday.com/story/news/nation-now/2014/05/15/school-segregation-civil-rights-project/9115823

Leachman, M., & Mai, C. (2014, May 20). Most states funding schools less than before the recession. *Center for Budget and Policy Priorities.* Retrieved from http://www.cbpp.org/research/ most-states-funding-schools-less-than-before-the-recession

Mathis, W., & Maul, A. (2013, July 16). CREDO'S significantly insignificant findings. *Center for Research on Education Outcomes.*

National Alliance for Public Charter Schools. (2014). *Students' names on charter schools waiting lists top 1 million for the first time.* Retrieved from http://www.publiccharters.org/press/ waiting-list-2014

National Alliance for Public Charter Schools. (2015). *Estimated number of public charter schools & students, 2014–2015.* Retrieved from http://www.publiccharters.org/wp-content/uploads/2015/ 02/open_closed_FINAL1.pdf

National Center for Education Statistics. (2013a). *Fast facts: Expenditures.* Retrieved https://nces .ed.gov/fastfacts/display.asp?id=66

National Center for Education Statistics. (2013b). *A first look: 2013 mathematics and reading.* Retrieved from http://nces.ed.gov/nationsreportcard/subject/publications/main2013/pdf/2014451.pdf

National Center for Education Statistics. (2014). *Homeschooling in the U.S. 2012.* Retrieved from https://nces.ed.gov/programs/digest/d13/tables/dt13_206.10.asp?current=yes

National Center for Education Statistics. (2015). *Selected statistics from elementary and secondary education universe: School year 2013–2014.* Retrieved from https://nces.ed.gov/pubs2015/2015151/ tables/table_03.asp

National Center for Education Statistics. (2016a). *Fast facts: Back to school statistics.* Retrieved from http://nces.ed.gov/fastfacts/display.asp?id=372

National Center for Education Statistics. (2016b). *Public high school graduation rates.* Retrieved from http://nces.ed.gov/programs/coe/indicator_coi.asp

New America. (n.d.). *School funding litigation.* Retrieved from https://www.newamerica.org/ education-policy/policy-explainers/early-ed-prek-12/school-funding/school-funding-litigation

Orfield, G., Frankenberg, E., Ee, J., & Kuscera, J. (2014, May 15). Brown at 60: Great progress, a long retreat and an uncertain future *Civil Rights Project.* Retrieved from https://civilrights project.ucla.edu/research/k-12-education/integration-and-diversity/brown-at-60-great-progress-a-long-retreat-and-an-uncertain-future

Ray, B. D. (2015, January 6). Research facts on homeschooling. *National Home Education Research Institute.* Retrieved from http://www.nheri.org/research/research-facts-on-homeschooling.html

Religion News Foundation. (2014, July 31). *School vouchers and the separation of church and state.* Retrieved from http://www.religionlink.com/tip_060731.php

Snyder, J. (2013, December 5). Why public schools outperform private schools. *Boston Review.* Retrieved from https://bostonreview.net/us/snyder-public-private-charter-schools-demographics-incentives-markets

Strauss, V. (2010, October 12). Study shows deep disparities in funding for schools. *Washington Post.* Retrieved from http://voices.washingtonpost.com/answer-sheet/equity/study-shows-deep-disparities-i.html

Toppo, G. (2006, June 20). Big-city schools struggle with graduation rates. *USA Today.* Retrieved from http://usatoday30.usatoday.com/news/education/2006-06-20-dropout-rates_x.htm

U.S. Department of Education, Office of Elementary and Secondary Education, Consolidated State Performance Report, 2013–14.

Wetzel, J. (2012, November 2012). Home-schooling goes under the microscope in Peabody study. *Vanderbilt University Research.* Retrieved from http://news.vanderbilt.edu/2012/11/homeschooling

Wihbey, J. (2015, March 26). Urban charter schools and student gains: 2015 findings from Stanford University. *Journalist's Resource.* Retrieved from http://journalistsresource.org/studies/society/education/urban-charter-schools-student-gains-2015-stanford-university

Made in the USA
Monee, IL
04 August 2021